PACIFIC
Paradises

PACIFIC
Paradises

The Discovery of
Tahiti *and* Hawaii

TREVOR LUMMIS

SUTTON PUBLISHING

First published in the United Kingdom in 2005 by
Sutton Publishing Limited · Phoenix Mill
Thrupp · Stroud · Gloucestershire · GL5 2BU

British Library Cataloguing in Publication Data
A catalogue record for this book is available from the British Library.

ISBN 0-7509-3893-5

Typeset in 10.5/15pt Photina
Typesetting and origination by
Sutton Publishing Limited.
Printed and bound in England by
J.H. Haynes & Co. Ltd, Sparkford.

To Sanji, again,
with love

CONTENTS

Acknowledgements   ix

Maps   x

PART ONE: DISCOVERY AND EXPLORATION

 1. Paradise Unveiled   3

 2. The Polynesian Pacific   15

 3. Expanding their Minds   23

 4. Tahiti: Sailors and Scientists   29

PART TWO: CAPTAIN COOK AND THE CONSEQUENCES

 5. Return to Tahiti   41

 6. Tahiti and the Tahitians   51

 7. Hawaii and the Death of Captain Cook   65

 8. British Hawaii and the Early Adventurers   77

 9. The Traders   87

10. The Bear and the Eagle   94

11. Hawaii and the Hawaiians   102

12. European Interlude   115

PART THREE: CHRISTIANS AND COLONIES

13. The First Missionaries   129

14. All at Sea   139

15. Holy War   144

16. The Inspectors   151
17. The Last Pagans   161
18. Hawaiian Eclipse   167
19. Tahitians Defeated   177
20. Reflections   187

     Notes   195
     Bibliography   202
     Index   206

ACKNOWLEDGEMENTS

The two main sources for any book of this nature are the contemporary records and memoirs of those who experienced the events, and the publications of fellow historians and scholars in other disciplines whose names and works are listed in the bibliography. I would like to express my gratitude to the staff of the British Library, the National Archives, the National Maritime Museum and the British Museum, whose unfailing good humour and expertise makes research in these institutions so pleasant. Writing is a solitary occupation and the practical support and encouragement from friends is much appreciated, and although such a list could be long, I would like to thank the following: Geoffrey and Wendy Bray, Paul Curtin, Gretchen Gerzina, Howard and Barbara Ginsberg, Tina Henderson, Michael Kustow, Daniel and Ariane Piot-Jonker, Jane Shallice and John and Patricia Wright. I am greatly indebted to Leo Daniel who nursed an ailing computer through every conceivable fault; without him the script would never have been ready for publication. The detailed comments and suggestions of my editors Christopher Feeney, Clare Jackson and Lucy Isenberg were invaluable. My greatest debt, however, is to my wife Sandra whose careful reading and perceptive comments removed many obscurities and infelicities and greatly improved the final result.

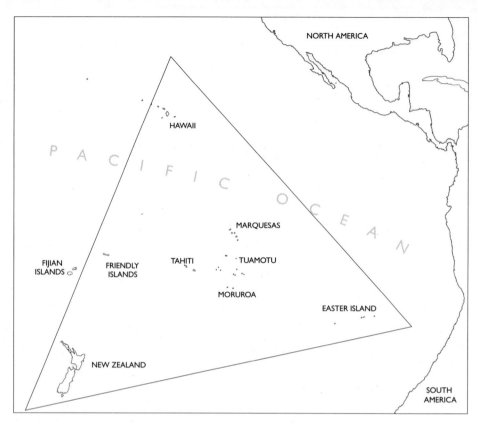

The Polynesian Triangle

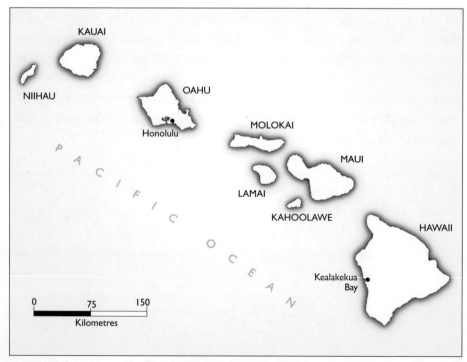

The Hawaiian Islands

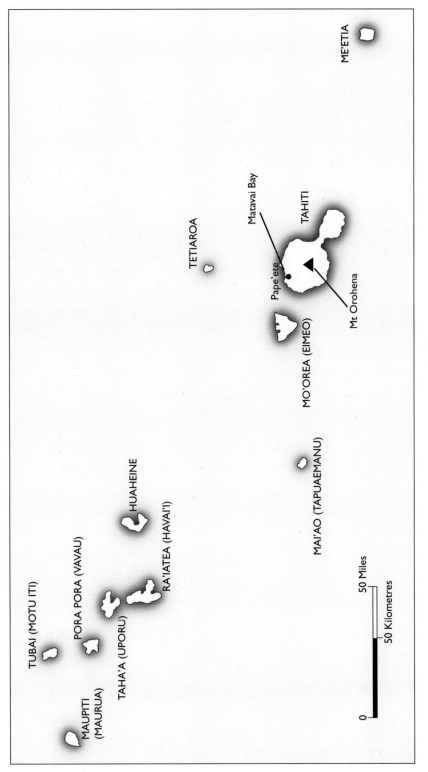

The Society Islands

ME'ETIA

TETIAROA

Matavai Bay

TAHITI

Pape'ete

Mt Orohena

MO'OREA (EIMEO)

MAI'AO (TAPUAEMANU)

HUAHEINE

RA'IATEA (HAVAI'I)

TAHA'A (UPORU)

PORA PORA (VAVAU)

TUBAI (MOTU ITI)

MAUPITI (MAURUA)

0   50 Kilometres

50 Miles

PART ONE

DISCOVERY AND EXPLORATION

Chapter 1

PARADISE UNVEILED

What we saw this evening at Sun Set, we now supposed we saw the long wished for Southern Continent, which has been often talked of, but never before seen by any Europeans.

George Robertson, Master of HMS Dolphin, 19 June 1767

On 18 June 1767 Captain Samuel Wallis, in command of HMS *Dolphin*, was sailing westward with a following breeze in the tropical South Pacific Ocean heading towards an area where a lookout thought he had glimpsed land the day before. But distant cloud banks often give the impression of being land and it was evening before the *Dolphin* was close enough for her crew to confirm earlier hopes. There was solid land ahead and the shoreline fell away into the distance on both sides with mountains towering in the background as far as the eye could see. This was no small scattering of coral islands, and the huge mass of the land made Wallis think that he had found the Southern Continent which geographers believed must exist in the southern hemisphere in order to balance the huge landmass on the northern half of earth. These were unknown waters – 17° 37 south latitude, 149° 27 west longitude – and it was a situation which called for some caution, for with a following wind the ship could easily have been driven on to reef or rock. On the morning of 20 June, George Robertson, the ship's master, recorded in his journal:

> we was obliged to lye too, the weather being so thick and foggy that we could not see the land altho within two leagues [six miles] of it, this thick weather made us all some uneasy for fear of falling in with some shoal, especially as we heard the sea breaking and making a great noise on some reef of rocks . . . in a short time the fog cleared up . . . and . . . saw breakers betwixt us and the shore, and upwards of a hundred Canoes betwixt us and the breakers all paddling off towards the ship, when they came within pistol shot they lay by some time and looked at our ship with great astonishment, holding a sort of Council of War amongst them.[1]

It was a tense meeting for both sides. The islanders had never before seen a European ship or Europeans, and the crew of HMS *Dolphin* were unsure how the inhabitants would react to this strange intrusion into their world.

Samuel Wallis was a 39-year-old Cornishman with a vast experience of tense situations gained in the European wars of the mid-eighteenth century which had seen him reach the rank of captain at the comparatively early age of twenty-nine. He remained calm and steady, determined to win the friendship of this unknown people. The men in the canoes threw green boughs into the sea and a chief gave a fifteen-minute speech which the sailors took to be a sign of peace – at least, they assumed he was a chief, but as his language was unknown to them they had only outward appearances and behaviour to judge by. Both sides were cautious as either could be intent on deception: however, the first bold soul ventured on board. Slowly more and more canoes approached and more and more men crowded on to the ship until Captain Wallis, fearing that his crew might suddenly be overwhelmed, ordered a cannon to be fired. This unaccountable and stunning noise cleared the ship of natives and induced the canoes to pull back a hundred yards. As the man who had been first on board dived over the side he snatched a midshipman's lace-trimmed hat: a well-deserved prize for his courage.

As this part of the coast offered no place suitable for a safe anchorage the *Dolphin* moved further along what one of the officers described as the 'pleasantest shore I ever saw' and which to the master appeared 'to be the most populous Country I ever saw, the whole shore side was lined with Men, Women, and Children, all the way that we sailed along . . . we was now fully persuaded that this was part of the Southern Continent'.[2] He was wrong. These Europeans were the first to discover Tahiti.

It was an anxious time for the master. 'At this time our Capt. and first Lieutn. was both bad, and about thirty seamen in the Doctor's list, some of which was so bad that he suspected Death to seize them soon, if timely relief was not found on this pleasant and delightful Country.'[3] They were desperate for water and for fresh food to combat the scurvy which was affecting so many of the crew. Water proved difficult to obtain as it was not simply a matter of rowing ashore towing some barrels to fill at the nearest stream. Before they dared venture ashore they needed to be certain that they would be permitted to do so, otherwise they might be captured or massacred. The actions of the natives confused them. The islanders traded any amount of fresh fruit, vegetables and meat with the strangers, but delivered only a few calabashes of water. Wallis and his officers did all in their power to establish friendly relations. They gave the islanders presents of hatchets, nails and other trade goods but still the Tahitians would not supply them with water; indeed they impounded the barrels which had been sent ashore in the hope that the natives would fill and return them. And yet pigs, poultry, fruit and produce of all kinds continued to be supplied. These sea-going islanders were only too aware of how crucial water was and they were using it, or the want of it, to force the sailors ashore. Eventually Captain Wallis had no choice but to send his men off in one of the ship's boats to try to collect water, but without success:

> The officers told me, that the inhabitants swarmed on the beach, and that many of them swam off to the boat with fruit, and bamboos filled with water. They said that they were very importunate for them to come on the shore, particularly the women, who came down to the beach, and stripping themselves naked, endeavoured to allure them by many wanton gestures, the meaning of which could not possibly be mistaken. At this time, however, our people resisted the temptation.[4]

Throughout the Pacific women were frequently used as a powerful strategic force in any contact with outside groups. Allowing voyagers from other islands friendly intercourse with the group's women could be a sign of acceptance, but it was also a means of placing strangers in a position where they could easily be overpowered. Had they been tempted ashore by the women or by their determination to secure water, subsequent events leave little doubt that they would have been taken prisoner or killed.

Wallis dare not leave the island without water; he tried again the following day:

> When the boats returned they brought us only a few calabashes of water, for the number of people on the beach was so great, that they would not venture to land, though the young women repeated the allurements which they had practised the day before, with still more wanton, and, if possible, less equivocal gestures. Fruits and provisions of various kinds were brought down and ranged upon the beach, of which our people were invited to partake, as an additional inducement for them to leave the boat . . . When they put off, the women pelted them with apples and bananas, shouting, and shewing every mark of derision and contempt that they could devise.[5]

The surf crashing on the beach was so rough the sailors had refused to land. They knew that by wading through it they would be unable to keep the powder in their muskets dry, and so would be defenceless once ashore, even if they had been willing to face such a huge crowd with dry powder. Captain Wallis realised that he would have to take water by force. He decided to shift his ship a little further down the coast and to anchor it broadside to the shore so his cannon could command the beach where a small river met the sea. There he would be able send men ashore under the shadow of his guns.

The line between success and failure on these expeditions, and of the life or death of all engaged in them, was a fine one. Twice during this operation the ship came in contact with the reef and, with only a little less good fortune or smart seamanship, could have been wrecked: another of those ships which disappeared, their fate unknown. The crew were busy at this move from five o'clock on the morning of 24 June, and their activity was paralleled by greater activity from the Tahitians:

> By eight o'clock, the number of canoes was greatly increased, and those that came last up were double, of a very large size, with twelve or fifteen stout men in each. I observed, with some concern, that they appeared to be furnished rather for war than trade, having very little on board except round pebble stones . . . more canoes were continually coming off from the shore, which were freighted very differently from the rest, for they had on board a number of women who were placed in a row, and who, when they came near the ship, made all the wanton gestures that can be conceived. While these ladies were practising their allurements, the large canoes, which were freighted with stones, drew together very close round the ship . . . As an attack was now begun, in which our arms only could render us superior to the multitude that assailed us, especially as a greater part of the ship's company was in a sick and feeble condition, I gave the order to fire . . . When the great guns began to fire, there were not less than three hundred canoes about the ship, having on board at least two thousand men; many thousands were also upon the shore, and more canoes coming from every quarter.[6]

Captain Wallis's account is bare and factual, but the role of the women in this attack and its partial success (for the natural instincts of the crew proved stronger than discipline) was noted by the ship's master: 'they brought off several Young Girls with them who Played a great number of Wanton Tricks, which took our Peoples Attention from other things, and immediately as our People and the Girls seemed friendly, a Signal was given by one of theirs Greatest Canoes, and in a second our Decks & Boats were full of large Stones which the Indians threw, and hurt several of our Men.'[7] After the attack had failed the natives withdrew inland leaving the beach empty, making it reasonable to risk sending a heavily armed party ashore to obtain water. As both Captain Wallis and the first lieutenant were ill, Tobias Furneaux, the second lieutenant, was given an honour and responsibility which would not normally have fallen to one of his rank. It was he who, mixing some of the pure river water with rum, drank a toast and took possession of the island in the name of his king: the island the inhabitants called Otaheite had been named 'King George III Island'.

The ship's company had only one day's respite. On Friday 26 June the Tahitians mounted yet another determined canoe-borne attack. Captain Wallis was impressed both with the accuracy and force with which the Tahitians threw stones weighing up to 2¼lb and the danger they posed to the life and safety of his crew. Having beaten off the canoes Wallis came to the conclusion that this constant warfare would be ended only by decisive action on his part. He resolved to impress the islanders by demonstrating just how far he could throw a much heavier missile. Elevating his cannon to maximum range he fired so that the shot fell into the crowd on the shore who, suitably astounded and terrified, fled inland. Wallis continued his account:

Having thus cleared the coast, I manned and armed the boats, and putting a strong guard on board, I sent all the carpenters with their axes, and ordered them to destroy every canoe that had been run ashore. Before noon, this service was effectively performed, and more than fifty canoes, many of which were sixty feet long, and three broad, and lashed together, were cut to pieces.[8]

It was a truly devastating act. Perhaps Wallis, intent as he was on preserving his ship against further attack, did not realise quite what the destruction of those canoes meant in terms of loss and labour to the Tahitians. To fell a tree large enough to make a 60ft canoe and to haul it to the coast was labour enough; to hollow it out, to carve the planks, to do all the felling and shaping with only stone, shell and bone tools meant that a large double canoe was a major investment requiring two or more years' arduous work. Later, a small group of Tahitians came down to the shore and left what was assumed to be a peace offering of hogs, dogs and tapa cloth. The sailors landed and took the hogs, released the dogs and, having no use for it, left the cloth, leaving their own gifts of axes and nails in return. In spite of the enormous value of metal to the Tahitians these were left untouched. Captain Wallis and his officers were puzzled. What did this refusal to touch the gifts of the Europeans mean? Eventually someone suggested that perhaps there was something symbolic about the gift of cloth and they had committed a breach of good manners by not accepting it. They observed that the Tahitians returned and left more hogs with the cloth. The sailors returned to the beach and took the hogs and the cloth – and this time the Tahitians scooped up the axes and nails with every indication of joy.

One important lesson had been learned. The Tahitians were not a poor bunch of savages willing to acquire European goods by any means. They were a civilised and cultured people who were too proud to exchange goods and services until their notions of correct behaviour had been observed. They held to these even though they had been subjected to unknown and terrifying weapons. There was fear and incomprehension on both sides and, no doubt, also ambition, greed and an eye for the main chance. Little by little visiting sailors would build up a vocabulary which facilitated the provision of their basic needs, but it was a much longer task to develop sufficient fluency to discuss more abstract concepts such as beliefs and customs. The Europeans had quickly learned that tapa cloth was an important symbolic gift which played a large part in Tahitian rituals and ceremonies.

After this exchange of gifts the natives kept their distance from the ship, allowing the sailors to land unmolested and to set up camp. The Tahitians were much subdued by the power of firearms and, although it seems extraordinary given what they had already suffered from the ship's cannon, Wallis claims that it was seeing a musket fired ashore which did most to impress them:

> It happened that walking out with his gun, after he [the surgeon] had seen the sick properly disposed of in the tent, a wild duck flew over his head, which he shot, and it fell dead among some of the natives . . . Several other ducks happening at the instant to fly over the spot where they were standing, he fired again, and fortunately brought down three more. This incident gave the natives such a dread of a gun, that if a musquet was pointed at a thousand of them, they would all run away like a flock of sheep.[9]

Nevertheless the sailors remained cautious, choosing a defensible situation with the beach on one side and the river on the other, and one well within range of the ship's cannon. It was almost a fortnight after they had arrived before the sick were even well enough to be taken ashore. Scurvy had come very close to causing the deaths of many crewmen. The effects of fresh water and provisions were, however, remarkable: 'The men were constantly served fresh pork, fowls, and fruit, in such plenty, that when I [Captain Wallis] left my bed, after having been confined to it near a fortnight, my ship's company looked so fresh and healthy, that I could scarcely believe them to be the same people.'[10] The pure water and bountiful food so freely obtainable was to impress all who came to Tahiti.

Captain Wallis remained cautious and did not give the natives open access to his camp, but kept them on the other side of the river from where they were called across in small numbers to trade their provisions. He placed the gunner in charge of all bartering as indiscriminate exchange would have driven up prices, and contact was greatly facilitated by an elderly man (presumably a chief) who performed a largely similar role on behalf of the islanders. When the old man who bartered with them did not appear for three days and no supplies were forthcoming, they feared that they had offended the natives in some way. Fortunately for them,

> On Sunday the 5th, the old man returned to the market-place, and made the gunner understand that he had been up the country to prevail upon the people to bring down their hogs, poultry, and fruit, of which the parts near the watering-place were now nearly exhausted. The good effects of his expedition soon appeared, for several Indians, whom our people had never seen before, came in with some hogs that were larger than any that had been yet brought to market. In the mean time, the old man ventured off in his canoe, to the ship, and brought with him, a present to me, a hog already roasted. I was much pleased with his attention and liberality, and gave him in return for his hog, an iron pot, a looking-glass, a drinking-glass, and several other things, which no man in the island was in possession of but himself.[11]

The orders forbidding individual barter or free contact with the handsome women put a considerable strain on discipline. Sailors not only disobeyed the rule against barter but stole lead and then tricked the natives into thinking it was iron by cutting it into the shape of nails. These impositions on the

Tahitians were not ignored and Lieutenant Charles Clerke's log contains this entry for Friday 26 June, 'Punished William Welch (seaman) with 24 lashes for defrauding the indians the day before'.[12] Compared to the twelve lashes William Bowman was given for the double offence of refusing to obey an order and of striking the coxswain some ten days later, it is clear that mistreating the Tahitians was considered a very serious offence. Yet, in spite of this element of trickery from the sailors, relations were obviously growing more cordial and there was now greater confidence in the peaceful intent of both parties.

Cordial relations of a different sort were to lead to thefts which put the ship in jeopardy of falling to pieces. 'While our people were on the shore, several young women were permitted to cross the river, who, though they were not averse to the granting of personal favours, knew the value of them too well not to stipulate for a consideration: the price, indeed, was not great, yet it was such as our men [were] not always able to pay, and under this temptation they stole nails and other iron from the ship.'[13] And not only loose nails lying about the carpenters' stores, but they took to extracting nails from the structure of the ship in such quantities as to threaten the safe working of the vessel. The Captain offered a large reward to discover who stole the nails, but without success. 'The commerce which our men had found means to establish with the women of the island, rendered them much less obedient to the orders that had been given for the regulation of their conduct on shore, than they were at first. I found it necessary therefore, to read the articles of war, and I punished James Proctor, the corporal of marines, who had not only quitted his station, and insulted the officer, but struck the Master at Arms such a blow as brought him to the ground.'[14] Reading the articles of war was a formal warning and reminder of the supreme and all-embracing authority of the captain and of his legal right to punish.

It was now thought necessary to look more diligently about the ship, to discover what nails had been drawn; and it was soon found that all the belaying cleats had been ripped off, and that there was scarcely one of the hammock nails left. All hands were now ordered up, and I practised every artifice to discover the thieves, but without success. I then told them that till the thieves were discovered, not a single man should go on shore: this however produced no effect, except that Proctor, the corporal, behaved in a mutinous manner, for which he was instantly punished.[15]

Corporal Proctor was something of a malefactor as a few days later the captain recorded: 'I was this day also obliged once more to punish Proctor, the corporal of marines, for mutinous behaviour.'[16] It would appear that Proctor, with his offences of deserting his post and striking a senior officer followed by mutinous behaviour, had given the Captain more than enough cause to have hanged him from the yardarm. On some ships such consistent indiscipline would have earned him 100 or even 300 lashes, sentences which could mean death. Captain Wallis, who usually ordered punishment of only a dozen lashes, was neither martinet nor tyrant. But his appeals and leniency were insufficient to maintain discipline against the greater attraction of the Tahitian women. Again, on Monday 2 July:

> in the afternoon it was discovered that Francis Pickney, one of the seamen, had drawn the cleats to which the main sheet was belayed, and, after stealing the spikes, thrown them overboard. Having secured the offender, I called all the people together on deck, and after taking some pains to explain his crime, with all its aggravations, I ordered that he should be whipped with nettles [short lengths of rope] while he ran the gauntlet thrice round the deck: my rhetoric, however, had very little effect, for most of the crew being equally criminal with himself, he was handled so tenderly, that other were rather encouraged to repeat the offence by hope of impunity, than deterred by the fear of punishment.[17]

He then gave orders that no man be allowed ashore save on the working parties collecting wood and water. But the repeated indiscipline, treated as it was with relative leniency, shows that in practice not all naval crews of the period were subject to overly brutal punishment even for serious offences.

On Saturday 11 July the gunner was trading on the beach when a tall woman of some forty-five years appeared. Because of the respect and ceremony she was shown by all the natives ashore he realised that she was the most important person who had so far made contact with the British, so when she indicated that it was her wish, he took her out to the ship. 'She seemed to be under no restraint, either from diffidence or fear, when she first came to the ship; and she behaved, all the while she was on board, with an easy freedom, that always distinguishes conscious superiority and habitual command.'[18] She noticed that Captain Wallis had been ill and made signs that he should go ashore to improve his recovery. Next morning he duly went ashore for the first time in order to return her visit and, as he was still weak, was carried by the natives over the streams and rough places in the path to what he believed to be the queen's house. It was actually the communal meeting house, a thatched building so imposing that Wallis had it measured and described. It was 327ft long by 42ft wide, and had thirty-nine pillars down each side and fourteen in the middle holding up the ridge which gave a head room of 30ft. The sides were completely open and 12ft high. He and two other sick men were each attended by four young women who massaged their limbs, which he reported as being therapeutic and much improved his health. One assumes that Captain Wallis was not a man of very imposing stature for on the return journey 'She had given directions to her people to carry me, as they had done when I came, but as I chose rather to walk, she took me by the arm, and whenever we came to a place of water or dirt, she lifted me over with as little trouble as it would have cost me to have lifted over a child if I had been well.'[19] The next day he sent the gunner back with presents for her; on his return the gunner reported that the queen had been entertaining at least a thousand people to a feast.

Such was the success of this initial contact between Captain Wallis and Queen Obearea that she returned for another visit to the ship and insisted that Wallis again visit her ashore. There she honoured him by tying around his hat a wreath of braided hair, which she indicated was her own work and her own hair. In return for her hospitality he made her various presents and 'I also sent the queen two terkies, two geese, three Guinea hens, a cat big with kittens.'[20] She wept when told that he intended to leave in seven days. The remaining week was a busy one with all hands engaged in preparing the ship for the long voyage ahead and in getting the last wood, water and provisions on board. When the Dolphin sailed it was to the tears of the queen. 'At 4 p.m. our good friend the Queen of the Island paid us another visit on board the ship, when we made her understand that we were to sail soon, she appeared to be very sorry and made signs to know when we were to sail. We told her by signs, at Sunrise the morrow morning, she immediately wept and appeared as much concerned as a women could be in parting with her Husband or Child.'[21] They had difficulty in making her leave the ship and when they did put her ashore she and her attendants slept all night on the beach.

On 27 July 1767 the Dolphin upped anchor at first light and 'About ten o'clock we got without the reef, and a fresh breeze springing up, our Indian friends, and particularly the queen, once more bade us farewell, with tenderness of affection and grief, as filled both my heart and my eyes.'[22] They sailed away to an outpouring of grief and what, to all appearances, was a genuine sorrow at their going. The queen was comforted only with many promises to return.

As Captain Wallis sailed for home with news of his discovery, a French expedition with the ships *La Boudeuse* and *L'Etoile* under the command of Count Louis de Bougainville also 'discovered' Tahiti quite independently the following year, unaware that the British had been there before them. They landed in a different chiefdom from the British, but like them, were much impressed by the beauty of the women and the free sexual mores of the people. Bougainville was a member of the French aristocracy and his description suggests that he was better educated than a practical seaman such as Captain Wallis. Bougainville named the island New Cythera after the one where, according to Greek legend, the goddess of love, Aphrodite, arose from the ocean. Bougainville is responsible for recording one much quoted incident which marked their arrival.

[They] pressed us to choose a woman and come ashore with her; and their gestures . . . denoted in what manner we should form an acquaintance with her. It was very difficult in such conditions, to keep at their work four hundred young French sailors who had not seen a woman for six months. In spite of all our precautions, a young girl came on board and placed herself upon the quarter-deck near one of the hatchways . . . The girl carelessly dropped a cloth which covered her, and appeared to the eyes of all beholders such a Venus as showed herself to the Phrygian shepherd, having, indeed, the celestial form of that goddess.[23]

Bougainville stayed only thirteen days, so had little time to learn much about Tahitian life. But one custom was obvious, how freely the sailors were shown unprecedented hospitality. They were offered food every time they went ashore and this generosity did not 'stop at a slight collation: they offered them young girls . . . Here Venus is the goddess of hospitality, her worship does not admit of any mysteries and every tribute paid to her is a feast for the whole nation. They were surprised at the confusion which our people appeared to be in as our customs do not allow of these public proceedings. However I would not answer for it that every one of our men found it impossible to conquer his repugnance and conform to the customs of the country.'[24] It was this comparison with classical culture as a much admired source of European civilisation that framed the rose-coloured perspective through which the well educated viewed Tahitian life. In classical Greece athletes had exercised naked; her pottery was decorated with erotic scenes and her citizens openly acknowledged the sensual dimension of humanity: here again was a society living without shame and with none of the Europeans' hypocritical social conventions concealing a basic natural activity. Paradise was beautiful, unveiled and unashamed.

Such was the first contact between Europeans and Tahitians and within it one can discern elements of experience which were to give rise to a mélange of romance and reality which in turn would fashion the popular perception of these islands. Here were lushly beautiful islands enjoying an idyllic climate, where bounteous nature not only enabled the population to feed themselves with little work, but provided them with surplus enough to give freely to strangers; the image conveyed was of beaches lapped by a warm blue ocean where the free sexuality of the people meant that they did little more than laze and make love and, after the initial hostility, of the islanders' good-humoured acceptance of their European visitors.

When Captain Cook discovered Hawaii a decade later on 18 January 1778 the story was similar. Before continuing with the experiences of those who followed Captain Wallis to Tahiti in 1767 it is as well to place him, and them, in context. Why was HMS *Dolphin* in the south Pacific? Why were Tahiti and Hawaii unknown to Europeans until the late eighteenth century? These issues can be better understood by taking a brief look back at those who had discovered the islands before them.

Chapter 2

THE POLYNESIAN PACIFIC

Man is known to have lived in the Pacific for as long as he is known to have lived anywhere.

Glen Barclay, A History of the Pacific . . .[1]

T he above claim for historical settlement could only be true of the western Pacific close to the Asian mainland where the first stretches of water were comparatively easy to cross, as the islands of present-day Indonesia were large and close to the continent. Mankind first spread over these islands setting out from what are now south China, Vietnam and Malaysia and then migrating in a westerly direction to the Philippines, Moluccas, New Guinea and the Solomon Islands, all of which were settled in early prehistory. To the south mankind reached Australia by similar short sea voyages and archaeologists seem to be continually pushing back the date at which human habitation commenced there. By contrast, New Zealand, the one other large landmass to the south-west, was not discovered and populated until about AD 1000, and then not, as one might suppose, by aborigines from Australia some 1,200 nautical miles away, but by Polynesians doubling back south-west from the distant Cook or Society Islands – a voyage of 2,000 nautical miles.

It is in fact incorrect to talk of Europeans discovering islands such as Tahiti and Hawaii, for they had all been discovered and settled long before by people travelling in nothing more than fragile canoes. The eastern Pacific is the largest expanse of water in the world and only sparsely sown with small islands. From Panama to Japan is a distance of over 8,000 nautical miles with little more than the Hawaiian Islands *en route*; by comparison, crossing the Atlantic from Gibraltar to New York is a mere 3,200 nautical miles. Even sailing diagonally across and down the Atlantic from the major ports of western Europe to West Indian destinations the distances rarely exceed 4,000 nautical miles – and the journey can be broken by calling at the Azores. And yet (the Vikings apart for the moment) it was not until the late fifteenth century that Christopher

Columbus, setting out from the Canary Islands, was hailed as a hero for venturing with his frightened crew into the unknown ocean as far as the West Indies. His ships may appear small to us now, but next to the canoes of the Pacific they were huge: they could carry months or even years of supplies; a canoe could carry comparatively little. That the Polynesians found and settled virtually every habitable island in an ocean much larger than the Atlantic, and did so centuries before Europeans dared venture even half the distance, serves as its own tribute to their navigational skills, seamanship and courage.

How the Polynesians discovered and inhabited the isolated islands remains something of a mystery. They had reached and settled on Easter Island by AD 500, and yet Easter Island is a tiny speck of land in the empty south-eastern quarter of the Pacific Ocean some 1,300 miles from other Polynesian habitation. When Europeans started visiting Tahiti it was apparent that the Tahitians knew about the other island groups and archipelagos to the west and north of them, clear evidence of previous contact between these groups, but it seemed any previous knowledge of New Zealand or Easter Island had long been forgotten, and the Hawaiian Islands were remembered only as a mythical place. But these three places – New Zealand, Hawaii and Easter Island – were the outlying points of an immense triangle of ocean over which the Polynesians spread and on whose myriad islands they settled.

Expert opinion as to when the Society Islands, of which Tahiti is one, were first settled varies, but between AD 700 and 800 would seem to be the most favoured date. It was long argued that Hawaii was then settled from Tahiti some two hundred years after Tahiti was first inhabited, but that opinion is now disputed. Goldman states that the previously commonly accepted view that Hawaii was populated from Tahiti is now untenable. 'The earliest occupation date for Hawaii is AD 124', whereas for Tahiti he puts it 'as late as 1100'. He argues that the Hawaiian Islands had been settled from elsewhere at the earlier date and that the Hawaiian/Tahitian connection was the result of Hawaii being 'invaded sometime in the twelfth century by Tahitians'.[2] However, this claim seems most unlikely as it is difficult to imagine how a sufficiently large army of warriors could have been carried by canoe across more than 2,500 miles of ocean.

Bellwood is also of the opinion that Tahiti was not the source of the original Hawaiian population, and suggests that Hawaii was settled from the Marquesas between AD 500 and AD 600; although he does agree with the generally accepted view that the inhabitants of the two island groups, Hawaii and Tahiti, albeit separated by so much ocean, were in regular contact during the twelfth and thirteenth centuries. On various evidence (for example, the name of one stretch of water in the Hawaiian Islands means 'The Path to Tahiti' and it was from there that the canoes oriented themselves at the start of the voyage) it is probable that the Hawaiians at least made frequent voyages to Tahiti at that earlier period. The practicality of such a voyage with the technology of the period was later put to the test:

> In 1976 a replica of a Polynesian double canoe (called the *Hokule'a*) was built in Hawaii and sailed from Maui to Tahiti with a Hawaiian crew and a Micronesian navigator. The canoe had no instruments, and the successful trip navigated by star positions and wave patterns over [more than 2,500 miles] took 35 days. It carried a crew of 15 men (plus two photographers), together with traditional foods and livestock, and all thankfully survived except for the taro.[4]

This was a remarkable achievement and an excellent sailing time; an eighteenth-century European man-of-war would have taken a comparable time to cover the distance. But this does little to substantiate the claim that Hawaii was settled from Tahiti; it shows only that wind and current mean the voyage from Hawaii to Tahiti is feasible. To prove that Hawaii could have been settled from Tahiti they should have sailed in the opposite direction.

It is one of history's small ironies that Captain Cook wrote the name 'Hawaii' long before he knew of the existence of those islands which he himself was to discover and where he was to die. While Cook was at Tahiti and attempting to understand the culture he enquired into their religion and was told (at the end of a long creation myth) that the gods created the first human, Eothe, but that ultimately all human beings were descended from three men and one woman. He wrote down what he was told: 'Eothe is said to have lived in an island (Heawaii) to the northward from which came hogs, dogs, fowls, etc.'[5] Cook took 'Heawaii', as he spelt it, to be a mythical place, such as the biblical Garden of Eden. Apart from the strange coincidence that Cook should have recorded this account, it serves rather to support Goldman's belief that Hawaii was settled before Tahiti. The myth names Hawaii as the source of their common livestock, the implication being that Tahiti was settled from Hawaii. Myths are not historical facts, but many of them contain a grain of truth.

The date at which the various islands came to be inhabited, although crucial for establishing the pattern of settlement, is in itself less remarkable than the fact that they were discovered and settled at all. What drove people, perhaps no more than twenty to a canoe, to venture out into the unknown in search of another land? What made them think that they would find land elsewhere? It was not until the fifteenth century that Columbus was bold enough to venture into the Atlantic, and he was not entrusting himself and his crew to a 3ft wide canoe only inches above the waves. 'The early Polynesians underwent hardships which few modern men could even visualise. The [2,500-mile] voyage from the Society to the Hawaiian Islands may occupy only a few inches on a map, but in a partially open canoe laden with men, women, children, animals and precious seed plants it must surely have been an appalling ordeal. The astounding fact is that the Polynesians reached virtually every island within the huge Polynesian triangle . . .'[6] One can only share in the admiration for their epic voyages, although it is doubtful that the evidence allows one to assume that they took children on these dangerous initial voyages of exploration and settlement. Such feats were probably undertaken mainly by the young and adventurous; children could be produced if and when the explorers arrived at a habitable destination.

It has been argued that the truly long-distance voyages to settle the eastern Pacific islands were largely the result of accident, when canoes were driven out into unknown territory by storms. Some, no doubt, were forced migrations as those defeated in wars had to flee their own island in order to save their lives. Although such events could account for some discoveries, the idea that natives setting out on unplanned voyages, not intentionally supplied with the maximum food and water, could survive a really long crossing by canoe is not very convincing. But whatever the impulse, Polynesians were skilled at detecting the presence of unseen land by the disturbance caused to the regular flow of the long ocean swell; they knew how many hundreds of miles from land certain seabirds would travel; they were skilled at seeing the almost imperceptible changes in cloud formation caused by warmer air rising over an island still invisible beyond the horizon. Indeed, their navigational abilities and skills may well have been superior to those of the Europeans before the chronometer allowed the latter to fix their longitude. Certainly, Polynesian tradition tells of men deliberately following the migration of birds in order to discover where they landed. Barclay's argument that 'They could not have followed birds to landfall, as has sometimes been suggested, because they would not have known where the birds were flying to, and they could not have seen the birds flying at night' is a weak one.[7] They knew the migratory birds which arrived from and flew back to the north were land birds, so they were confident that if only they could follow their direction they must come to land of some description. As for not seeing them at night, that is totally unnecessary as migratory birds do not all pass one point in a single night; others come along the next day, and the next – and once one has found the line of flight, one can simply continue to sail in that direction. Also, as it has been established that Polynesian canoes could make trips of up to 3,000 miles with their plants and animals (which also needed food and water) from one island to another, it follows that exploratory *return* trips of about 1,500 miles were not impossible.

It is significant that the Polynesians not only discovered and populated all these habitable islands but they also carried with them the seeds, plants and animals upon which they relied for their sustenance: 'All the major food plants and animals were introduced into Polynesia by man.'[8] The islands in the Pacific Ocean were young in terms of geological time and appeared after the major continents drifted apart into roughly their present position. Essentially they are the tops of volcanoes which rose out of the ocean and although they developed vegetation, insect and bird life they had mostly not evolved to sustain larger animals. The only large mammals found, and only where conditions were suitable, were seals and similar sea mammals. These islands were thus free of the dangerous animals and poisonous reptiles which made life in so many tropical countries a trial and a danger. Apparently many of them did not even have mosquitoes until European ships brought them: to live in the tropics free of mosquitoes as well as having no predators or snakes made for a pleasant and relaxed existence. An even greater advantage for Europeans was the healthy atmosphere free of most of the diseases that had proved so fatal to them in other tropical regions. During Captain Cook's first voyage he had no deaths from sickness until the ships reached Batavia (Indonesia) on the way home where the 'bloody flux' (dysentery) took the lives of thirty men. The healthy climates of Tahiti and Hawaii made them paradises indeed.

That all the food plants growing on these islands when the Europeans arrived had been transported there by man only leads to further debate about the settlement of these islands. Virtually all the foodstuffs on which the population relied had their origins in the western Pacific. Their pigs were the small Chinese type, as were the edible dogs. Their vegetables – yams, taro, bananas, sugar cane, gourds and so on – were also from the western Pacific. The one exception was the sweet potato which is of South American origin. In 1947, Thor Heyerdahl sailed a balsa-wood raft, the *Kon-Tiki*, of the type used by the Peruvians, from South America to Polynesia to prove the theory that the Polynesians came originally from South America. This theory, although arguable, has not found general favour save in the case of Easter Island where it is believed that South Americans and Polynesians both settled. From there the sweet potato could have been taken to the rest of Polynesia. But it is noteworthy that during the sixteenth century the Spanish made several voyages of exploration into the Pacific from their possessions in South America so it is conceivable that they introduced the plant to the islands. Between 1527 and 1595 expeditions from Peru or Mexico discovered the Solomon Islands, the Marshall and Marquesas Islands. Europeans have been criticised for transplanting species from one continent to another – and this has occasionally been disastrous as in the case of rabbits to Australia – but it was a process familiar to the inhabitants of the Pacific from the time of their earliest settlements. When Europeans took their plants and animals with them on similar voyages they were following a practice as old as mankind.

There was one huge difference, however, to the long-term effect on the environment between European and Polynesian settlement. When Europeans first began to settle and colonise islands around the world these were as lush, fruitful and fertile as Tahiti and Hawaii, their indigenous populations living in harmony with nature and her resources. But the clearing of forests for monoculture of crops such as sugar and cotton and the felling of trees both for building and fuel soon created environmental problems. As Grove's meticulous study of the origins of environmental thought from the seventeenth century demonstrates, it was the rapid degradation of lush tropical islands under western capitalist development which stimulated the growth of environmentalism.[9] Early disregard for nature's balance led to exhausted soil, erosion, the drying up of springs and streams and the need to pass and enforce protective laws. Once those islands – and other places – became part of the world commodity market the lands were degraded, early examples being the Canary Islands, Madeira and then, post-Columbus, a number of West Indian islands as forests there were cleared for plantations of sugar, cotton, tobacco and indigo. Other islands such as St Helena in the south Atlantic and Mauritius in the Indian Ocean which had become busy ports of call for ships to take on water, wood and provisions when bound for the Cape of Good Hope, India and beyond, were already degraded. And yet the Polynesians had inhabited islands since time immemorial without precipitating any of these problems: they had kept their environment intact. This was in some measure because they were not then part of an ever growing globalisation of market forces, but also because they kept their numbers in check. The result of uncontrolled population growth on small areas can be seen in the example of Pitcairn Island which the descendants of the *Bounty* mutineers and their Tahitian women were eventually obliged to leave because it could no longer support their numbers. It only took some thirty years for them to so deforest their island that soil erosion seriously affected the inshore fishing grounds. The water table had also been lowered and streams and springs were providing less water. As with other islands, this was partly due to Pitcairn becoming part of an international market supplying ships with food, fuel and water: in so doing the Pitcairners were, in effect, increasing the population of the island. Forty years after they settled there Pitcairn had to be abandoned.[10] This was not simply due to market forces, and clearly it is possible to have sustainable agriculture; the problem was also one of culture. The Pitcairners were no longer living according to traditional Polynesian belief and practice which had sustained island life over many generations.

It is possible that no major political power or religion was capable of restricting or controlling the growth of commerce and the destructive powers of the market; but these flowed out and over the world largely from Europe. The underlying Christian culture of Europe held that mankind was not only made in the image of God; but also that God had given mankind dominion over the natural world: a basic world view which legitimised any treatment of the natural world. The Polynesian world view was very different. Mankind was not above nature, but simply part of it: nature had to be preserved. Taboos protected the environment against overuse. The Polynesians practised agriculture, but not with a degree of exploitation that would degrade it. The world was holy: one could not use even a leaf from a tree without the appropriate appreciation. Polynesians even discovered and colonised tiny coral atolls without overpopulating them; as for the larger islands like Tahiti and Hawaii, although inhabited by them for centuries they were still in pristine condition. This harmonious state struck the early European visitors so vividly as they were examples of mankind and nature in happy balance.

By contrast Europeans found justification for their actions in the Bible. Certainly in both Tahiti and Hawaii the missionaries were anxious to stimulate commerce, if only to save the people from what they saw as sinful idleness. Many North American Indians had been dispossessed of their tribal territory on the grounds that they did not cultivate the earth, and the implication was that they had less right to it than those who would do so. Although Grove records the efforts of a handful of scholarly Europeans to put in place schemes to combat the desecration of the earth in various places, the sum total of successful action was woefully small. Not that one should be over-critical of those early pioneers; in our present age the degradation of the environment is far more serious, yet still the political will to take action remains totally inadequate. The impact of unspoilt Pacific islands, and particularly of Tahiti, on scientists such as Joseph Banks, the naturalist on Cook's first voyage, or on Johann Reinhold Forster and his son George Forster who sailed on Captain Cook's second, or on Philibert Commerson who arrived with Bougainville, was particularly strong. Both Joseph Banks and Captain Cook expressed the regret that they could see, even from those early and brief contacts, that the islanders were not to enjoy their tranquil lives, in balance with nature, for much longer.

Having discovered every possible island, the Polynesian voyages of discovery and colonisation had ceased by the time the Europeans arrived in the eighteenth century. Where island groups were comparatively close together, their inhabitants now undertook voyages of only 250 to 300 miles, mainly trading objects of exceptional value. Their voyages often bore comparison with those of Europe's boldest early sea-rovers, the Vikings, who found their way in similar length island hopping stages from Norway to North America via the Shetlands, Iceland and Greenland long before Columbus. But the effect of climatic changes during the Little Ice Age in about the fifteenth century, which cut contact between Norway and America, might also account for the breaking of contacts between Hawaii and the rest of the world, and the memory of them drifting into the realms of legend during over three hundred years of isolation.

Chapter 3

EXPANDING THEIR MINDS

Thus accustomed to live continually immersed in pleasure, the people of Tahiti have acquired a witty and humorous temper, which is the offspring of ease and of joy.

Louis A. de Bougainville, A Voyage Round the World (1772)

During the eighteenth-century Enlightenment philosophers and scholars had been questioning and examining the extent of man's knowledge of the world and scientific enquiry was coming to question, even replace, the old religious and secular certainties. As the gaps in knowledge became evident, there was a desire to collect the missing information or to solve the intellectual problem. There was a movement throughout western Europe to systematise and catalogue what was known – Chambers' Cyclopaedia was first published in 1728; the French started publication of Diderot's *Encyclopédie* in 1751; the *Encyclopaedia Britannica* was published in Scotland in 1768 – each compendious work of scholarship testifying to the growing public interest in knowledge of the world. The voyages to formerly uncharted parts of the globe had revealed a range of flora and fauna, hitherto unsuspected, which required examination and classification: the French naturalist Buffon's *Histoire Naturelle* set out to do just that and its first volume was published in 1749, the work eventually running to over forty volumes.

So highly esteemed had the voyages of exploration become that at the outbreak of the War of American Independence in 1775, in which the French, Spanish and Dutch joined the American colonists against Britain, the King of France ordered the French Navy not to attack Captain Cook's ships but to leave them to go about their scientific business. Benjamin Franklin, in Paris soliciting French aid in the struggle for independence from Britain, issued the same instructions to American ships – but the American Congress failed to ratify this generous exception. The academic world was also to show its internationalism during the French Revolution. Bougainville, the French commander who had 'discovered' Tahiti just a little later than Captain Wallis, was in command of another expedition in the Pacific when the Revolution started in 1789. On his return to Europe he refused to land at a French port and hand over the results of the voyage to the revolutionary government because he and the expedition had been commissioned by the King of France. Instead, he landed in England and the entire collection of native artefacts and specimens was sent to London. The French agent in London duly contacted King Louis XVIII who instructed that Queen Charlotte was to choose whatever she wished and that the rest should be awarded to the British Museum. But Sir Joseph Banks, its director, refused to accept it and sent it all to France because, as he put it, the philosophers of the two nations were not at war, thus matching the French gesture in leaving Captain Cook outside the conflicts of war. Nevertheless, Sir Joseph was strongly criticised by William Cobbett, the anti-French radical writer, when he addressed as 'Citizens' the directors of the National Institute of France, in a profuse acceptance speech at his election as a member of their society and in which he expressed his admiration for a country which even during the horrors of the Revolution he still respected. Politicians and the military were usually as one in prosecuting wars; the intellectuals of Europe were still united in the search for knowledge.

As the eighteenth century progressed, scientific interest came to extend beyond the physical nature of the earth and its fauna and flora to include the study of cultures. The islands of the Pacific revealed a variety of people with contrasting manners and mores, and all very different from Europeans. There was debate (bearing essentially on Christian belief) as to whether mankind was born innately wicked or whether he was born good and subsequently corrupted by civilisation. This was exemplified in Rousseau's theory of natural upbringing and education and his concept of the 'noble savage' as superior in manners and morals to his European counterpart. Philibert Commerson, a medical doctor and naturalist who had served with Bougainville as the botanist aboard La Boudeuse, was spellbound by what he saw on Tahiti and gave his enthusiastic support to Rousseau's theory. He would not accept any criticism of the Tahitians or their way of life, dismissing even their perpetual thieving as being no crime on the grounds that theft can exist only where there are property rights, and those, Commerson argued, do not exist in a state of nature and in a society where everyone is given what they need to live.

I can assure you that it is the one spot upon the earth's surface which is inhabited by men without either vices, prejudices, wants, or dissensions. Born under the loveliest skies, they are supported by the fruits of a soil so fertile that cultivation is scarcely required . . . Some blighting censor might discover in all this [sexual freedom] nothing but debauchery, horrible prostitution, and the most shameless cynicism; but he would grossly deceive himself, failing to recognise the condition of Natural Man, born essentially good, tainted by no prejudice, and following without mistrust and without remorse the sweet impulses of his instincts, always sure guides, for they have not yet degenerated into reasons.[1]

There can be no more overt example than this of the 'noble savage' school of thought. Commerson did, however, suffer an embarrassment while in Tahiti.

He had a young assistant who had robustly performed his manly duties throughout the voyage. The moment this assistant stepped ashore, however, the Tahitians were not deceived for a moment by his all-concealing European clothes. Immediately they identified him – as a woman. The assistant, Jeanne Baré, had in fact aroused some suspicion among the ship's crew by never appearing undressed at any time. Although, as his valet, she shared Commerson's tiny cabin, he made the rather unbelievable claim that he had been entirely unaware of the deception. But whatever the doctor's prior knowledge of his assistant's gender, she became the first European woman known to sail around the world. Bougainville described her as being about twenty-six years old and neither pretty nor ugly. She stayed with Commerson as his companion and assistant until his death on the island of Mauritius in March 1773, after which she retired to France.

Commerson's view of the Tahitians was even more favourable than that of Captain Wallis, as the French were given a peaceful and hospitable reception from the start, presumably due to their healthy respect for the power of the musket and cannon which the Tahitians had learned from their earlier experience with the British. There was one unfortunate incident when three natives were killed by bayoneting and the four soldiers held responsible put in irons, but the natives did not attempt to retaliate, they simply left the area and fled inland. Bougainville had to go inland himself and make amends to the chief before contact and trade could be resumed. When the French left, good relations were so well established that the chief insisted that a native named Aoutourou accompany them to France.

The idea that each Pacific island society had developed independently on their respective islands away from any corrupting influence led to the belief that studying these groups could elicit fundamental knowledge of the forces which shaped human nature and society. The islanders were considered more varied in their patterns of behaviour than Europeans:

> manners of civilised nations bear strong resemblance to each other; whereas, in countries which science or the arts of refinement have never reached, we observe a wonderful disparity. Some are found in that state of darkness and absolute barbarism, from the view of which humanity gladly turns aside, while others, by the mere force of natural good sense, have not only emerged from this gloom, but have nearly obtained that order, propriety, and good conduct, which constitute the essence of real civilisation. Such a people, who do honour to the name of man, have been brought to the knowledge of Europe by the events which attended the catastrophe which is here to be related.[2]

That catastrophe was the wreck of the *Antelope* in August 1783 upon the Pelew Islands. These islands, located to the east of the Philippines, were scarcely known atolls. The ship, the *Antelope*, struck a reef but did not sink immediately and the crew were able to ferry ashore useful quantities of stores and tools to an uninhabited islet. There they were visited by the king of the islands who befriended them and ensured that they were fully supplied with provisions. The crew built themselves a small vessel in which they sailed to China where they were sure of finding British ships and a passage home. The king of the islands sent one of his sons to sail with them: like so many the son was to die of disease in London before he could be returned home. The behaviour of these islanders had confirmed the image of the noble savage, full of generosity and kindness, uncorrupted by the viciousness, greed and violence engendered by 'civilised' cultures. It duplicated, even surpassed, the amiable behaviour found at Tahiti and confirmed everything the Romantics wished to believe about the essential goodness of man. This was partly the product of French atheism which rejected the Christian view of humanity. Christians believed that mankind was conceived in sin and that life was little more than a proving ground for the demand of forgiveness and the granting of grace. They believed that man should earn his bread by the sweat of his brow and women put forth children in sorrow. In living one had to make amends for the sins of the fathers which were visited upon the children from generation unto generation. The discovery of the isolated islands of the Pacific far from the demands of commerce and civilisation seemed to undermine the Christian religion and confirm the philosophical view. In the Pacific mankind did not lose much sweat in gaining all the necessities of life, nor was childbirth necessarily difficult, and people were, on the whole, good-natured and easy going. The concept of sin was virtually unknown.

As more islands were discovered it was realised that not all islanders were as agreeable as the Tahitians or those of Pelew. Many were fierce and warlike, brutal to their enemies and harsh to elements in their own societies. The loss of another vessel in New Zealand some twenty-five years later, in 1809, led a contemporary to a very different conclusion from the one above.

Certain philosophers have asserted, that man in savage life presents an image of genuine innocence and simplicity, and that all powers and feelings are then most happily unfolded. Such theories have been confuted in the most decisive manner, by modern observation. Savage man has been found not only stained with all the crimes to which the most highly civilised society is incident, but abandoned to a fury and frenzy of passion, of which even its most depraved members are never guilty. Of this a dreadful instance is now to be recorded.[3]

The instance in question was the burning of the *Boyd*, a ship which had left the River Thames on 10 March 1809 with convicts bound for Australia and, having discharged her unwilling passengers at Sydney, had then proceeded to New Zealand to load timber. There she was attacked by Maoris and the crew killed or captured. Then, and the aspect of the encounter which most horrified Europeans, 'the victorious party proceed[ed] invariably to that most dreadful consummation, the tearing to pieces and devouring the flesh of their unfortunate captives.'[4] Cannibalism excited particular horror, as it was one of the strongest European taboos. As was often the case the natives would suddenly, for whatever reason, stop killing their enemies and let them live; on this occasion they spared the lives of a woman, two children and a young boy. They were later rescued by another ship and were only too able to testify to the events. Indeed, Captain Cook had permitted Maoris to cook and eat human remains on board his ship in order that he could swear by the evidence of his own eyes that they were cannibals. The native New Zealanders had the most fearsome reputation and seemed always prepared to slaughter the crew of a ship if they could catch them off guard. The Maoris lived in fortified villages and were constantly at war, one tribe with another. On being chided by a European for eating a slain enemy, a Maori responded with the information that had his enemy been the victor it was he who would have been eaten. The Tahitians and Hawaiians denied ever being cannibals, and there is no evidence to suggest that they were: Polynesian culture appears to have lost most of its more brutal aspects as it migrated west.

But, apart from possible shipwreck and slaughter, there was a more immediate and mundane problem to overcome before these remote islands could be visited without undue threat to the well-being of all on board, sailors and scientists alike. The long voyages to such regions entailed the risk of sickness and death from scurvy. Even in the late eighteenth century this was still a problem. Indeed, it was these new long voyages far from home which had created the problem. The enfeebled state of Captain Wallis and his crew when they discovered Tahiti was due to the same scourge. And yet, at one level the cure was simple – fresh vegetables. Their masters were beginning to learn to treat ordinary sailors as rather more important than expendable labour by paying more attention to hygiene, and by shortening their hours of work. In home waters sick or dead seamen could be replaced; on a long voyage where a ship was to be away for two or even three years, letting men die through neglect and indifference could jeopardise the safety of the ship. Long voyages remained the hard and dangerous experience they had ever been, and men continued to suffer from scurvy on badly managed ships, but one lethal consequence of long weeks at sea was no longer inevitable.

The discovery of Tahiti in the south Pacific and then Hawaii in the north Pacific meant that European sailors now knew certain landfalls where they were sure of receiving virtually all the fresh provisions they required. The great expanse of the Pacific no longer had to be crossed unaided and unsupplied. Not only was there plenty of food to be had (not always so with small coral islands where food was often barely sufficient for the inhabitants), but the occupants were normally friendly and welcoming. Europeans could now travel and occupy the area; and they started to do so with scientific discovery in mind.

Chapter 4

TAHITI: SAILORS AND SCIENTISTS

This may well be called the Cytheria of the southern hemisphere, not only from the beauty and elegance of the women . . . what poetic fiction had presented of Eden, or Arcadia, is here realised . . . and the fair ones ever willing to fill your arms with love.

George Hamilton, surgeon on HMS Pandora 1790–2

C aptain Wallis returned to England knowing that this new land was not the Unknown Continent he had been sent into the South Seas to find. But to be so plentifully supplied with fresh produce of all kinds from just one location was an immense advantage which in itself made Tahiti an important discovery. Many of the small islands and archipelagos throughout the Pacific had enough food only for themselves and so could supply ships with very limited provisions. In addition, after the initial clash the islanders were far friendlier and less warlike than the inhabitants of many other Pacific islands. But that was about all that was known. The British had learned little or nothing of the social and political organisation of the island apart from the evident authority of the female chief they encountered, whom they took to be the queen, for they did not realise that the island was split into many chiefdoms. Nor had they learnt anything of the social structure, or of the islanders' religion and beliefs. To a captain and crew sick with scurvy who had spent months surviving on a diet of salt beef, biscuit and lentils, those latter questions were of considerably less interest than fresh food, safety ashore and the complaisant women they had found.

Scientists, however, were concerned with other issues. As was mentioned earlier, scientific opinion held that there must be a substantial landmass in the southern hemisphere to balance that in the northern hemisphere; a good logical and mathematical deduction which was to have ships sailing across mile after mile of empty ocean for year after year before the theoreticians in their studies – it would be an affront to call them ivory towers – became convinced of their error. The search for this supposed continent was, of course, partly stimulated by the prospect that it might contain a variety of riches and commercial opportunities, but was also motivated by a scientific drive to know more about the world, to be able to measure it more accurately and to examine and classify its natural phenomena. At the time Wallis discovered Tahiti, plans were being formulated in London to send a scientific expedition into the Pacific, where it would set up a base on some suitable island, in order to observe the transit of the planet Venus across the face of the sun. The transit of Venus, properly measured, would allow astronomers to calculate its distance from the earth and, as progress in the science of navigation depended on ever more accurate knowledge of the stars and planets, it was urged as a practical benefit. The Royal Society persuaded the Admiralty, through an appeal to the king, to make a ship available for the expedition. They also pointed out that virtually all the great powers of Europe were setting up observatories for this same purpose and that Britain could not afford to fall behind in a branch of science so closely linked to navigation and to the efficiency of the navy. King George III needed little persuasion. He had come to the throne in 1760 as a young man of twenty and was an enthusiastic supporter of voyages of discovery and scientific progress. In 1761 Britain had sent one expedition to St Helena to observe an earlier transit of Venus across the face of the sun – without result, for the day had proved overcast. Another expedition had been despatched to Sumatra for the same purpose, but that had remained stuck at Cape Town owing to the danger posed by the French fleet during the Seven Years War (1756–63). The year 1769 was calculated to afford the last opportunity for a long time to measure this astronomical event (it would not occur again until 1874).

This time the authorities decided to send three expeditions; one to Hudson's Bay, another to North Cape in Norway, and a third to the south Pacific. However, just where in the south Pacific was difficult to decide. The Solomon Islands and the Marquesas had been discovered by the Spanish in the late sixteenth century but no one had reported seeing them since. No one could even be absolutely sure that they existed as it would not have been the first or last time that mariners, desperate to send word of some success to their backers, had reported land where none existed. If these island groups existed (as they did), there was no guarantee that an expedition would find them again as given the earlier period's low level of navigational technology, discoveries were liable to have been recorded in wildly inaccurate positions. And even if found in time and their locations proved suitable to make the observation, there was no guarantee either that the natives would not be unremittingly hostile. Captain Wallis's discovery of Tahiti solved the problem. He had been able to set up his instruments ashore and to fix the position of Tahiti with sufficient accuracy to ensure that it would easily be found again. Tahiti's ability to supply abundant provisions and the friendship exhibited at Wallis's departure convinced the British that this island would be the most suitable base for their observatory in the South Seas.

James Cook was chosen to command the voyage. And, exceptionally, in an era when patronage was vital for securing employment and in the army commissions and promotions were bought and sold as were benefices in the Church of England, James Cook was selected on merit. For, although many an army officer of the period needed to know little more than how to die bravely, handling a sailing ship called for competence over a range of skills. Patronage played its part in the navy too, but even the most aristocratic and privileged entrants started as midshipmen and learned the duties of a seaman aloft and below. But, of course, those destined for high command because of birth and family connections were not necessarily the best seamen and navigators, if only because their promotions were so rapid that they never thoroughly mastered every branch of seamanship. Like high-ranking army officers, they were there to command rather than to grapple with everyday tasks. But any ship needed expert handling if it was not to founder in foul weather at sea or to be wrecked onshore. The responsibility for handling the ship safely was the business of the ship's master, a separate and distinct position from that of ship's captain. This distinction was rooted in history dating from when kings had few specially built men-of-war, hiring merchant vessels to serve as ships of war as and when they were needed. These ships were hired with their civilian master and crew who actually navigated and worked the ship, while the captain of the soldiers put on board to do the fighting commanded the ship in the military sense of ordering where it went and which enemy it engaged. Hence, in the eighteenth century a man-of-war carried both, a captain and a master.

The captain was in supreme charge and his responsibilities were awesome; it should be remembered that in those days it could take a year or longer for a government to reply to a message or query from a captain. For example, when Captain Cook was killed it took a year for the news to reach London, having been sent via Alaska, across Siberia, Russia and Europe. Captains needed to exercise discretion in following their own judgement. Effectively acting as diplomats in distant parts of the globe, laying title to newly discovered lands or by defending British interests against a foreign ship, an ill-judged step could risk starting a war. In general, they had to be the embodiment of their country, so it was not surprising that important and sensitive commands were often given to admirals whose families were part of, or connected to, the class that also controlled government.

Ships' masters were drawn from an entirely different social class. They did not hold commissions, they were mere warrant officers. Responsible for ensuring that the hull was sound, and maintaining and working the masts, rigging and sails, they did everything that the captain of a merchant ship would do. Often they had gone to sea as sailors in the Royal or Merchant Navies, working up to be masters' mates and boatswains, and often master's rank was as far as they progressed in the Royal Navy. After six years of naval service, they were permitted to sit an examination and receive their commission as lieutenants, but this usually required the patronage of someone of influence with the Admiralty, and it also meant a drop in pay.

When chosen for this important voyage James Cook was not even a commissioned officer. Born the son of a farm labourer, he had worked his way up to become a ship's officer in the coastwise trade carrying coal from the Tyne to London. An honest occupation and no small achievement, but in June 1755 he threw that away and volunteered for the Royal Navy as an able seaman. In the days when the press-gang was necessary to crew His Majesty's Navy, volunteers as capable as Cook were rare, and he took a calculated risk in hopes of quick promotion. The risk paid off as he rapidly worked his way up to master's mate and then master – warrant officer rank – and while serving in that capacity in Newfoundland and Canada, earned a high reputation as a skilled navigator and chart-maker. He had played a leading part, too, in navigating and charting the route up the St Lawrence River which enabled the British under General Wolfe to move their troops up river and capture Quebec. By a strange coincidence Louis de Bougainville, who was to precede him to Tahiti and the South Seas, was fighting with the French as aide-de-camp to General Montcalm and acquitted himself with great bravery against the British. Cook's more mundane although perhaps more valuable service in providing skilled pilotage, accurate charts and maps was recognised by some senior officers seamen enough to appreciate the skills and ability these tasks required.

Cook never stopped studying and improving his knowledge of astronomy and mathematics to add to his practical abilities. He was given command of a small vessel and employed to chart the coast of Newfoundland. It was, for much of the time, hard, cold and dangerous work which called for an almost instinctive feel for shoals and rocks, tides and currents, something for which his years of working along the dangerous east coast of England had supremely fitted him. Although never given the lieutenant's commission his contribution to the victory over the French had merited, he was earning 10s a day as master (twice the pay he would have started at as a lieutenant) while his independent command allowed him to return home to his wife and family regularly. His charts were being published and his reputation as a surveyor of exceptional ability was growing.

The vessel chosen for the voyage was a lowly merchant ship. Small, slow and lightly armed she would not attract 'gentlemen' captains eager for command of larger men-of-war with their opportunity for winning glory and taking prizes. She was, in fact, a Whitby cat of the type in which Cook had learned his trade. The task ahead also called for a competent navigator, surveyor, chart-maker and astronomer; the commander had to be steady and diligent – it was a command tailor-made for Cook. However, he was still only a warrant officer and already forty years old, but his sheer ability had won him supporters in the Admiralty and after due consideration he was commissioned lieutenant on 25 May 1768. Two days later he took command of the *Endeavour*.

The ship chosen for the voyage was specially bought by the Admiralty for its strength and capacity rather than for speed for she had capacious holds and a flat bottom which could safely take the ground. In round figures she was 106ft long overall, 98ft along her lower deck and 29ft at her widest. She was rated at 369 tons and drew 14ft of water fully laden. The Admiralty refitted her with unaccustomed care and expense. The most essential work was to protect her hull from the teredo worm found in tropical waters and which could bore its way through the ship's timbers, destroying their strength. As a protection those timbers were covered with tarred felt and with thinner planking fitted over that, the outside planking itself being further protected by large flat-headed nails. Thus the worms had few chances of finding the outer planking and, when they did, they would be deterred from attacking the inner planking by the layer of tarred canvas. In the event of the outer planks becoming too worm-eaten to provide protection, they could be replaced without great difficulty. The size of the ship meant that she could be beached if necessary and careened to clean and repair her bottom, in a way which a larger man-of-war, such as a frigate, could not.

Originally it was planned to have a complement of seventy men, a large number for such a ship; but, as seemed almost inevitable on most of these voyages, this was increased to eighty-five, thus adding to the overcrowding. The crew came from all corners of the British Isles with the odd stray hand from America, Venice and Brazil. Admiralty instructions ordered Cook to leave London for Portsmouth where his crew would receive an advance on their wages to permit them to buy whatever they needed for the voyage. Able seamen were paid £1 4s 8d a calendar month, which was not very generous even by the standards of the day, but the advance would have been welcome. In order to discourage men from deserting it was customary to withhold six months' pay, and it was not unusual for men to be owed two or more years' wages. Cook objected to enrolling only one man sent, a cook who had had his right hand amputated, but he had to accept him because maimed seamen were given preferential treatment in that capacity: it saved the Admiralty from paying them a pension. Two of Cook's signings may well have drawn objections from the Admiralty had not custom meant that they turned a blind eye to what was common practice. Cook signed on his two sons, one a servant to Second Lieutenant Hicks and the other as an able seaman, the two being aged six and five at the time and not intended to cruise beyond their mother's apron strings. It meant, however, that if they did choose to make the navy their career and really did go to sea at fourteen or fifteen they would be able to sit their examination for second lieutenant in a very short time because they would have – on paper at least – the requisite number of years' service.

Apart from the crew there was the scientific party among whom the outstanding figure was Joseph Banks. He was the moving spirit behind the enterprise for it may never have been organised but for his commitment. Only twenty-five years old, Banks was already a Fellow of the Royal Society and a rich man able to indulge his taste for travel and botany. He was reputed to have spent £10,000 of his own money on the expedition; he went at his own expense and paid for his party. This consisted of two artists, one particularly skilled in botanical drawing which was absolutely essential for recording the details of all the varied specimens of fish, birds, animals and plants they would encounter, the other more adept at figure painting and landscape; a secretary (no sinecure given the labour involved with quill and ink); and four servants, two of whom were negroes. Dr Solander, a Swedish botanist who had studied under the famous Linnaeus, and like Banks, a Fellow of the Royal Society, accompanied him. With them went all the paraphernalia necessary for capturing, preserving and storing their specimens. The Royal Society appointed Mr Green as the astronomer of the party.

Captain Cook's orders instructed him to win the friendship of the natives and to treat them well, while being on his guard against treachery. Further orders were contained in a sealed package which instructed him that on leaving Tahiti he was to proceed south in order to search for the Southern Continent. If found, he was instructed to chart it, to bring back information on the fertility of the soil and what it produced, and to make descriptions of the flora and fauna and to collect the seeds of all the native trees and plants. If it were inhabited, he was to form an alliance and trade with the inhabitants and to take possession of it in the name of the King of Great Britain: no mean ambition for one small ship and less than a hundred men. If he did not find the Southern Continent, the orders continued, he was to explore as much of New Zealand as the condition of the ship, the health of his crew and their remaining supplies would permit. Before returning he was to confiscate any journals that had been kept and forbid the crew to say where they had been in order to keep their discoveries secret until the Admiralty was ready to publish them.

In addition to his official instructions, a plea came to him and to the other officers and gentlemen of the party from Lord Morton, President of the Royal Society. This is interesting because it is indicative of a change in opinion as to how the inhabitants of newly discovered lands should be treated: the expedition leaders were urged

To exercise the utmost patience and forebearance with respect to the Natives of the several Lands where the Ship may touch. To check the petulance of the Sailors, and restrain from the wanton use of Fire Arms. To have it still in view that sheding the blood of those people is a crime of the highest nature . . . They are the natural, and in the strictest sense of the word, the legal possessors of the Several regions they inhabit . . . They may naturally and justly attempt to repell intruders, whom they may apprehend are come to disturb them in the quiet possession of their country.[2]

Given that the African slave trade was then at its height with all that that implies in terms of human degradation and the inhuman way in which Europeans were prepared to view and treat those with black skins, it shows a profound change in attitude towards the inhabitants of these new discoveries and of lands yet to be found. It is noteworthy that similar sentiments were included in instructions given to French and Spanish expeditions around this period.

With this injunction to treat the natives well, on 30 July 1768 the *Endeavour* sailed out of the Thames for Plymouth. From there, after some additional work on the vessel and a delay caused by unfavourable winds, they set sail on 25 August. As was not unusual, shortly after sailing they encountered a westerly gale which carried away one of the boats and several dozen poultry. Happily, a goat that had survived the entire voyage with Captain Wallis and had been embarked again to supply the officers with milk proved old salt enough to keep safe. They arrived at Funchal on 12 September where they loaded over 3,000 gallons of wine and replenished their stores of water and food. Each man was also issued with 30lb of onions against the scurvy. In theory the food allocation in the navy was plentiful enough as each man was given a daily ration of 1lb of biscuit, and allowed either 1lb of salt pork or 2lb of salt beef on alternate days, and there was a seemingly adequate weekly issue of dried lentil and oatmeal. While it lasted there was also a ration of butter and cheese. In home waters men received a gallon of beer a day. On long voyages to the south a pint of wine or half a pint of brandy or rum was issued instead of beer; similarly, rice and olive oil would replace other unobtainable items. In fact the captain could order rations to be cut at any time, and the actual amount of food issued often bore little resemblance to the official scale. Food was often issued on the basis of six rations for eight men, or even four rations for eight men, thus cutting the scale in half. This might be the result of the length of time a voyage was taking and the need to preserve some supplies against unforeseen circumstances, but it was often perceived by the crew as a means of putting money in the purser's pocket. The quality of the food was also often inferior, the meat being tainted or mostly bone so that quantities did not reflect what was actually edible, as a result of corruption practised between the contractors who supplied the food and the naval dockyards.

At Funchal a master's mate was drowned while anchoring and a replacement was impressed from an American ship which happened to be in harbour at the time: such was often the fate of seamen. The unfortunate American doubtless lost all his back pay from his previous employment and any hopes of seeing his homeland for years. After six days in harbour they sailed. They crossed the equator on 25 October and Cook allowed the 'Ancient Custom of the Sea' when all those who had never crossed the Line were ducked in the ocean, the officers and gentlemen of the party being permitted to buy their exemption with bottles of rum. In all it was a rather drunken frolic: not a bad way of relieving tensions and settling in the crew. Cook was to permit similar occasions and, if at sea on Christmas day for example, would take in all sail and let the crew get as drunk as they cared to. 'Cook, although he was a disciplinarian, never bothered to struggle against the inevitable.'[3] With a ration of half a pint of spirits a day it was easy for seamen to save a little each day until they had enough for a binge.

They had pleasant sailing on their run to Rio de Janeiro where they arrived on 13 November. While there four men were flogged and another drowned – he being replaced by a Portuguese from Rio. On 7 December they were again at sea headed for Cape Horn. Cook anchored on the east side of Tierra del Fuego from 15 to 20 January 1769 and the crew cut wood, refilled the water casks, and collected quantities of wild celery to add to their diet against scurvy, while the scientists went ashore botanising. There they encountered a few natives to whom they gave beads and whom Cook, in common with most previous observers, described as the most miserable of people. In spite of icy winds and snow the men were naked and the women scarcely less so. The freezing weather caused another tragedy. Joseph Banks and his servants lost their way while exploring and were obliged to spend the night ashore without proper shelter, as a result of which his two negro servants froze to death. Cook, as usual, spent his time charting the coast. And then, eighty-three days after leaving Tierra del Fuego, they hove to in Matavai Bay, Tahiti.

In terms of the general health of the crew it had been a good voyage. Cook had been unlucky to lose four men in accidents, and just before they arrived at Tahiti a marine committed suicide overboard after being harassed by his companions for a petty theft. His miserable and lonely death underlines how powerful was the will of the crew: once one was excluded from the collective fellowship the prospect of spending months, or even years, as the butt of others could make life insupportable. But the rest of the crew were healthy and it was quite exceptional that none had suffered from scurvy or died of sickness. The care Cook took of his men, and his insistence that they eat fresh foods where possible, had had a noticeable beneficial effect. Seamen were conservative where food was concerned and often preferred their customary diet of salt beef and ship's biscuit to fresh food. Back at Funchal a live bullock had been purchased, and one seaman and a marine had each received twelve lashes for refusing to accept their meat ration as *fresh* beef. Later in the voyage Cook opted for other means than flogging to make them eat what he deemed good for them:

The Sour Krout the Men at first would not eate untill I put in practice a Method I never once knew to fail with seamen, and this was to have some of it dress'd every Day for the Cabbin Table, and permitted all the Officers without exception to make use of it and left it to the option of the Men either to take as much as they pleased or none at all; but this practice was not continued above a week before I found it necessary to put every one on board to an Allowance, for such are the Tempers and disposissions of Seamen in general that whatever you give them out of the Common way, altho it every so much for their good yet it will not go down with them and you will hear nothing but murmurings gainst the man that first invented it; but the Moment they see their Superiors set a Value upon it, it becomes the finest stuff in the World and the inventor a damn'd honest fellow.[4]

This judicious mixture of persuasion and indulgence in permitting the occasional drunkenness rather than relying on flogging (although he never hesitated to use that as well, resorting to the cat-o'-nine-tails more frequently than the infamous Captain Bligh) meant that Cook was particularly successful in winning the respect and loyalty of his men. That he was a superb seaman gave them the added confidence that if anyone could take them into the unknown and bring them back alive, it was he. Confidence in their commander was an invaluable asset in maintaining crew morale, and through that, crew discipline. Captain James Cook was to command three expeditions to the Pacific and in addition to earning the loyalty of his crews was to merit his reputation as the world's foremost explorer. On this first voyage to the Pacific he ordered the anchor to be dropped on 13 April 1769, his first landfall on a Pacific island and his first contact with Polynesian society. It was just over eight months since they had left England: the first European sailors and scientists to be there by intent had arrived.

PART TWO

CAPTAIN COOK AND THE CONSEQUENCES

Chapter 5

RETURN TO TAHITI

All these visitors – perhaps intruders is a better word – were going to make their separate contribution to the transformation of the Tahitians, whether by firearms, disease or alcohol, or by imposing an alien code of laws and morals . . . at the time of Cook's arrival they were probably happier than they were ever to be again.

Alan Moorehead, The Fatal Impact *(1987)*[1]

At Matavai Bay the *Endeavour* anchored close to where the *Dolphin* had lain two years earlier. This renewed the British connection and it proved most successful as the Tahitians gave them an immediate welcome. Cook, his officers and crew, the scientists, artists and their assistants were to remain from 13 April to 13 July 1769, three months during which they had the time and initiative to learn a little of the language and a good deal more about the place and people.

The old Tahitian man who had been so useful to Captain Wallis as organiser of the trade in provisions recognised his opposite number, Mr Gore, who had sailed on the *Dolphin* and was again deputed to act in the same capacity. The experience of Captain Wallis had been that the Tahitians desired iron above all things, so the *Endeavour* was well supplied with nails and iron implements. Like Wallis, Cook also laid down the rule that no man was to trade for provisions, in order to protect the rate of exchange. No iron or cloth was to be bartered for anything other than food. Sailors being sailors and in reach of willing women, Captain Cook's restrictions on their using iron in return for favours granted were hard to enforce and, as with the *Dolphin*'s crew before them, the ship's company turned its hand to stealing nails, this time from the stores rather than from the ship itself. 'One of the theives [*sic*] was detected but only 7 nails were found upon him out of 100cwt and he bore his punishment without impeaching any of his accomplices. This loss is of a very serious nature as these nails if circulated by the people among the Indians will much lessen the value of Iron, our staple commodity.'[2]. Even allowing for whatever devaluation the sailors' actions caused they really had little reason to complain of the rate of exchange. One bead the size of a pea was sufficient to buy four to six coconuts or breadfruit, and one nail would buy twenty. Such nails were 4½in long and cost 3s 4d a hundred in England. Not that Cook was over impressed with breadfruit on first acquaintance, finding it rather sweet and tasting a bit like a mixture of wheat bread and Jerusalem artichoke. Joseph Banks, being less habituated to the hard tack than professional sailors, was in no mood to be critical. For when at one period during their stay supplies of breadfruit became scarce and they had to go back to eating ship's stores which were full of weevils, he wrote: 'But what makes any refreshments of this kind [breadfruit] the more acceptable is that our bread is at present so full of vermin that notwithstanding all possible care I have sometimes had 20 at a time in my mouth, every one of which tasted as hot as mustard.'³ Such was already the rotten state of the stores on which they would have to live for month after month throughout the rest of the long voyage of exploration and on their return journey.

Joseph Banks was the expedition member who showed most confidence in the natives and who immediately took a walk inland to search for the 'palace' of the queen, and the queen herself, but found no trace of either. Obearea, whom Captain Wallis had taken to be the queen of the island, had been only a chief and Banks learned that Tootahah, the present chief of the district, lived 3 miles down the coast. Cook, Banks and some others then had themselves rowed down the coast to meet the chief, to exchange presents and generally to try to establish the right atmosphere for their intended stay. They were received with great ceremony and friendliness and it was quite clear that they were welcome. If not for their own sake they were valued as the one source of iron, and for their possession of the awe-inspiring technology of firearms. Like governments all over the world the local chief hoped to acquire this priceless metal and these superior weapons for himself. Once the formal welcome was over the women made themselves available with customary generosity: 'After this ceremony was over we walked freely about several large houses attended by the ladies who showd us all kind of civilities our situation would admit of, but as there were no places of retirement, the houses being intirely without walls, we had not an opportunity of putting their politeness to every test.'⁴. The women sometimes forced them on to their sleeping mats in the houses but, by Banks's word, they were all too shy to take advantage.

They may have held back on that occasion, but Captain Cook is reputed to have been the only man who did not have a Tahitian mistress. Certainly, most did not hesitate for long and the first case of venereal disease among the crew of the *Endeavour* was reported five days after the ship's arrival, so it must have been caught virtually on the first day. By the time they left half the crew had been infected. The islands had been free of this scourge before the Europeans discovered them. When Cook reported this on his return to England it started an argument about who was responsible. Captain Samuel Wallis was adamant that none of his men contracted the disease there, nor did they take it there: 'the reproach of having contaminated with that dreadful pest, to a race of happy people, to whom its miseries had till then been unknown, must be due either to him [Bougainville] or to me, to England or to France; and I think myself happy to be able to exculpate myself and my country beyond the possibility of doubt.'[5] He makes a good case. On the outward voyage of the *Dolphin* the last man on the sick list was discharged on 27 December 1766, some six months before arriving at Tahiti; the first man to go sick with venereal symptoms was on 26 February 1768 six months after leaving Tahiti, and the man was known to have been infected in Cape Town. It is only just, however, to acknowledge that Bougainville was equally certain that his crew were not responsible. One of them was mistaken.

If erotic pleasures were an easily available and a habitual part of Tahitian behaviour the Europeans were also immediately subjected to another persistent dimension of Polynesian society – theft. During the entertainment and banquet given on their first visit to the chief two of the party had their pockets picked and lost a pair of opera glasses and a snuff box. The chief gave orders for these items to be returned and they duly were – save that only the empty case of the opera glasses was returned and not the glasses. Joseph Banks took a very firm line on this and showed that he was not prepared to overlook the theft, so eventually the chief took Banks a mile to recover the lost articles from the thief. Yet even then Banks was obliged to give a few beads as a present to ensure their return. Incidents like this give grounds to question the usual claim of the absolute power of the chiefs – the right to life and death – when they had so much difficulty in making their subjects obey them in even a small affair such as this. Unless, of course, the chief was party to the thefts.

Once they had cemented relations with the chief the British set about securing themselves ashore. They built a fort taking advantage of the sea and the river, as Wallis had done, to enclose a space where they not only secured their water supply, but also established a defensible refuge for those working ashore should the need arise. It was also the base for the astronomical observations. In setting up the fort they took every precaution not to offend the natives and did not cut down so much as a bush without specific permission and prior purchase of all the trees they felled and used. Captain Cook did his best to maintain good relations and the crew was forbidden to cheat, molest, or strike a native in any way whatsoever. When a group of natives complained to him that one of his crew had threatened to kill a woman because she refused to part with a stone axe he coveted, Cook invited the offended natives on board to witness the man's punishment in order that they should know that he was willing to protect them and their interests. The Tahitians watched with some puzzlement as the offender was tied up to the rigging, but with the first stroke of the cat-o'-nine-tails they were so horrified that they burst into tears and begged that the punishment end. Cook refused their request. That these people were so surprised and shocked demonstrates that they were quite unused to the cruel punishments which were so commonplace in Europe. That the whole affair was caused by a sailor's determination to obtain a stone axe also suggests that the seamen were aware that such exotic items could be sold at a great profit back in Britain.

But theft remained a constant problem and the ship had been there for only two days when a native was shot and killed while running off with a musket he had snatched from a sentry. This gave Joseph Banks an opportunity to observe the Tahitians' burial customs and for a little scientific observation: 'I visited the Tomb or Bier in which was deposited the body of the man who was shot. I lifted up the cloth and saw part of the body already dropping to peices [sic] with putrefaction about him and indeed within all parts of his flesh were abundance of maggots of a species of Beetle very common here. Such an advance of putrefaction in 8 days for it was no more since he was shot is almost past credit but what will not a hot climate and plenty of insects do.'[6] Given their custom of exposing the dead until there was just the skeleton remaining it is not surprising that Banks complained that flies were an absolute nuisance. His artists were obliged to paint enclosed in mosquito nets which covered them, their easels and their specimens, as the flies would otherwise eat the paint from the paper and totally cover the fish or other specimen being recorded.

At the beginning of May the expedition suffered a disaster. The astronomical quadrant with which they were to take their observations of Venus, a major aim of the whole enterprise, was stolen. It had been stored in a hut which had a continuous marine guard, and that hut was within the fort which was also continually guarded by sentries. It was not a theft which could be ignored; the object had to be recovered whatever the cost in good relations. Banks was a favourite of the Tahitians and was fearless in going alone among them. He set off in hot pursuit but without success and eventually sent back for reinforcements because he was afraid that he might be passing into the territory of a different chief and of encountering a population who had not seen Europeans before.

Back at the fort and ship Cook ordered the detention of some of the chief Tahitians to serve as hostages for the return of the quadrant. This had the desired effect: the quadrant was returned, a little bent, but reparable. Chief Tootahah, however, complained of rough handling by the ship's boatswain when he was detained – an incredible insult and loss of face, for chiefs were held to be sacred by their people. Once released he ordered them not to trade with Cook or his men. The British were left isolated; no one came to trade provisions the next day, or the day after, or the day after that. On the fourth day, Mr Banks managed to purchase a few breadfruit as a personal favour, but it was clear that the British could not expect food from anyone unless they could regain the goodwill of the chief. On the fifth day, Captain Cook, Banks and others were obliged to visit the chief with suitable gifts, apologise and sue for his goodwill. He received them seated in dignity and, in full view of hundreds of his people, accepted their presents – more likely viewed as tribute – but did not display any warmth towards them. They had been promised a dinner with the chief, but he changed his mind and although the food was cooked he ordered that the dinner must take place on the ship. Captain Cook and his party had no choice but to obey and instead of being feasted as honoured guests by the chief in front of his people, they were obliged to leave the chief's residence without the customary hospitality of being offered food, and to return to their ship to honour the chief as their guest. Having demonstrated his power – to the Europeans as well as to his own people – and after being given yet more gifts the chief was eventually satisfied. This reconciliation had immediate effect for as soon as his people knew that their chief was on board ship they recommenced the supply of every kind of provisions. At the time the British were unaware of it, but they had just felt the force of a chief's right to impose a taboo – in this case forbidding any supply of food until the insult to him was expunged – which because it had religious as well as secular force few people would break.

Nevertheless, thefts continued to be the main source of friction: while working ashore every tool and item of equipment had to be constantly watched and protected. Finally, bedevilled by a stream of petty thefts, Cook impounded twenty-five large canoes which had arrived from another island loaded with semi-cured fish, refusing to release them until a long list of stolen goods was returned. This was a policy unpopular with everyone as it was clearly unjust to penalise the owners of the canoes, who had had nothing to do with the thefts. The result was the return of some of the items, a breach with the chief and the imposition of a taboo against trading with the Europeans which once more immediately cut supplies. Again Cook was obliged to seek the chief's goodwill and conciliate him. No European ever worked out a really satisfactory method of dealing with theft; failure to do so was eventually to cost Captain Cook his life.

While they were at Tahiti Cook and Banks circumnavigated the island in a pinnace and Cook, industrious as ever, made a chart of the island. Before they left the area Cook also sailed to the other islands in the group, now known as the Society Islands, and found that although the islands were frequently at war with each other they shared the same culture. Moving around the island, they saw for the first time the great *marae*, a large level area which had been walled and the walled area filled with earth like a terrace and which was used for religious ceremonies. The one which they came across was the largest in Tahiti and was of recent construction, showing that the culture was still vigorous. This particular *marae* had a series of eleven terraces, each one set within the the one beneath so that it was stepped rather like an Aztec pyramid, each step some 4ft high. Its sides at ground level measured 267 by 71ft and were faced in white coral squared into slabs. The upper terrace was paved with coral. The amount of earth which had had to be carried (for they had no wheeled vehicles) to fill this area, and the amount of coral which had had to be cut and shaped without metal tools, reveals a considerable amount of collective energy. The party also saw evidence that warfare was common on the island for at a number of places human jawbones were hanging up as trophies of war; something they were to see again in greater profusion at the islands of Raiatea and Bora Bora which had recently been at war. According to some accounts, battles were brief and bloody and if their chief was killed his warriors immediately fled and, although life was rarely spared during the fighting or for a few hours afterwards, the slaughter was brief; but other accounts state that the victorious side devastated the lands of the defeated, killing women and children without mercy. How wars were conducted before the arrival of Europeans is difficult to ascertain. For example, Cook tried to discover how many casualties the Tahitians had suffered from their fight with the *Dolphin*; some said ten, others up to thirty, while still others used an expression meaning 'hundreds'.[7] Whatever the number, it was evident that European superiority in terms of weapons of war had made a strong impression and kept the Tahitians from molesting them.

Most of what the Europeans learned of Tahiti was gained by direct observation and experience. One of the first things they noticed was that some items of Tahitian manufacture were better than anything produced in Europe. Tahitian fishing lines were much admired as being finer and stronger than the best silk ones of British manufacture, as was the Tahitians' skill in shaping their huge canoes without iron tools and their ability to bind the planks into a watertight whole. They were also made aware of their own low standards of personal hygiene. Eighteenth-century Europeans were not noted for their fondness for soap and water so the cleanliness of the Tahitians came as a revelation: they washed twice a day in running water and were prepared to go quite a long distance to find a suitable stream for their ablutions.

Some activities, however, were not so self-evident and trying to interpret actions with only a limited, albeit growing, command of the language was still a formidable barrier to understanding. The Europeans saw that houses had no walls and nothing was guarded and yet there was apparently no, or very little, theft among the native inhabitants, so it was clear that strangers came under a different moral code. One puzzle is how the Tahitians had learned to steal objects from a person's pocket more skilfully than even London pickpockets. George Forster speculated that there was little theft within the community because it was a society with no money and everyone was fed and clothed in much the same way. He wrote that there was less difference in living standards between the highest and the lowest in Tahiti than there was between a tradesman and a labourer in England. Indeed, his observations and those of others convinced them that it was a society with very little crime of any sort and even fewer punishments. Joseph Banks noticed that food had to be shared even by the most powerful in the land, and during a shortage of meat, wrote that 'Even their most principal people have it not every day or even week, tho some of them had piggs that we saw quartered on different Estates . . . when any of these kill a hog it seems to be divided almost equally among all his dependants himself taking little more than the rest',[8] a startling difference from European custom where the tables of the aristocrats groaned under the weight of luxurious food while many of the poor lived with the pangs of perpetual hunger. Rather strangely, Cook and his men were not introduced to kava, the one intoxicating drink, which was drunk mainly by the chiefs. They believed that the Tahitians drank nothing but water and coconut milk. Unlike the stereotype of natives being introduced to alcohol for the first time and immediately becoming addicted to and made frenzied by 'firewater', most Tahitians disliked its taste, whether wine or spirits, and very few would touch it after their first taste.

Abstract ideas and religious beliefs are virtually impossible to grasp without a full command of language, and a month after his arrival Banks was still unsure whether Tahitians had any form of religion: a strange blindness in a country where religious taboos permeated every aspect of daily life, nor did he realise his error before he left. Yet he was so liked by the people that a priest connived with him so that he could take part in and observe a mourning ceremony. This involved stripping naked and being covered with blacking along with the female mourners to join the procession. Ceremonies of death and burial were religious in Europe so the parallel should have been easy to draw. But, without language, it is difficult to distinguish between religious belief and social custom. It was noted that 'The men who visit us constantly eat with us of our provisions, but the women never had been prevailed on to taste a morsel; today however they retired sometime after dinner into the servants apartment and eat there a large quantity of plantains, tho they could not be persuaded to eat with us, a mystery we find very difficult to account for.'⁹ Clearly it was not yet realised that this refusal to eat was an example of religious observance which forbade men and women to eat together. To the Tahitians men were sacred and women were secular. In Tahiti the gender divisions went deeply into everyday life and behaviour. Because food went inside the body it was potentially the most polluting substance, so men could not eat food prepared by women. Also certain foodstuffs were the food of male gods and could be eaten only by men.

Given the length of time the British were on the island it is surprising that they seem to have had few encounters with the activities of the *ariori*. The *ariori* were members of a society, which was joined by selection, and although recruited mainly from the chiefly classes, was open to all and selected its members, male and female, mainly for their physical beauty and skills in dance and drama. They were responsible for the sexually explicit displays for which they are mainly remembered. In fact the *ariori* were so important a part of Tahitian culture that they lived at public expense in return for their religious services and their role as entertainers. There was complete sexual liberty between members, who were not allowed any descendants, any babies born to them being killed at birth. If any of them decided to keep a child he or she was expelled from the order. The journals from the *Endeavour's* visit do not refer to any outrageously indecent displays – Banks mentions coming across a group of five male *ariori* whom he regarded as strolling players, although he was aware that being an *ariori* gave certain privileges and penalties. Nevertheless he failed to appreciate just how deeply the *ariori* were involved in religious ritual and life.

The British detected no separate profession of doctors, very little in the way of medicine and disease and felt that such contagions as there were existed in only mild forms, with the exception of yaws. These were open tropical ulcers and people who had them seemed simply to ignore them and attempt no remedies. There was also a mild form of leprosy which was recognised to be contagious so that those who suffered from it were obliged to live in houses built in remote places although they were supplied with food by the rest of the community. It was evident that society cared for the sick. The treatment came from priests and relied on prayers and ceremonies. 'If he [the patient] recovers, they say the remedies cured him, if he dies, they say the disease was incurable, in which perhaps they do not much differ from the custom of other countries.'[10] Like their medical contemporaries in Europe, the Tahitians also bled people, presumably the harm done to the patient being similar in both parts of the world. The priests also had a monopoly of tattooing and male circumcision: the first was done for ritual reasons and personal ornament and the second for hygiene: 'Circumcision had been adopted merely from the motives of cleanliness; it cannot indeed properly be called circumcision, because the prepuce is not mutilated by a circular wound, but only slit through the upper part to prevent its contracting over the glans.'[11] It was a disgrace to bear neither tattoos nor the marks of circumcision. But the new maladies imported by the Europeans neither priests, prayers nor customary hygiene could cure.

If this first deliberate British expedition to Tahiti gained only limited knowledge of the language, religion and culture, it did reach some conclusions about the physical aspects of the place. The foremost consideration was that the size and fertility of the island made it a sure source of provisions for any ship calling there. It was ideally located to refresh weary crews after their rounding of Cape Horn and had a healthy climate. It was in the interests of a maritime power such as Britain to cultivate good relations with the inhabitants. On their side the inhabitants were equally keen that the British should return. Four years later, during his epic voyage into Antarctic waters in search of the Southern Continent, Captain Cook twice returned to Tahiti to refresh his crews; he also stayed there for six weeks on his third and final voyage. By this time he, and a number of officers and men who repeatedly sailed with him, had become familiar with the language and were more at home in Tahitian society. In Europe their accounts of Tahitian life fed the European imagination: the free sexuality of the people was to prove grist to the mill of the Romantic Movement, and the breadfruit tree was seen as manna for those who wanted cheap food in other parts of the tropics. After Cook's voyages of exploration and scientific enquiry it was the breadfruit tree which was to provide the next major contact and significant change in the island's affairs by Europeans. Cook noticed that their visits had had an irreversible effect on the islanders in that they now relied on iron tools – one never saw a stone or bone chisel and traditional stone axes had become a rarity. He already felt that the islanders would come to regret the European intrusion into their lives.

In 1789, twelve years after Captain Cook's last visit, the island was to play host to Captain William Bligh and the crew of HMS *Bounty* for five months while they collected and potted their breadfruit trees. After the mutiny a number of the crew – some mutineers and others whom the mutineers detained – lived on Tahiti for nearly two years, before they were captured by the infamous Captain Edwards and transported on HMS *Pandora*. A year later, in 1792, Captain Bligh returned, again to collect breadfruit trees for transplanting in the West Indies, but this time with two ships and a complement of marines to guard against mutiny. These repeated visits inevitably had an impact on individuals both on ship and ashore. But what of Tahitian society itself? The journals and records left by those sailors and scientists who stayed long enough to learn something of the natives' daily lives, especially from the long stay of Captain Cook and those who sailed with him, and of Captain Bligh and the mutineers who lived there contain much information on traditional Tahitian life. These sources have been greatly expanded by the work of anthropologists and historians and it is from this amalgam that descriptions of Tahitian society as it was before the arrival of European missionaries are drawn. Although the increasing contact with sailors and the growing number of traders, deserters and other flotsam and jetsam of the maritime world inevitably had some effect on traditional society, the change was slow and unintended, as, on the whole, the sailors were quite happy to leave Tahiti as it was, and the scientists likewise to do their work and leave. Once the missionaries arrived it was a different story. Because they came with the sole intention of destroying traditional Tahitian religion, customs and values, theirs is a tale which requires separate telling.

Chapter 6

TAHITI AND THE TAHITIANS

In fact Tahitian life generally was pervaded by the most exemplary love, attachment, respect, obedience, filial duty, serenity, good taste, and felicity.
J.C. Beaglehole, The Endeavour Journal of Joseph Banks . . . *(1962)*

Tahiti is only one among the group of what are now known as the Society Islands – Mo'orea, Huahine, Bora Bora, Raiatea, Tahaa and Tahiti were the main ones – which spread over 200 miles of ocean. Tahiti is the largest and was the one most frequently visited by Europeans and it became the best known and recorded, although Mo'orea, nearest to Tahiti, is only 9 miles away and its people were much involved in Tahitian society, politics and wars. Tahiti suffered the most frequent and intense European penetration, so its culture and fate can serve as an example and a precedent for the fate of the remoter islands.

Tahiti itself is shaped rather like an hour glass with two large, mountainous, circular areas joined by a low-lying isthmus about 1¼ miles wide which was often used as portage for canoes to save them from having to travel right round the island. The largest part of the island is about 21 miles in diameter and the smaller about 12. Both mountainous sections have land rising to over 5,500ft, each with four peaks over 6,500ft. These central mountains provided ample catchment areas for small rivers and streams which flowed down across the fertile coastal plain and into the sea every 1½ to 2 miles around the entire island. The plain was extremely fertile, crops needed only a minimum of labour, the lagoons and seas were full of fish and the Tahitians did not have to work very hard for food. To European seamen arriving at the island after long weeks of arduous voyaging as they dipped down into the cold southern ocean and faced the hard and risky passage around Cape Horn to come back up into the Pacific, and as the weeks at sea turned into months of hard graft, sustained only by scant and monotonous food, it was little wonder that the green and beautiful island of Tahiti appeared to rise out of the sea as a veritable paradise: a land so perfumed that it could often be scented long before it was sighted.

The Tahitians were seen as an intelligent and physically attractive race. After the initial contact they proved to be friendly, good humoured, hedonistic and generous. It might be argued that given the superior armed might that the men-of-war possessed the islanders had little alternative; and it is clear that superior military technology was ultimately to prove a decisive factor. But although superior arms were an important dimension in relationships it was not a crucial one until much later. On other Polynesian islands the inhabitants proved to be fierce and warlike and resisted the incursion of Europeans until the late nineteenth century and even into the twentieth. If the Tahitians had been so minded they could have fought the Europeans every time they set foot on shore, or simply starved them out by refusing to trade and withdrawing to the interior until they had gone. The Europeans were accepted because they possessed goods which the Tahitians desired.

Although there appeared to be a common culture European visitors commented on the existence of two noticeably different physical types. Modern research suggests that the islands were already inhabited when the Polynesians arrived in the seventh century and that the original inhabitants were defeated by the incomers and became the lower class – the *manahune* – the tenants and serfs of the invader. The invaders divided into (or arrived as) two ranks of feudal lords: the *arrii* the highest class, from which the paramount chiefs were chosen, and their followers, the *raatira*, the lesser chiefs: in European terms, the *arrii* might be termed the aristocracy and the *raatira* the landed gentry and proprietors. The word *manahune* occurs only on one other Polynesian island, Hawaii, a fact which reinforces the link between the histories of the two places. However, in Hawaii the original inhabitants (if they had indeed existed) were remembered only in folklore, as an earlier race of dwarfs who had built some of the stone structures surviving from a previous era. In either case, by the time the Europeans appeared on the scene they were effectively all the same people.

Some basic facts, such as the size of the population, are impossible to establish with any degree of confidence. Captain Cook estimated the population of Tahiti to be 240,000; George Forster, who accompanied Cook's second voyage, considered it to be 120,000. Only thirty years later, in the late 1790s, the missionaries assessed the population at a mere 16,000. The number of people in a crowd is notoriously difficult to estimate. Cook saw a Tahitian fleet of some three hundred war canoes carrying about eight thousand warriors preparing to attack the neighbouring island of Mo'orea, which suggests a sizeable population of women, children and old people in that chief's district. But none of those giving an estimate had penetrated the interior; the numbers living inland were pure guesswork, and to judge based on the situation at the seashore was fraught with problems. Districts that appeared populous and prosperous on one voyage could be virtually deserted on the next as the people would readily flock to the area where these intriguing strangers were anchored only to return to their usual habitations when they left. Most recent research calculates that the population was about seventy thousand at the time of European discovery.

Everyone agrees on one thing, that after the arrival of the white man the population went into sharp decline. The first European-style census which should have given fairly reliable figures was taken in 1857 counted just 7,212 Tahitians including those of the sister island of Mo'orea: the population of Tahiti itself had been reduced to around six thousand. A happy, well-fed, people living comfortably with a great deal of leisure, filling all their needs from their own self-contained environment for hundreds of years had been almost totally destroyed in fifty to sixty years. This was partly due to the intensification of civil warfare, partly to the introduction of European diseases against which they had no immunity, and partly to sheer demoralisation as their whole culture was denigrated.

James Morrison, who had been boatswain's mate on HMS *Bounty*, a literate, intelligent man who had previously served both as a gunner and midshipman, lived on Tahiti for over eighteen months after the mutiny; he learned the language and took a keen interest in all that happened around him. He is a well-informed witness especially as he lived there when there were no European ships to excite the people and change their daily routines. According to him there were seventeen districts each one with its paramount chief, six of whom remained in alliance, as were another three, these two groups customarily accepted the same king, while others did not. There were about a dozen families on Tahiti, all much intermarried, whose lineage went back to great men of the past or to the gods themselves, and whose members could aspire to kingship. Theirs was a complex and shifting system of political and dynastic alliances. A paramount chief had the power of life and death over criminals and also the right to seek those who had offended in a sub-chief's territory, but there were limits to the centralisation of power as he relied on his sub-chiefs to support him in any conflict with other paramount chiefs. He always needed their goodwill because they could decide to join him in a war, or not, as they chose. Unlike the medieval kings of England who could dispossess disloyal subjects, a paramount chief had no greater claim to the loyalty of those under him than they cared to give: governmental power effectively rested with the local chiefs. The king governed through a council of chiefs with special officers for various functions, but as lesser chiefs always had the potential to refuse the wishes or orders of their chief, authority was quite diffuse: an unstable political situation.

Although the local chiefs had considerable power – they could requisition labour, food and material, as well as raise troops – it seems to have been exercised lightly. One aspect of their power was their authority to impose a taboo: they could forbid the harvesting of certain plants, the killing of certain animals, or the fishing of sections of a lagoon. And while this power was usually only exercised for a brief period to ensure ample supplies for forthcoming feasts on ritual occasions, it gave them strong powers of conservation – essential to island living. It also gave them some hold over the Europeans, as they could – as Cook discovered – invoke a taboo to prevent people from trading with those who displeased them. Taboos and religion permeated Tahitian life to a degree which meant that the great and the lowly lived under much the same regime. To western ears the word 'taboo' has taken on an aura of mystery and magic, but for those who lived in that society it simply meant 'forbidden'. And although chiefs had the authority to impose some taboos, they themselves were restricted and circumscribed by taboos which controlled and limited their behaviour. The sacred and the priests were in many ways more influential in Tahitian society than the secular and the chiefs. In terms of everyday life the basic division was between the masculine and the feminine: this meant that there were strictly defined and separate spheres for men and women. Thus certain foods and drink were forbidden to women because they were the province of a male god, and women were excluded from certain offices and rituals. Perhaps this helped the British captains and Tahitian chiefs to accept each other so readily; after all, English women could not take holy office save in a community of women, and they could not even sit and drink port with the men after a meal.

The early voyagers were not well informed on Polynesian gods, although they did understand that there was a supreme god who could not be given material form beneath whom was a whole hierarchy of gods of war, fertility and so on, down to the particular gods of each home which were essentially the spirits of dead ancestors. So complex was the religion and 'so numerous were the gods of Tahiti that the early missionaries came to the conclusion that there were almost as many of these immortal souls as there were people on the island.'[1] The Polynesian religion and its gods will be described more fully later, but that it included human sacrifice was evident from the earliest contacts.

Human sacrifice was the most repellent aspect of the religion. While the obligation to sacrifice a human being was limited to the paramount chiefs, such were the demands of ritual that by the time a male child of a paramount chief became a man five people would have been sacrificed. There would be others later in his life and at his death. The other most common demand for human sacrifice was to the god of war. The number of human sacrifices was related to the amount of warfare, and as wars and their intensity increased with the European presence so the number of sacrifices to the god of war escalated. Victims were always male and usually killed by a blow with a club to the back of the neck, one of the corpse's eyes then being offered to the gods and the other to the chief. Apart from wartime and the killing of prisoners during it, the number of ritual sacrifices and how oppressive this practice was to a chief's subjects is difficult to judge. James Morrison was in Tahiti five months before the first human sacrifice was required. He was allowed to witness the ceremony which demanded the maximum number sacrificed at any one time, that for the investiture of a new king, when each chief of a district had to provide one man: 'the human sacrifices offered this day were 30, some of which had been Killed near a Month. These were the First that had been offered since our coming to the island. They never offer Men but such as have committed some great Crime Nor then, but on particular Occasions.'[2] There was no barbaric ceremony in which the unfortunate sacrifice was bound and waited his fate in a ritual before the god. When the chief's men went out to find a sacrifice they ambushed some criminal and killed him on the spot. The demand for thirty from the whole island seems to have put something of a strain on the system if month-old corpses were offered, particularly when one recalls the advanced state of decomposition of a corpse after only eight days as witnessed by Joseph Banks. Clearly, some 'sacrifices' were of those already dead. Women were never sacrificed.

Although murder was a crime so rare that some European observers claimed that it did not exist, murderers were executed, serving, at a suitable occasion, as the human sacrifice at an appropriate ceremony. The main sanction against criminal or antisocial elements seems to have been an informal system of marking offenders out as a suitable choice when a human sacrifice was required. Even then the chosen victim could escape his fate by fleeing to sacred ground where it was forbidden to kill, and staying there until the occasion had passed. Given that criminals were chosen, despatched suddenly and not arrested and held captive to suffer the stress of dwelling on their inevitable end, this custom was rather more humane than the incarceration and public execution of criminals in the England of the day.

In Tahiti individuals were born sacred. 'From the moment of birth a child was looked upon as a highly sacred being, . . . the mother, having handled the sacred child, could no longer touch her own food but had to be fed by another person. Should that person . . . touch the child, he or she immediately came under the same taboo. Should the baby reach out and touch anything, it too became sacred and was immediately appropriated to the child's use.'[3] Not even a royal baby in Europe was so sacred that it owned everything it touched. Clearly, this sacred being had to be secularised so that the child could interact easily with its parents and kin; sharing, for example, their food without making it sacred, and enabling it to mix with the rest of the population. This secularisation was conferred through a series of religious ceremonies after which the child was tattooed on the arm as a visible mark of conformity. The children of chiefs remained sacred for much longer than those of their people, until in fact they had a child themselves and it became head of the household. This is why some chiefs had to be carried everywhere, otherwise every piece of land they walked on would become theirs. They had servants to feed them otherwise the meal they were sharing with other people would become sacred and exclusively theirs.

Perhaps the most remarkable thing about Tahitian social and family arrangements was that, 'the Child is as soon as born the Head of the Family and the Honor and Dignity of the Father is transferd to the first born Child whether Male or Female, and before these rites are performed the Parents are not thought worthy to partake of its food'.[4] Being head of the family meant 'they lay no restraint on their Children because they are the Head of the Family and therefore do as they please'.[5] Tahitian childhood was thus remarkably free and unfettered and devoted to play. A number of games were familiar to the Europeans such as flying kites, stilt-walking and cat's cradle. The young girls had dolls complete with umbilical cord which they would 'deliver' after a suitable interval of imitating labour pains. Children spent much time in the water as they learned to swim almost as soon as they could walk, and surfing was a sport for all ages and both sexes. As children grew older they joined the adults in their work activities as and when they felt ready. It is not easy to appreciate how children were controlled and socialised:

one can only assume that it was achieved through their role within the whole community, because each child would be cared for by virtually anyone, and did not necessarily return home to eat or sleep. There was, too, the strong pattern of obligatory and acceptable behaviour provided by taboos.

Socialisation was a matter of communal rites; girls came to puberty at between eleven and twelve years of age, and boys a year or two later. It was at this stage of their initiation into adulthood that they had their buttocks tattooed black, covering an area similar to a pair of male swimming trunks. These rituals were enforced and Joseph Banks records watching a tearful thirteen-year-old girl undergoing the prescribed tattooing while being firmly held by two women. Boys were circumcised at a similar age. Children were free to follow their sexual inclinations at whatever age they chose without restraint. But, if one incident is indicative, it would appear that they were free from enforced sex. A gang of some half dozen *Bounty* mutineers were using their firearms to intimidate the Tahitians and to win influence with the chiefs. The Tahitians tolerated them, or were in fear of them, until one of the mutineers, Mathew Thompson, had sex with a young girl against her wishes. He was immediately severely beaten by her brother and the crowd that gathered outside his house was so hostile that he and his friends were forced to flee to a different district. It seems significant that the bad behaviour of this group had been left unchecked until Thompson's crime: that was intolerable. Such was the power of their muskets that when they arrived in their new district one of the group, Charles Churchill, was elected chief when the Tahitian chief died or was perhaps murdered. Churchill was then murdered by Thompson. But by then the Tahitians had had enough and executed Thompson. Interestingly, they did not harm any other Europeans.

A child's free life continued through adolescence until such time as he or she chose a partner and decided to marry. Morrison, however, denied that the Tahitians were as dissolute as many visitors believed. He was not gainsaying the truth of the visitors' reports, but merely stating that 'their whole system was overturned by the arrival of a ship, their manners were there as much altered from their Common Course, as those of our own Country are at a Fair.'[6] He goes on to say that iron was as valuable to them as gold to us, and that had visitors to Europe given quantities of gold to those who pleased them, then there would be many willing to sell themselves for such riches. He observed that, as in Europe, it was the aristocracy who were the most dissolute and that the common people were much more restrained. He does not deny that ordinary Tahitian society was very sensual but implies that such behaviour was normally ritualised: 'The Single Young Men have also dances wherein they show many indecent Gestures which would be reproachable among themselves at any other time but at the dance, it being deemed shameful for either Sex to expose themselves naked even to each other and they are more remarkable for hiding their Nakedness in Bathing than many Europeans.'[7] Tahitians bathed twice a day and both men and women cared for their appearance, having pierced ears for wearing flowers as well as earrings fashioned from shell, seeds and similar decorative elements.

The degree of respect and care taboos placed on adults in their dealings with babies and children seems, at first glance, to be in sharp contrast with the widespread custom of abortion and infanticide. The right to decide whether or not a baby would live or die was usually left to the woman herself, although if a new-born baby cried out before it was smothered it won the right to live as it had to die before it drew breath. A man could demand a baby's death only if he was an offended husband and his wife's child the result of adultery. The one general exception to this was in certain cases of a misalliance between classes: the offspring of a union between a higher chief and someone of lower class were not allowed to live. This applied equally to the offspring of male and female chiefs. In spite of their revulsion at such openly acknowledged infanticide, all observers agreed that Tahitian children were well-cared for and raised with much affection, and probably had the most carefree life of children anywhere.

The reputation for lasciviousness, sexual licence and infanticide which so outraged and horrified Europeans was mainly attributable to the *ariori*. The *ariori* were recruited from among the most beautiful and physically perfect men and women and had to undergo a long apprenticeship in singing, dancing and dramatic performance. They lived promiscuously and any children conceived by them were not allowed to live, for 'only the top rank was allowed to transmit its titles and honours down a descent line. All other ranks were held to obligatory infanticide and so denied the honour of descent.'[8] When first encountered the Europeans took them to be the most dissolute of all the islanders, whereas they played an important role in the most solemn religious ceremonies. They were in fact an essential part of Tahitian life and their religious functions aside, provided the most sophisticated as well as popular entertainment. To be chosen to become an *ariori* was a great honour for anyone from the common people as, when they retired, they were granted the rank of *raatira* and given land.

The majority of them, however, were recruited from among the chiefly classes and in becoming an *ariori* they renounced all rights of inheritance. One *ariori* explained to Captain Bligh that they lived like that because there were too many children. There can be little doubt that to keep population in balance with the limited resources available to an island people some form of population control was a necessity. But as only the *ariori* had an absolute ban on producing children and as they were drawn mainly from the chiefly class, it was more likely a method of preserving the position of the chiefly clans. Only one child could inherit the position of chief, therefore if his siblings joined the *ariori*, the wealth and power of the family would not be divided and dissipated. As the *ariori* owned no property the rest of society was obliged to keep them. They were in the service of one chief and moved around his districts, and their arrival was welcomed by the ordinary people in spite of the food and other resources they would consume, as they brought with them the power and blessings of the gods as well as a welcome break in routine.

Apart from providing the dramatic ceremonial spectacle on religious days and customary festivals, the *ariori* provided entertainment. They performed the most indecent dances, and gave displays of sexual prowess and variation. It is difficult to assess how frequently the really lewd performances occurred. Joseph Banks, who moved freely among the Tahitians on Captain Cook's first visit to the island, never saw one. Captain Bligh, however, described three male *ariori* performing one of these entertainments which culminated in individual displays:

> the whole business now became the power and capability of distorting the Penis and Testicles . . . The Second [performer] brought his stones to the head of his Penis and with a small cloth bandage he wrapt them round and round up to wards the Belly stretching them at the same time very violently until they were near a foot in length which the bandage kept them erect at, the two stones and head of the Penis being like three small balls at the extremity. – The Third person was more horrible than the other two, for with both hands . . . it however afforded much laughter among the spectators.[9]

Dance was an essential component of Tahitian enjoyment of life and displays ranged from bare-breasted dancers through to those clad in elaborate costume not unlike Victorian clothing, heavily covered from shoulders to ankles, although the dancers might well disrobe at the end of the performance in order to present themselves to the guests of honour. George Hamilton, surgeon of HMS *Pandora*, the ship sent out to arrest the *Bounty* mutineers, was one such guest and described a dance given by two women and the dress they were wearing as

> Something resembling a turkey-cock's tail, and stuck on their rumps in a fan kind of fashion, about five feet in diameter, had a very good effect while the ladies kept their faces to us; but when in a bending attitude, they presented their rumps, to show the wonderful agility of their loins; the effect is better conceived than described. After a half an hour hard exercise, the dear creatures had remued themselves into a perfect fureur, and the piece concluded by the ladies exposing that which is better felt than seen; and, in that state of nature walked from the bottom of the theatre to the top where we were sitting on the grass.[10]

The *ariori* also gave theatrical performances and their satirical plays could rebuke those rulers who transgressed the customary exercise of power or social mores. Finally, and very importantly, the men were expected to be in the forefront of any war which their paramount chief undertook. In other words the *ariori* fulfilled a strange mixture of military, religious, political and social functions which linked the priests, chiefs and people in a common culture.

Even for the ordinary people sexual relations within marriage were comparatively open and tied to the male system of special friendships. A *taio* was a friend of a formal kind, perhaps blood brother is an apt description. A married woman was expected to be faithful to her spouse. But *taios* could have sexual relations with the wives of friends, as could a man's natural brothers, so married women retained a number of males with whom to enjoy sex even after marriage. Married men were under similar, if somewhat less rigorous restrictions. Marriage seems to have been a purely personal matter, entered into and dissolved at the will of the partners, although most marriages were stable. If a couple did separate, their possessions were divided and the man took the male children and the woman the females. The man remained responsible for his previous wife and family until she found another partner, although given the ease with which the community fed those in need this was not a very onerous obligation.

Tahitian society was very strictly divided by gender. Men and women had their own areas of competence and one could not do the tasks allotted to the other. Homosexuality was accepted and a man could, if he wished, live as the 'wife' of another man without any stigma: he was simply redesignated as a woman and lived and worked under those taboos affecting women; the male status of his 'husband' was not affected. (The author has come across no references to lesbianism although, given the lack of erotic inhibitions, it is difficult to believe that it was unknown.) Because society was structured by gender it was easy for the male visitors to observe and record the lives of men, but not so easy to observe those parts of a woman's life which did not intermesh with men's.

Food and meals were the subject of many taboos: 'A man could not eat anything prepared by a woman, and the women could not touch the food of the men, unless they were near relatives who had undergone the special *amo'a* ceremony that allowed them to do so by removing certain taboos. Neither could the sexes join in partaking a repast, so they ate separately.'[11] These taboos meant that men were responsible for much food preparation and cooking and for the large earth ovens – many Europeans who tasted the results cooked in them claimed this to be the finest method in the world. The meat was pork, chicken or dog. The Tahitian pig was a small animal weighing up to about 110lb and was of Chinese origin; its flesh was adjudged excellent, although Captain Cook considered dog meat superior: he said that it tasted like lamb. Such dogs were raised for food and lived on a vegetarian, mainly fruit, diet; unfortunately the breed died out as introduced species interbred with them. Meat was not commonly eaten every day and the diet was largely fish, with breadfruit, coconuts, bananas, yams, sweet potatoes and taro as the basic vegetables.

Kitchen equipment was simple. All implements were of wood, stone or shell, and slivers of bamboo and sharpened shell served as knives, rock was used to make pestles and mortars, vegetables were grated with pieces of coral. Fingers were used for eating and very few domestic implements were required. As the Tahitians had no metal or earthenware they had no fireproof cooking utensils. Occasionally liquids were heated by having hot stones dropped into them, and the same method was used to set blancmange-type puddings. Food was usually served on a large leaf, although the homes of chiefs might possess one or two carved wooden platters, or even more rarely a wooden stool to sit on. Most possessions and foodstuffs were stored in baskets made from reeds, leaves or vines and hung from the ceiling out of reach of the ever-present rats. These were small rats which the Tahitians otherwise ignored, even feeding them titbits on occasion as they served as necessary scavengers to devour the kitchen scraps. Large sections of bamboo were used to store oils and liquids as were gourds, and coconut shells served as drinking vessels. But however cooked and served, food was something to be shared with those who wished to eat and everyone was obliged to share their food, however little, with those who asked for it. Specialist items could be exchanged. For example, fishermen would agree to supply a family with fish for a given period in return for hogs or similar produce, 'but their Principal Method [of trade] is by Gifts and Presents to each other, and it is not Common to refuse the Greatest Stranger any thing he stands in need of whether Food raiment or any thing else'.[12] No one, not even the poorest, went hungry in Tahiti, nor did they beg; they were fed as of right and custom.

Food supply was seldom a problem, although on Cook's second voyage he found provisions, particularly meat, were in short supply as a result of a civil war then taking place. Also, as with any agricultural system, adverse seasonal conditions could delay or diminish a crop; but in general the Tahitians kept their population and food sources in comfortable balance. The flat coastal area was like a huge unplanned garden with breadfruit, coconut, bananas and fruit trees mixed together with yam, sweet potatoes, taro and sugar cane, each scattered dwelling with its own small garden plot. They had fruits the Europeans likened to plum, apple, chestnuts and almonds. The loose soil required little digging and a shell on a stick served as a spade. Full-time fishing from canoes was a male preserve, although women fished freshwater streams and anyone could collect shellfish or spear fish from a reef.

These native plants and animals were added to by virtually every ship which called. Captain Wallis had left turkeys, geese and cats as a casual gift. Subsequent visitors took carefully selected items. Captain Bligh, for example, planted oranges, pomegranates, quince, fig, pineapples and maize for food; he introduced a variety of livestock, and planted fir and similar trees to give future European sailors better timber for planks. Because he appreciated how much the islanders loved scents and flowers, on his second voyage Bligh took them English rose seeds.

The clothing for both sexes was much the same: a wrap-around skirt and a poncho, which rested on the wearer's shoulders. On the few occasions when it was cold enough two or three ponchos would be worn belted into the waist with a sash. Clothing denoted status. The upper classes wore a single rectangle of cloth draped around the shoulders, the middle classes a similar garment tucked around the body under the arms. These were often richly dyed and patterned. Weaving was an art unknown to the Tahitians, instead they used tapa, a cloth made from the bark of the paper mulberry, breadfruit and types of fig tree. Tapa was produced in several different qualities, the best being highly prized and used extensively as gifts and ritual offerings to chiefs and other dignitaries. Its main drawback was that it could not be washed as it fell apart when wet, so it had to be replaced with new as it became soiled. This meant that the making of tapa was an endless task for the women. The bark from the appropriate trees had to be soaked and softened and then beaten out with mallets across a wooden beam in overlapping strips.

As tapa making was labour intensive and the responsibility of women they were the ones to gain most by the introduction of woven cloth from Europe. This was much sought after and many a sailor lost his shirt to his love. It was the relationship between *women*, particularly perhaps lower-class women and Europeans which was to prove a potent solvent of Tahitian society. Simply by granting sexual favours (which as a class-conscious society the women from the families of chiefs did not do unless to an officer) lower-class women could gain unimagined wealth. As they often lived on the ship for days or even weeks sharing the crowded accommodation of the crew, they must have broken taboos on cooking and eating, and doubtless many others. They learned, and others learned from them, that these taboos could be broken without punishment from either chiefs or gods. That knowledge was to be crucial in undermining the authority of their own culture.

Although Tahiti was a self-sufficient society, it had regular contact with other islands that involved small-scale trade. The Tahitians would take tapa cloth, wooden bowls and stools out with them to be exchanged at other islands for coconut oil, nacre and pearls. Canoes were their supreme artefact. Constructed with magnificent tall carved prows the single hulls were up to 90ft long, but no more than 3½ft deep and of about the same width. To create such a canoe – to fell the huge trees, hollow out and shape the hull and add all the elaborate appurtenances and decoration – using only stone axes, shell and bone implements was a major undertaking. Double canoes were made by lashing two of these together thus prefiguring the modern catamaran. In these they would trade as far as the Cook Islands, some 600 miles away, on normal voyages.

The endemic civil wars between the chiefs are a subject on which the early reports and historical comment are confusing. They agree that wars were quite common, but some argue that they were largely matters of display and did not involve many casualties, others that warfare was merciless. Certainly armies would indulge in economic revenge by destroying by 'barking' all the breadfruit and other food trees, thus condemning their enemy to five or six years of economic hardship until newly planted trees started bearing fruit. Here again the *ariori* had a predominant role as they were not only expected to be in the front rank of warriors but their supposed influence with the god of war was held to be crucial. The priest was considered more important than the chief on these occasions.

The advent of the Europeans changed the nature of Tahitian warfare. The possession of even a few muskets and cannon could be decisive in achieving victory and so chiefs tried to acquire these new and terrifying weapons. This led to an arms race throughout the Pacific islands, making chiefs submissive to the demands of foreigners, and anxious to induce European sailors to desert their ships and serve as mercenaries in their wars. That the British made Matavai Bay their customary anchorage in Tahiti led to the growing strength and importance of the chief of what had previously been a minor district. If having a foreign ship stay in one's area was a sure road to enhancing a chief's power, it was also something of a vicious circle in that to supply all the provisions demanded a chief needed to control ever larger areas of land – thus intensifying the pressure for war and conquest. The disadvantage to the chief was that the Europeans could always threaten to leave his district and go to trade in that of another, thus strengthening a rival. As power began to rely more and more on owning muskets, influence shifted decisively to the European visitors who were the sole source of the powder and shot, without which the muskets were useless. Any chief ambitious for power needed to maintain good relations with the Europeans, and as the British were the most regular visitors, they were the most influential. The decision of the chiefs of Matavai Bay to remain fast friends of the British led to a decisive change in the balance and complexion of Tahitian power and politics.

Chapter 7

HAWAII AND THE
DEATH OF CAPTAIN COOK

On Tahiti, servility was shown by baring the breast, and on Tonga and Hawaii by the more extreme form of prostrating oneself before the ruler.
                                    I. *Goldman*, Ancient Polynesian Society[1]

In late 1777 Captain Cook and his men were once again at Matavai Bay overhauling their ships, *Resolution* and *Discovery*, and taking on provisions ready to sail north. It was Cook's third Pacific voyage. He was at the peak of his fame, acclaimed by all the great seafaring nations – friend and foe alike – as the greatest navigator and explorer of his time or, perhaps, of all time. During his previous two voyages he had beaten his way back and forth across the southern Pacific Ocean from the tropics to deep into the Antarctic ice to prove that there was no great inhabited continental land-mass to be discovered. He had circumnavigated New Zealand and had discovered new islands, but above all it was his skill as a navigator and his charts which were exceptional. During these long and arduous voyages which strained ships and men to their limit, he had also proved uncommonly successful in preserving the health and lives of his crew. No small reason for this was his habit of returning to Tahiti for the winter season so that his men could be restored to health by the bountiful food of the island, and their morale and humour raised by the welcome they were given.

This time he was under orders to search for the Northwest Passage, that elusive sea passage from the Atlantic to the Pacific which was believed by some to exist via the Polar seas across the north of Canada. Searching for it from the Atlantic end had cost the lives of many men and had wrecked many ships: now Cook was to try from the Pacific. Many such crews must have viewed their forthcoming hardships in the icy wastes of the northern latitudes with grave apprehension. At its best it was going to be a cold and miserable experience with the great risk of being trapped in the ice to add to the normal hazards of gale, rock and reef. The ships might not return. The men were comfortable under a balmy tropical climate, enjoying the delights of Tahiti and the contrast with what they were about to face could hardly have been greater. But they were there to obey orders – and there was another incentive. Parliament had voted £20,000 to the crew of the ship which first succeeded in finding a Northwest Passage, a prize worth striving for, and with Captain Cook as their commander they could not be in more experienced hands. At all events, as they left their Tahitian friends and lovers they had no other expectations than that their next landfall would be the imposing coast of Canada or the barren rocks and icy wastes of Alaska.

They had sailed close to 3,000 miles north when on 18 January 1778, land was unexpectedly sighted: it was Oahu, one of the Hawaiian Islands. As they closed with the land wind and current prevented them from going ashore and carried them on to the next island in the chain, Kauai. Here Cook brought the ships to anchor in Waimea Bay close to a river for easy watering. He had chanced across a group of islands which promised to be even more populous, lush and exotic than Tahiti and an even better source of provisions in an even emptier quarter of the ocean.

The ships came to anchor at a well-populated area and the ships were greeted by thousands of Hawaiians. These strangers had obviously come from somewhere. But where? The Hawaiians knew of no other lands. Their geographical knowledge was limited to their own island chain. Their religion taught them that somewhere out in the boundless ocean was the home of their gods and where their dead also dwelt, their folk tales held that their ancestors had come from beyond the seas. According to their own religious and cultural beliefs these visitors could only be gods or ancestors returning to them. Here one might find some similarity with the mental world of the ancient Greeks, many of whose gods came back to earth and lived in various guises, even consorting with human beings, who in turn might be taken to the home of the gods. The separation between god and human was not of beings at opposite poles of existence as in a monotheistic religion. At all events, as a society very conscious of power and rank they accorded Captain Cook the highest honours and prostrated themselves when he walked ashore. The Hawaiians must have been as overawed as modern men would be at the sight of visitors from another planet, but Polynesians were pragmatic people and the white strangers – *Haoles* – had their corporeal status put to the test by being offered women, and their response was human enough to convince most of the common people that these were indeed men. Kauai, however, was only one of a chain of islands and news of this strange event took time to be relayed to the other islands and, no doubt, lost no strangeness in the telling.

Whatever the fascination of this island group, Cook could not stay to explore and chart his new discovery, although it was clearly of major importance. If the Northwest Passage was to be found he needed to reach the edge of the ice fields by way of the Bering Straits with the spring. After two weeks his ships continued on their voyage having been so unexpectedly refreshed with plentiful food and compliant women. But ports are places to be left and Cook and his men suffered all the hardships, dangers and discomforts of trying to find their way along the Alaskan coast, through the uncharted Aleutian Islands to the ice packs and beyond before being stopped by a barrier of endless ice. There was no alternative but to turn back. The return voyage tested men and ships to the limit. The ships' masts had been strained under the weight of ice which had formed on the rigging and sails; and the network of ropes, stays and tackles were stretched and weakened by being alternately soaked then frozen. Captain Cook may have been disappointed at his failure to add yet another achievement to his tally, but as they turned on their tracks to return to the Hawaiian Islands to refit and replenish, many a sailor must have been cheered at the thought of the warm comfort that awaited them there.

This time their landfall in November 1778 was the rocky east coast of Maui, another of the chain of Hawaiian Islands and, in search of a sheltered bay which could provide safe anchorage, the ships coasted slowly south. During this time they were supplied with fresh food by the many canoes which came out to trade with them, and although Cook at first ordered that no women were to be allowed on board his orders were increasingly ignored as more and more women came to live on the ships. From Maui the two ships continued to sail south finally discovering the island of Hawaii, the largest and most important in the group. Still searching for a safe haven, they felt their way down the east coast, rounded the south coast and moved up the west coast until they reached Kealakekua Bay. It offered the first safe anchorage so Cook ordered the ships in. This was a sound decision based on pragmatic seaman-like criteria, but through a number of coincidences it was to prove an unfortunate choice. The ships had been seven long weeks coasting along the shores without touching land, their every movement watched from the shore and reported on by those who supplied them with food. The population was at a fever pitch of excitement and the authorities – chiefs and priests – still unsure of anything concerning these mysterious strangers. Would they land? Where were they from? What was their purpose?

On his initial visit the divinity of Cook had been debated and treated with some scepticism by the islanders of Kauai. The authorities on Hawaii knowing of the earlier contact only by hearsay were less certain. But there were omens for the priests to interpret. Firstly, both of Cook's visits coincided with the season of *makahiki*, a time sacred to the god Lono, when war was taboo and no work done. It was the period when taxes were paid and when everyone joined in a round of festivities and sporting competitions. Secondly, Cook did not land until he found Kealakekua Bay – the name of the bay means 'The Pathway of the God'. The long search for this particular landing place was considered most significant. For Lono had been a remarkable man who was deified long after his death and he had been last seen on earth leaving that very bay in his canoe. That Cook should have chosen that place to land convinced many that this god had returned to his home. Thirdly, the ships' tall masts with their square sails hanging from the yards looked to many Hawaiians like the sacred emblem of their god Lono – a tall pole with two long sheets of tapa cloth suspended from a cross-piece. Could it be that this god was returning to them? That so many religious aspects should come together seemed to some Hawaiians to be beyond coincidence. The religious expectations and hopes aroused by the return of a god can well turn to bitter disappointment when such faith is found to be unjustified. Captain Cook landed in complete ignorance of why he was accorded such enormous respect; he knew nothing of the religion and culture of these people save that they were obviously Polynesians; although whether they would be like the aggressive, cannibalistic Maoris, or the agreeable Tahitians was an open question. It was difficult enough for him to feel his way into the political power structure, to discover who were the most important chiefs and to whom he should accord the greatest respect and favour without trying to live up to anyone's expectations of his divinity. Misunderstandings and cross purposes were virtually unavoidable.

In near contemporary Europe it was widely accepted that the honours shown to Cook were the result of the Hawaiians' belief that he was a god returning to them. Indeed, just five years after Cook's death the poet William Cowper reflected in a letter on the Captain's death, blaming it on the revenge of the Christian God: 'God is a jealous God and at Owhyhee the poor man was content to be worshipped . . . though a stock or stone may be worshipped blameless, a baptized man may not. He knows what he does, and, by suffering such honours to be paid him, incurs the guilt of sacrilege.'[2] In later years the American missionaries attempted to suppress a cult of Cook on the islands on similar grounds. If the Hawaiians felt some doubt and confusion over the secular or sacred aspects of Captain Cook the degree of confusion is still a matter of historical debate. The argument for him being received as a god is presented at length by Sahlins.[3] Briefly, he argues that Cook's arrival coincided with the Makahiki Festival, an annual celebration during which Lono, god of fertility, replaces Ku the god of war. After a period Lono is again exiled. Cook (unwittingly) also appeared to fulfill this part of the native belief by leaving at the appropriate time. But when the ship lost its foremast he was forced to return; this, Sahlins argues, made Cook's death inevitable: as a personification of Lono he had to be defeated and destroyed. Instead of 'Lono' leaving in his vessel, he had not only come back at an inappropriate moment, but he then tried to capture the king and take him to sea, thus reversing the whole ritual.

A more recent and perhaps more convincing argument is presented by Obeyesekere.[4] He maintains that the respect paid to Cook was due solely to his position as a chief. Chiefs had certain sacred attributes in the way European kings were God's anointed and subject to sacred ritual. Cook was accepted not as a returning god, but was accorded great honour as an important chief and, perhaps, as possessing some of the sacred spirit. As at Tahiti, religion permeated every dimension of society hence the arrival of beings from beyond the horizon presented the priests with the greatest difficulty, for if these strangers were ordinary human beings then the basis of their religious view of the world was wrong. Just as Pope Paul V had rejected Galileo's observation that the earth went round the sun in 1615 (Galileo was forced to recant again in 1633 under Urban VIII), so they did not want to accept a new truth that conflicted with their own account of the universe. Captain Cook was welcomed ashore with great ceremony by Koa, an important priest, and taken up a *heiau* (a sacred place of worship) and even up the oracle tower, its holy of holies. The ceremony there has been taken to indicate that Cook was worshipped as a god, but a more probable interpretation is that Cook was put through a ritual in which he unknowingly worshipped Lono. Here it might be added that Cook had given no sign of being in the least religious: he rarely held services on his ships, and would not have priests on board.

It was the priests' world view and their credibility which were most endangered by the appearance of mere mortal men. Initially they were more generous than the chiefs in ensuring that the ships received plenty of provisions, and it was they who were most attentive to Captain Cook and tried to elevate his status in the eyes of the Hawaiians. Certainly, the customary extremely low obeisance which was made to Cook was also made to Charles Clerke, captain of HMS *Discovery* and whom the Hawaiians also received as a great chief. These honours were much the same as were accorded to their own chiefs and were necessary if the ship's officers were to meet and socialise with the chiefs on an equal footing. Interestingly, such obeisance was not made on board ship, only ashore where Hawaiian culture held sway.

The king of Hawaii who had been visiting the island of Maui when the British ships arrived, hastened to return and presented Cook with feathered cloaks and headdresses, the most prestigious and expensive gifts possible, as well as with other symbolic artefacts. James King, lieutenant on HMS *Resolution*, felt that the king had separate interests from the priests and he took the lead in seeing that the two ships were plentifully supplied with all the provisions they could desire: 'The Hawaiians heaped gifts of all kinds on the English, and the weary sailors accepted all the offerings. Many women came on board the ships and David Samwell reported, "We live now in the greatest Luxury, and as to the Choice & number of fine women there is hardly one among us that may not vie with the grand Turk himself". In return for their favours the sailors gave the women scraps of iron, scissors, beads, and mirrors.'[5] It was an exchange of favours pleasing to both parties.

But the sailors' lives were not all feasting and fornication. The ships had been badly strained and the hulls had to be caulked and the masts and rigging stripped and overhauled. Cook received every assistance from the authorities, both secular and religious. It was important to take precise measurements of latitude and longitude, which could most reliably be done from the shore. When he chose a site for an observatory to take observations of the sun and stars, one of the chiefs, Palea, had some houses near the ships demolished to give him a clear field, also making the area taboo to keep the natives from interfering with the work. Kealakekua Bay was a highly populated area where thousands of Hawaiians had their houses. The decision to observe these strangers, to treat them with a great deal of reverence and respect, and do their best to supply their needs reveals a wise and controlled response to the unknown. The Hawaiians were intent on learning just what account these strangers would give of themselves.

Shortly after the ships' arrival, one of the seamen, William Watman, died. He had sailed with Cook on his previous voyages and, although only an ordinary crew member, Cook accorded him an unusually impressive funeral complete with marines with reversed muskets and all the panoply the ship could provide. Whether this was solely in honour of the man himself or was an opportunity to impress the Hawaiians is a moot point. In any case, the Hawaiians wished also to pay their respects by sacrificing a pig at the grave. Cook refused to let them. That night a group of them honoured the grave according to their customs. Differences in culture and customs on both sides were perhaps inevitably most evident at such solemn occasions, occasions which were, above all, expressed in religious ritual. The seamen took no notice of the system of taboos which were the absolute bedrock of Hawaiian religious, social and political authority. They broke taboos and yet suffered no ill-effects from gods or men. Not only that, but they encouraged islanders to break them too. The British camp ashore was placed under the taboo that no islander should enter it. But the seamen enticed women into the now sacred enclosure and these women prospered. The women were the main beneficiaries of the sailors' largesse, receiving precious cloth and metal in return for their liaisons.

Like the Tahitians the Hawaiians were not given to unnecessary work. They raised sufficient stock and grew sufficient crops to supply themselves from one harvest to the next. Suddenly being required to feed the crew of two ships began to prove a noticeable drain on food resources. Not only were the ships' crews taking their daily food but the Hawaiians were replenishing their stores for the long ocean crossing ahead. In addition, the ships had attracted thousands of Hawaiians to the area and they too needed feeding. If the very human appetites of the visitors had thrown serious doubt on their sacred nature, the Hawaiians made no attempt to steal from the ships or molest the crews, in fact they supplied much food without any return payment. But as well as reducing the amount of food to meet local needs before the next harvest, supplying all the provisions meant extra work for the common people, and they did begin to hint that it was time for the ships to leave.

The timing was agreeable to the British: the sailors had overhauled the ships and Cook sailed on 4 February 1779, having stayed a month. The priest, Koa, who had changed his name to Britanee in honour of the strangers, sailed with them while they stopped once more along the coast to fill their water casks and then, finally, amid expressions of goodwill on both sides, the ships made for the open sea. Again, they were sailing to the north, to spend a summer searching for the Northwest Passage before returning home. Had the voyage proceeded as planned, Captain Cook could have returned home to enjoy the acclaim of yet another remarkable discovery and to an honoured and comfortable retirement. But before they had cleared the island the foremast of the *Resolution* was split by a sudden squall. It was decided that the only sensible course was to return to the safe anchorage of Kealakekua Bay and there unstep the mast, float it ashore and effect the necessary repairs.

Their return was not welcome. When the two ships re-entered the bay the British were astounded at the change. Instead of the thousands of islanders living there only a few days earlier the place was now virtually deserted. King Kalaniopuu had placed a taboo on the area. This was common practice where an area of the land or sea had been heavily used as it gave the vegetation ashore and the fish in the sea time to regenerate. It was an essential power when living on an island with finite resources; once the area had recovered the taboo would be removed. Nevertheless, the king arrived to receive Captain Cook but there was not the same open-hearted welcome which had marked his first visit. The people were much less helpful and respectful and were now prepared to steal anything they could in the manner of other Polynesian islanders. It was these thefts that were to lead to the death of Captain Cook and his men.

It happened that Captain Cook was ashore with a party of marines settling one dispute over thefts when the *Discovery* fired its cannon at a canoe in which some other thieves were fleeing. Cook and his marines ran along the shore in an attempt to catch the thieves as they landed and, failing to cut them off, tried tracing them inland only to realise that they were being misinformed as to their whereabouts. On returning they learned that the incident had developed into a serious fracas. The master of the *Discovery* had sent a party ashore to seize the offending canoe, which happened to belong to Chief Palea who had shown such friendship to Cook and his men when they first arrived. Feelings were running high but Cook and Chief Palea restored order. But it was an uneasy order and, as events during the night were to prove, the Hawaiians were now determined to steal from the ships whatever they could lay hands on.

They were extraordinarily skilful thieves. At dawn the next morning the *Discovery*'s cutter, moored virtually alongside her, had gone. This was indeed a serious theft; ship's boats were essential for exploring and charting strange waters, for moving to and from the shore, and, in case of fire or wreck, were their lifeboats. Immediately, Cook ordered that the bay be blockaded so that no canoes could leave. He took nine marines under the command of Lieutenant Molesworth Phillips and in two boats they were rowed to the village of Kaawaloa where the king lived. Cook intended to use the tactics which were commonly employed throughout the Pacific: these were to invite the king (or important chief) on board and then hold him hostage until his subjects returned the stolen object. Cook went to the king's house and, after talking to him, invited the king to spend the day aboard the ship. The king appeared willing and walked with Cook and his men down to the beach.

The Hawaiian people were not as amenable as their king. As the British walked to their boats, the natives crowded around their king, pleading with him not to go, and once they reached the shore they forced the king to sit down. Nearby, Lieutenant Molesworth Phillips drew his marines up in a semicircle with their backs to the sea to protect an escape route and called the ship's boats close into the shore ready to embark. Estimates suggest that there were over twenty thousand Hawaiians gathered around the centre of the drama. It was a very hostile crowd, part of which started arming. Accepting that he would have to leave the king ashore, Cook moved towards his boats. It is unlikely that he would have been harmed had not a native runner arrived with the news that the British had killed a chief who had tried to evade the blockade. This enraged an already excited crowd – one man threatened Cook with a dagger. Cook was armed with a double-barrelled musket but, according to his custom, one barrel was loaded only with small shot which was intended more to intimidate than to cause serious injury. When he fired, the pellets bounced harmlessly off the man's woven matting armour. Emboldened, the Hawaiians pressed closer. Cook fired the other barrel killing one man; Lieutenant Molesworth Phillips fired killing another; and the marines and the crew of the two boats drawn close inshore opened fire killing and wounding more – all to no avail as the crowd closed in. Just as Captain Cook reached the water's edge he was felled with a blow from a club and then stabbed. 'On seeing him fall, the islanders set up a great shout, and his body was immediately dragged on shore, and surrounded by the enemy, who snatching daggers out of each other's hands, showed a savage eagerness to have a share in his destruction. Thus fell our great and excellent Commander.'[6] Lieutenant Molesworth Phillips reached the safety of the boats and then, although seriously wounded, immediately jumped back into the surf to rescue one of the marines. Once the two were back on board the sailors hauled on the oars to pull the boats a safe distance from the shore. Four of the marines were left dead on the beach.

The whole incident was witnessed from the ships but the crews were powerless to intervene. The *Resolution* fired two of its cannon at the crowd on the beach which now dispersed – perhaps more in shock at the turn of events than at the ineffectual bouncing of two cannon balls. Off the beach

Lieutenant Molesworth Phillips, commander of the marines, called for the boats to go in to retrieve the bodies. Lieutenant Williamson, the naval officer in charge of the boats, refused to do so. Enraged at this refusal, Lieutenant Molesworth Phillips accused him of cowardice and threatened to kill him, but to no avail. The seamen were under Williamson's command and as the boats rowed the stunned survivors back to the ships the bodies of Captain Cook and the four marines were left where they had fallen.

How can the event be explained in the light of the previously good relationships? It is simply unbelievable that the mass of people suddenly started large-scale, systematic thefts without the tacit knowledge and approval of their chiefs, if not under their actual instructions. Perhaps they came to the conclusion that these strangers had been treated rather too royally and given little in return. At all events, the mood of the ordinary people had changed – perhaps with good reason. It may have been the king, chiefs and priests who granted supplies to the ships, but it was the ordinary Hawaiian who had to labour to produce all that was required. They had already given enough and when the ships made their unforeseen return they were intent on gaining substantial items by fair means or foul. It is also difficult to accept the view that the king was willing to accompany Cook to his ships when he was forced to sit down by the people. Every account we have of the relations between a Hawaiian king and his subjects emphasise the supreme, arbitrary power of the king. His word was life and death. It was forbidden to let even one's shadow touch the king; it was compulsory to uncover one's shoulders on passing his house, and to prostrate oneself when a king's servant went past carrying the king's property. Who would dare to *touch* him against his will? It is more likely that the king had no intention of going with Cook, but did not want to challenge him with an outright refusal, and so let a popular demonstration appear to be the cause of his non-compliance. One certain thing is that Cook's death was unplanned, unforeseen and in the long run, perhaps, regretted.

Cook's second-in-command, Charles Clerke, inherited an unenviable situation. The Hawaiians could not be left with any lingering doubts or hopes; they had proved all too decisively that these strangers were mere mortals. Clerke needed to act quickly. The observatory and its equipment ashore were under the charge of William Bligh (later to win fame and notoriety as Captain of HMS *Bounty* and Governor of New South Wales) and some marines, who were also now attacked and were lucky to survive until reinforcements strengthened their position. It would have been humiliating to have to abandon all the instruments of the observatory by simply sailing away, but even that option was not open to them. The foremast and sails of the *Resolution* were still ashore, and they could not sail until those had been recovered and installed. Symbolically they could not leave the body of their late commander in the hands of his killers. The death of Cook had been a shock to both sides. It is unlikely that either side wanted the trouble over thefts to end in bloodshed. A truce was agreed.

On the night of the truce the Hawaiians approached the hostile ships and said they had come to return Cook's body. The bundle was swung on board and unwrapped: it was a parcel of flesh – flesh which had been cut from the bones of Captain Cook. The British were horrified and outraged at this mutilation of the commander they had so respected and admired; but it was being returned by the priests as a mark of respect and they promised to recover more of Cook's remains. There was clearly a division of opinion among the Hawaiians as the great majority continued to celebrate their 'victory'. For two days after Cook was killed they were seen on the beach dancing around in Cook's uniform, and one chief taunted them by circling the ships in a canoe while wearing Cook's hat. Left to the officers the affair would have been resolved peaceably, but the crews of the *Resolution* and *Discovery* approached Captain Clerke in a body demanding permission to take their revenge. Stepping into the shoes of the commanding figure of Cook was a testing position, to have absolutely refused the crews' thirst for revenge at that point could have poisoned relations between him and them, and put his authority under strain for the rest of the voyage. He compromised by saying that if they met hostility the next day when they were to go ashore to collect water they could use all means to defend themselves. When the marines and sailors went ashore and some stones were thrown they responded by going on a rampage, destroying villages and killing indiscriminately. Some 200 houses were burned, temples destroyed and some 50 Hawaiians killed or wounded. In decorating the bows of two of their boats with the decapitated heads of their victims the British showed a barbarity at least equal to that of the islanders.

In fact, according to most accounts, the Hawaiians had shown the corpse of Cook the greatest respect. They traditionally removed all the flesh from the bones of their great chiefs. Cook's bones were then buried in a secret place so that no one could desecrate the grave or show him any disrespect. If the great man had been loved as well as respected for his eminence, then parts of him would be kept in the homes of other great men for a period of time. It is claimed that this great honour had been accorded to Captain Cook. His head had been sent to the king, other parts of his body, mainly bones, had been placed in the care of other great chiefs. The bodies of the four slain marines had been similarly honoured by being so distributed to lesser chiefs. It was this distribution of body parts, which meant that it took four days for them to be collected, before with great dignity, and in the full ceremonial regalia of his red feathered cloak, a high chief 'returned the hands, skull, arms, and leg bones of the captain'.[7] Captain Clerke, anxious to re-establish good relations, did not insist on the return of the marines' body parts.

But there is another Hawaiian version, which says that Cook's intestines were used to rope off the space for a cock-fight and his hands were put on sticks and used as fly swatters. Such disrespect of a slain enemy was common throughout Polynesia, so this account cannot be brushed aside. Certainly Cook's death was not mourned as the death of a god – if only because there was no ritual for such an event. But neither was he mourned as a beloved chief. When chiefs died people went about naked and many would knock out one of their teeth as a sign of mourning. There was none of this after Cook's death. That was celebrated as the death of an enemy – the blowing of conch shells, the parading his clothing around the ship – so the immediate defilement of his corpse seems most likely. If the Hawaiians changed their minds and decided to respect his remains it was only through the efforts of the priest and chiefs. Whatever the subsequent history of Cook's remains – and they do reappear in the island's history – the short-term change of mind may well have been accorded to force rather than affection.

Once the remains had been returned a taboo was placed on the bay, so there were no islanders on the shore to witness the funeral. Cook's remains were sewn in a hammock for burial at sea, and on 21 February 1779 they were plunged into Kealakekua Bay to a ten-gun salute and the tears of many of the crew. After the ceremony the taboo was removed, and once more the ships were plentifully supplied with all types of provisions. Amid mutual expressions of goodwill and assurances that the incident was closed, the ships sailed the next morning, stopping at the islands further north where the few women who had lived on board throughout the conflict finally went ashore. As they returned to their people the ships again headed north to spend another season in the futile attempt to find the Northwest Passage before returning to England.

Chapter 8

BRITISH HAWAII AND THE EARLY ADVENTURERS

Cook himself had noted that 'Spain may probably reap some benefit by the discovery of these islands, as they are extremely well situated for the Ships sailing from New Spain [Mexico] to the Philippine Islands to touch and refresh at.'

Glen Barclay, A History of the Pacific . . .[1]

Cook's observation on the potential advantages of his discovery for Spain cannot be denied. Indeed, some have argued that in fact the Spaniards had discovered the islands long before Captain Cook. Since 1556 Spanish galleons had been making an annual voyage from Mexico to the Philippines. Because of the prevailing winds and currents these voyages ran south of the Hawaiian Islands outward bound and north of them homeward. Given how frequently ships were blown off course by adverse weather, it does seem rather strange that in over two hundred years the Spaniards should never have stumbled across these islands. Some suggestion that they did was a chart taken from a captured Spanish ship showing a group of islands in the appropriate latitude but with a large longitudinal error – an error not unusual among early navigators. Those who support the view that the Spanish did chance upon the islands argue that they kept their discovery secret, and never revisited them because they did not want other countries to know about them, as other nations, or pirates, might use them as a base to prey on Spanish possessions and shipping. This seems a rather weak argument, as no one was better placed to make a base of them than the Spanish themselves, nor did any other nation have so great a need of it.

On the other hand, later archaeological evidence from Hawaii includes an iron implement and woven cloth from a late sixteenth-century burial – material not produced in Hawaii and so certain proof that these fragments arrived there through some external agency. But all such evidence, including the ethnological and the anthropological, from the island could be explained by a single shipwreck, news of which might never have reached the outside world. The islands on the chart are not so easily accounted for and one is left with the question: if the Spanish knew about the islands, why did they never take advantage of them? They would have been a convenient place of replenishment and refuge on the long and difficult return voyage from the Philippines to established Spanish possessions in the New World and would have made trade with the Philippines less costly and risky. If they knew of them and wished to keep them secret, placing them on charts, however inaccurately, was not the best way to conceal such information. And why put them on the charts carried by ships if they were forbidden to go to them? That knowledge of them, if so widely shared within the Spanish seafaring world, would hardly have remained secret from one generation to the next. Certainly, any previous contact must have been very ancient as Cook wrote that he had never encountered any people anywhere who were so astounded at their arrival. If the islanders had been visited by Europeans, it must have been so long ago as to have disappeared from folk memory and oral tradition.

The most likely explanation for the scraps of cloth and fragments of iron is that of a shipwreck in the distant past, or of even only a few survivors being washed ashore in a small ship's boat and being integrated into the community. In addition to an unusual incidence of red hair among the islanders, Hawaiians were the only Polynesians to have adopted crested helmets, daggers and cloaks in the European style. And these were made with enormous trouble from tiny feathers in red and yellow, the colours of the Spanish flag. It could take a decade to collect the feathers for the cloak of major chief as it required 400,000 or so, which in turn required the feathers from 80,000 birds. The yellow feathers were taken from a bird which had only a tiny patch of them and they were so valuable that they were trapped, plucked of that one colour and then released to regrow those feathers. The colours symbolised honour for the Hawaiians and it was accorded to Cook in great measure when any earlier possible connection with Spain had long been forgotten.

Whatever the truth of possible early Spanish involvement it was the British expedition which brought knowledge of the existence of these islands to the wider world. After this strange intrusion into their lives the Hawaiians resumed their traditional interests. The eight main islands were divided between four warring chiefs, who each strove to bring all the islands under the control of a single head, and within each island civil war was not uncommon as ambitious chiefs fought for supremacy. Their wars, alliances and betrayals read much like the history of medieval Europe. Their internal affairs, however, were not to remain their own concern for long. As the islands are among the most isolated in the world, thousands of miles from land, very few ships crossing the north Pacific would fail to call there to replenish their supplies once news of their existence was published.

Initially there were not many ships to take advantage of the discovery. The west coast of America was only lightly settled and commerce went south to Mexico or right down to Cape Horn and then back up to the eastern side of North America. There was no established trade across the Pacific to Japan and Asia. Cook's two expeditions may have failed to find the Northwest Passage, but he did chart much of the coast of present-day Canada and Alaska and compile a report on the resources of the area. The items of most immediate commercial interest were furs. These could be obtained from the Indians of north-western America at the cost of a few trade goods. As those same furs were highly prized in China and very expensive, it was obvious that there were staggeringly high profits to be made by transporting them from one side of the Pacific to the other. This was proven by the crews of the *Resolution* and *Discovery*. After the death of Captain Cook they continued the voyage in search of the Northwest Passage under the command of Captain Clerke, who was the most experienced of all the Pacific explorers, having first sailed round the globe as a midshipman on the *Dolphin* with Captain Byron before serving under Captain Cook on all three of the latter's voyages until he died of consumption off the coast of Kamchatka. Saddened by his death the expedition then returned home by way of China and the Indian Ocean. In China the seamen were offered such high prices for the few furs they were taking home that the new commander, Captain Gore, was faced with a near mutiny as the men demanded to return to North America for a cargo of furs which would have made their fortunes. One of the officers estimated that even the limited number of furs on board left the crews richer by some £2,000; a seaman was paid about £15 a year. Clearly, there were fortunes to be made from even one successful voyage. Sandalwood was also highly prized by the Chinese and in Hawaii it grew in abundance. Furs and sandalwood were sufficient to attract men to what was a very risky enterprise. For, although merchant ships were armed, they were not men-of-war and had only small crews. Wherever a vessel stopped to trade the crew ran the risk of being murdered for possession of their ship and its contents.

Soon after the return of the *Resolution* and *Discovery* in October 1780 a British corporation was formed to trade in furs. Captains Portlock[2] and Dixon were chosen to command the *King George* and the *Queen Charlotte*, and in 1786 were among the first to arrive on the Canadian coast and at Hawaii from commercial interests. Both men had sailed with Captain Cook and were no strangers to the Pacific. They returned the following year; this time they shared the trade with another English vessel. The Hawaiians were eager to learn from this growing number of strangers and to take advantage of them. They were particularly keen to obtain firearms which, as they had learned from their clash with Captain Cook and his men, they knew could be decisive in their internal struggles. The only way they could obtain these was by force, theft or trade. The chiefs realised that resorting to force and too much theft would simply deter ships from coming to trade and, as in Tahiti, that the only practical way of obtaining arms and, more importantly, a continual supply of gunpowder, was to protect the foreigners so that they would chose to trade in their chiefdom. Good relations with these westerners meant power. So although the paramount chiefs tried to keep trade and negotiations with the Europeans in their own hands, they had difficulty in controlling rebel or ambitious chiefs who challenged their authority and who were prepared to take a ship by force if the opportunity arose.

Strangely enough, in view of Cook's death and the treatment the Hawaiians had received at the hands of his compatriots, the British were the most popular visitors. The Hawaiians were highly intelligent and curious about the wider world these visitors had revealed and they wanted to see for themselves where these foreigners came from and went to: they clamoured to be taken aboard the ships and to join the voyagers. John Meares, who reached Hawaii in 1787 in command of an English trading vessel, described his experience on Kauai:

> Presents were poured in upon us from chiefs, who were prevented by the multitude from approaching the vessel, and the clamorous cry of 'Britanee, Britanee', was for a long time vociferated from every part, and without ceasing: nor can their silent grief be described, when it was made known among them, that Kaiana, a prince of Atooi [the island Kauai], was the only one selected to the envied honour of sailing with us.[3]

It was no wonder that Meares selected Kaiana. The chief was shrewd, intelligent and able. He was an imposing figure, nearly 6ft 6in tall and powerfully built with an air of authority. During the voyage to China, Kaiana endeared himself to the English captain. Having sold his furs in Canton

Captain Meares loaded Chinese goods for England, but he did not abandon Kaiana until he had managed to arrange for him to travel on board a ship bound for the north-west coast of America, from where the Hawaiian would be able to secure a passage back to to his home. He was shipped off with considerable possessions which came to him as gifts collected for him by the English inhabitants of Canton. Most of the Hawaiians who travelled with Europeans at this time were treated with a good deal of concern for their welfare, and care was taken to return them to their homeland. The admiring comments on their appearance and character demonstrate that racism, at least of a crude kind, was absent at this early period.

From the north-west coast Kaiana and his possessions were returned to Hawaii in December 1788 with one Captain William Douglas, another entrepreneur, who had command of two ships and had joined the profitable fur and sandalwood trade. The ship touched first at Hawaii. There Kaiana learned that during his absence enemies had taken control of his homeland of Kuaui: he could not return. Since the days of Captain Cook the single island of Hawaii had been united under one chief who took the title King Kamehameha.[4] An ambitious man, he aimed to bring all the Hawaiian Islands under his rule. In the long run he was to succeed and found a dynasty which was to remain in power until the monarchy was abolished. He knew that he would need the help of western technology and skills to achieve his ambition. Prince Kaiana had won a reputation as a great soldier before his voyage to China and now that he had returned with a number of muskets and quantities of gunpowder and shot he could be a valuable ally, so the king offered him lands and power if he would stay on Hawaii. Kaiana accepted. Captain Douglas even did Kaiana the service of sailing to his native island to fetch his family back to Hawaii.

King Kamehameha was envious of the size and strength of western ships and the ease with which they could sail from island to island; the Hawaiian Islands stretch some 600 miles from end to end and European ships were as superior to canoes in their ability to carry men, cannon and cargoes as firearms were to native weapons, and almost as essential if the whole chain was to be conquered and controlled from one island. The king tried to persuade Captain Douglas to leave him a number of firearms and a carpenter to supervise the building of a fleet on the European model. At first Douglas refused, but the king and Kaiana persuaded him to change his mind. They pointed out that Captains Portlock and Dixon had supplied the king's enemies with arms and also left behind a man – John Mackey – who could use them.

They were liable to be defeated unless he should do the same for them. Captain Douglas needed his friends to stay in power if he was to continue to trade profitably, so he gave them not only muskets but also a swivel cannon which was mounted on a large double canoe. The arms race had begun in earnest.

It cannot be said that Captain Douglas was well rewarded for his efforts. The Hawaiians continued to be far more dangerous than the Tahitians and were always ready to seize a ship if the crew dropped their guard. Their main method of taking a ship was to swim out at night and silently cut the anchor cable in the hope that the vessel would drift ashore where it could be pillaged. In spite of the considerable services Douglas had rendered, his cables were cut three times as he moved around the islands. Both sides employed the carrot and the stick. Douglas managed to recover two valuable anchors only by bribing a local chief with the gift of more arms while also threatening to burn his village. Simultaneously with their attacks the Hawaiians also encouraged individual crew members to desert, offering them land and women as inducements. Sailors were accustomed to using firearms, spoke the English language and were at home with European ways, so could be an asset to the chiefs on whose lands they agreed to settle. Men were tempted to desert by these offers; provided they were willing to risk their lives in support of one side in the island wars, they could enjoy a life of power and plenty rather than that of a common sailor, living on hard tack for miserable pay. Many did try to desert, although captains usually recovered their men by the customary and simple expedient of taking some important person hostage until they were returned.

Relationships with trading vessels were conducted on a different basis from those with men-of-war. The chiefs knew that they could not possibly take a well-armed and heavily manned naval vessel. However, commercial shipping was more vulnerable and the temptation to take the ship rather than to trade with it was ever present. Both sides were looking to their own interests, both sides had things the other wanted, so contact always continued – but each watched the other, always ready to take whatever advantage circumstances might offer. Such an atmosphere was bound to lead to tragedy.

Tragedy duly arrived in the shape of Captain Simon Metcalfe of the *Eleanora* and his son Thomas commanding the *Fair American*, the smaller of the family's two ships. During the outward voyage from America in 1790 the ships lost contact, and the *Eleanora* under Simon Metcalfe was the first to arrive. Landing initially on the north coast of Hawaii he was subjected to the customary thieving and, determined to stamp it out, took strong measures against it. On the first occasion he beat one chief with a rope's end – a humiliation not to be forgiven and an insult that would be repaid. He then lost a longboat and the crewman guarding it, whereupon he refused to trade with anyone and fired his cannon at those canoes which tried to approach the ship, killing a number of people. When islanders then swam out and tried to steal the copper sheathing from the hull of the vessel, Simon Metcalfe retaliated by landing and burning their village. He then sailed on to Maui always asking for news of his stolen boat. When, having taken on water for what he thought was the last time, he decided to accept its loss and was about to sail away, he was given the name of the chief responsible for the theft. He put about and returned.

The chief said that he would return the longboat in exchange for one musket with eight charges of gunpowder and the seaman who had been guarding it for the same. Captain Metcalfe agreed and handed over two muskets with sixteen charges. But he was tricked. He was then given the broken keel of his longboat and a thigh bone from the sailor – the sailor having been murdered and the longboat broken up for the metal it contained. Metcalfe extracted a severe revenge. He pretended that the incident was closed and resumed trading, telling the islanders that the port side of the ship was taboo but they were welcome to trade on the starboard side. All his cannon were moved to that side and each cannon loaded with 100 musket balls and assorted nails and pieces of iron; the ship was then trimmed so that the cannon tilted down into the sea close to the ship. Having attracted a great throng of canoes, Metcalfe gave the order to fire. Some hundred men and women were killed on the spot and twice as many died shortly after of their wounds. The Olowalu Massacre had taken place. Captain Metcalfe hauled his anchor, sheeted home the sails and resumed his voyage.

Meanwhile his son Thomas Metcalfe had just arrived at the same place on the north coast of Hawaii where his father had beaten the chief. The *Fair American* was a small ship with only six crew. The chief's revenge was swift: at a given signal Thomas Metcalfe and his crew were set upon and killed or hurled into the sea. The ship's mate, Isaac Davies, put up a terrific fight; once in the sea he tried to escape in a canoe, but the native manning it beat him with a paddle until he fell unconscious and lay as if dead. The schooner was plundered, towed inshore and set on fire to recover the iron used in its construction. When the canoe containing Davies reached the shore and the Hawaiians discovered that he was alive his attackers simply left him to his own devices. One native chose to nurse, feed and shelter him.

Shortly after Thomas Metcalfe and his men had been killed the *Eleanora* arrived in Kealakekua Bay with Simon Metcalfe still hoping to rendezvous with his son. King Kamehameha had by then been informed of the death of Thomas Metcalfe and the burning of his ship and knew that if news of his son's death reached him, Metcalfe would take his revenge. He placed the ship and its crew under a taboo so that no Hawaiian could visit it and let slip the news. A member of the crew, John Young, who had already made one voyage to Canton and back with sandalwood, knew the Hawaiians well and had hitherto always enjoyed friendly contacts with them. He said that whereas men could usually go ashore and mix with the natives without trouble or fear, 'I did not feel any particular desire to go on shore, as neither the Indians nor their manners were pleasing to me, although I entertained no particular dislike of them.'[5] But he was unlucky enough to be ashore shooting birds on the day the king placed a taboo on contact with the ship. When he returned to the beach, normally a hive of activity with canoes, fishermen and swimmers and from where anyone would have ferried him out to his ship, it was deserted. All the canoes had been taken far inland away from the beach and there was not a soul to be seen. Unnerved by the sudden disappearance of all the natives and by the eerie emptiness of the bay, although in fear of his life, eventually sheer desperation and hunger forced him to walk inland. He approached a house and was immediately offered food and shelter with customary Hawaiian hospitality, although it was clear that there was something terribly out of the ordinary afoot. The next day, to his horror, he watched as his ship hauled up its anchor and crowded on sail: he had been abandoned. He was not molested, the islanders continued to feed him, but he was left in this uncertain situation for two more days until someone told him that there was another white man nearby. That man proved to be Isaac Davies, still recovering from his wounds.

The king had reprimanded the chief for burning the ship and for killing her crew, if only because he wanted the goodwill of the Europeans. Nevertheless, he gained one advantage. Davies and Young, the two survivors of these ghastly events, could handle muskets and were taken into the king's service. Their fire power was to prove decisive in many battles. Indeed, they were kept so busy firing and recharging their muskets, that they could not always keep place in the forefront of the battle. When this happened, one of the chiefs (whom the British nicknamed Billy Pitt because they felt he was as influential as the British Prime Minister), a huge, strong man, would put one of them on his shoulders, run up to the front of the battle where he would shoot an enemy and then return that man to recharge his musket while he

HMS *Dolphin* attacked. 1767. Captain Wallis and his crew were given a hostile reception when they first discovered Tahiti. Most notable is the chief's canoe in the foreground. These war canoes could be as long as ships such as the *Discovery* (100ft) used by Captain Cook on his voyages. *(British Library)*

Women making tapa, 1769. Spinning and weaving were unknown in the islands. Cloth was made by preparing and beating the young bark of certain trees with mallets across a wooden beam. It was the principal labour of women before the introduction of European cloth. *(British Library)*

Tahitian dancers, 1777. Dancing was the main cultural art of the Polynesians. The elaborate costumes worn by the two women are made from the finest quality tapa. *(British Library)*

Vaitepiha Valley in Tahiti, 1777. This beautiful landscape illustrates why Tahiti made such a favourable impact on European visitors. Fertile as well as dramatic, while lacking the poisonous reptiles, predatory beasts or deadly diseases common to most tropical regions, it appeared as a veritable terrestrial paradise. *(British Library)*

A *marae* in Tahiti, 1769. These structures were holy ground. Each terrace built inside the other in steps 5ft high, was earth filled and faced with white coral. This sketch is by Herman Sporing, the artist on Cook's first voyage. One measured by Cook and Joseph Banks was 71ft long and 267ft wide. *(British Library)*

A house at Hawaii, 1779. Note the dramatic landscape behind the building. In 1819 the French artist Jacques Arago described the domestic buildings of Hawaii as the most comfortable he had seen on any island group during his crossing of the Pacific. (*British Library*)

Death of Captain James Cook, 1779. Captain Cook is shown in a heroic pose fighting to the last. John Webber, the artist on board HMS *Resolution* at the time, depicted Cook facing the other way and struck from behind while holding out a hand as if to stop his marines from firing into the crowd. *(National Maritime Museum)*

War canoes of Tahiti, 1774. The artist, William Hodges, witnessed the impressive preparations for an invasion of the island of Moorea by the chiefs of four of Tahiti's districts. Captain Cook estimated that 4,000 men were involved. Painted in Hodges's London studio, it is a romanticised composite. The more dramatic island of Huahine forms the background, instead of the historically correct Tahiti. *(National Maritime Museum)*

The *Resolution* and *Discovery* in the ice. This shows the other side of Cook's voyages of discovery. Months were spent in Arctic and Antarctic waters in conditions which tried men and ships to the limit. (*National Maritime Museum*)

This Rowlandson cartoon of 1815 shows that not all contemporary opinion approved of missionaries. The 'benign image' on the shield is projecting rays named 'Intolerance, Bigotry, Injustice, Oppression, Vice'. There are references to the Church of England, Nonconformity and Roman Catholicism. (*British Library*)

Children mining, from the Children's Employment Commission of 1842. In contrast to Hawaii and Tahiti, Britain (and the rest of Europe) treated huge numbers of its people to lives of endless drudgery. These children toiled in narrow coal seams dragging heavy tubs of coal. The child on all fours is a girl. (*British Library*)

The poor house at Datchworth, 1769. This is an extreme example of the callousness and indifference with which the poor were treated in Britain. The severe treatment of the poor seeking charitable relief often meant that people died of malnutrition rather than enter a workhouse. Such treatment of the needy would have been unthinkable in Tahiti or Hawaii. (*British Library*)

carried the other one forward. Davies and Young also operated the cannon which the king acquired and were instrumental in winning many battles for him. The two men were fortunate in that they happened to back the winner and both became respected advisors to the king, who rewarded their services with chiefly status and grants of land. Young went on to become the king's most trusted advisor and was left as the governor of the island of Hawaii over all the other chiefs when the king was absent on any of the other islands. Such was the wild swing of fortunes possible during this period. Ordinary sailors and adventurers could lose their lives or gain their fortunes with equal ease and as much uncertainty.

At this time most ships calling at the islands were American and the Hawaiians were not only often cheated by these traders and sold inferior merchandise, but the growing numbers also posed a most serious foreign threat. The king soon came to understand enough of the geography of the world and the respective strength of the navies involved to set the direction of his foreign policy. He sought the friendship of the British as the most powerful European naval power, who could protect him against too much American influence and prevent the islands being annexed by any other European power. His opportunity to promote this policy came when the British sent out a naval expedition under orders to re-establish British control of the north-west coast (Canada) and evict the Spanish who were laying claim to it, as well as to chart the coast and record its flora and fauna.

Captain George Vancouver was placed in command of the expedition's two ships – the *Discovery* (not Cook's old ship) and the *Chatham*, which sailed from Falmouth on 1 April 1791. Sailing via the Cape of Good Hope and New Zealand, they anchored in Kealakekua Bay, Hawaii in March 1792 to be received by Chief Kaiana as the king was absent. Vancouver did not wait for the king to arrive but pressed on to do his duty on the coast of Canada. The king was disappointed but was sure to have another chance to negotiate with the British and in January 1793 the British duly returned. Captain Vancouver was not a great admirer of the Hawaiians. The only men he allowed to board his ship were the chiefs and he would not let his own men wander freely about the shore. But, noting only that their contact with 'civilised' Europeans had made the women more immoral than ever, he placed no limit on the number of women who came out and stayed on the two vessels.

Captain Vancouver's caution was understandable. It was not his first visit. He had served as a midshipman with Captain Cook on both his second and third voyages of discovery and Kealakekua Bay held bitter memories. The old king, Kalaniopuu, who was ruler at the time of Cook's death, had died in 1782. The new king was Kamehameha whom Vancouver recalled as a fierce and ambitious chief. The throne had in fact passed to Kamehameha's cousin, the old king's son, but Kamehameha had rebelled, killed his cousin and defeated all the chiefs who had opposed him in a long civil war. Finally he had united the one island of Hawaii under his control in 1791. In the event, Vancouver found him a much softer and more agreeable personality than he recalled; in any case, now was not a time to remember old injuries; he had been sent into the Pacific to take possession of the coast of Canada and to re-establish British influence in the region. He interpreted his orders from the British government as authorising him to negotiate as he saw fit and he decided to include Hawaii in his sphere of action. It was a meeting of minds. King Kamehameha wanted a powerful European protector. At the king's instigation and with the agreement of a council of chiefs, the king ceded his possessions to the British Crown. On 25 February 1793 Lieutenant Puget went ashore, raised the flag, fired a salute and took possession of Hawaii for Great Britain. In return, as ruler of a British client state, Captain Vancouver supplied the king with muskets and ammunition and had his carpenters build him a European-style ship, thus making him the most powerful of the islands' kings.

That same year King Kahekili, ruler of the middle four islands of the chain, died and his kingdom was split by a civil war as his son and brother battled for the inheritance. It was the chance King Kamehameha had been waiting for and, using his new ship and firearms, he invaded, quickly overrunning two of the islands. The other two did not resist for long. Now only the northernmost island, Kauai, was not under Kamehameha's control. He then spent six years consolidating his existing kingdom, controlling trade and building up his wealth and armed force. He tried to conquer Kauai several times without success, his main problem being the difficulty of transporting a large enough army of warriors by canoe across the 75 miles of dangerous ocean between Kauai Island and the king's newly conquered territory of Oahu Island, that island itself well over 130 miles from his home island of Hawaii. Gradually he recruited European carpenters to supervise the building of more European-type ships capable of making the crossing laden with many hundreds of warriors at a time so that he might successfully engage his enemy. Through his control of trade with westerners he acquired a formidable arsenal. Only Kaumualii, king of Kauai and the minor island of Nihau, remained independent of his direct control: an independence which was not to last.

Chapter 9

THE TRADERS

They are of a lively disposition, friendly towards each other, open-hearted and generous; extremely superstitious, and not inclined to labour; seldom working more than two or three hours in the day, unless on some important occasion, or when at work for the king.

Charles Barnard at Hawaii, 1815

In the years which followed trade developed in intensity as various other countries pressed their claims to territory in and around the Pacific. The ownership of much of the north-west coast of America was in dispute and largely based on the claims of earlier explorers. Britain had laid claim to the area which now constitutes the west coast of Canada. Spain had old established settlements in California which were also witnessing an influx of American ships and traders. In the infant United States, President Thomas Jefferson was already asserting that it was his countrymen's 'Manifest Destiny' to occupy the continent from coast to coast, to which end he had financed the land expedition of Lewis and Clark across the west to the Pacific, thus establishing a claim to Oregon. In 1815, after the Napoleonic Wars, during which France had effectively been excluded from the world's oceans by the power of the Royal Navy, the French were now establishing their presence – and colonies – in the region. But whatever the claims or the nationality of the intruders, one result was that the west coast of the continent was becoming increasingly commercialised and westernised. The rights of the indigenous Native American Indians were completely ignored and they were soon to fall under the control of one or other of the foreign powers. Ironically, the British government refused to confirm Captain Vancouver's acceptance of Hawaii as a British possession. At the time Britain wanted no more colonies or responsibilities.

One possession in the region undisputed by other European powers was Russian sovereignty over the Aleutian Islands and Alaska. They comprised a huge inhospitable area where anyone, apart from the region's native

Indians and Eskimos, found it difficult to survive. The Russian outposts had
to be supplied by ships sailing from the Baltic; a journey circling two thirds
of the earth, from northern Europe south down round South Africa's Cape
of Good Hope then back up north to Alaska through 200° of latitude. The
Russians desperately needed a nearer and more reliable source of fresh
provisions. Governor Baranov of Alaska had tried to ensure a regular
supply of fresh food by founding a farming colony on the coast of
California, but this was never successful and produced little or no surplus to
support the Alaskan colonists.

The commercial development of Hawaii offered the chance of a more
reliable source and the king of Hawaii, not one to let slip a commercial
opportunity, wrote to Alexander Baranov, head of the Russian-American
Company in Alaska, that he would be happy to supply the Russians with a
whole shipload of supplies once a year. In response, in 1808 a Russian ship
from Alaska arrived for a load of salt with which to cure the valuable pelts of
the fur trade; on board they had a young Scotsman, Archibald Campbell, who
passed into the king of Hawaii's service, as had so many Europeans before
him. Campbell is an interesting figure, in so far as the roundabout means of
his arrival at Hawaii serves to show not only the freedom of the times, but
also the attraction which those islands exerted and the strange collection of
men who became important chiefs and powerful advisors to an absolute
monarch. It also illustrates the hazards of seafaring life.

Archibald Campbell was twenty-one years old when he arrived at Hawaii.
Born near Glasgow in 1787, apprenticed aged ten to a weaver, he had run
away to sea aged about thirteen, sailing on the *Isabella* which was trading to
the West Indies. In 1804, while his ship was at Madeira, he had been forcibly
pressed into service on the frigate HMS *Diana*. He served in the Royal Navy
under duress for two years before managing to desert while at Plymouth,
signing aboard an East Indiaman which sailed for China in convoy with nine
others. He left Britain expecting to be away for no more than two years: it
was to be six before he saw Scotland again. The voyage out was uneventful
and he gained promotion to sail-maker's mate and duly arrived at Wampoa
on 18 January 1807 after a passage lasting nine and a half months. He was
there for six weeks before his employers sent him to Canton. At Canton were
a number of American ships which were desperately short of crew, and
seamen were induced to desert their ships and sign with them by offers of a
cash bounty and higher wages. At first Campbell refused these blandishments
(after all, he would be forfeiting almost a year's wages), but finally he agreed

to sail on the *Eclipse* from Boston under Captain Joseph O'Kean with his crew of twenty-eight, for no other reason than that her ultimate destination was Hawaii, a place he wanted to see.

The ship was on charter to the Russian-American Company, bound first for Alaska before going on to Hawaii. On the voyage north they tried to trade at Nagasaki, but the Japanese absolutely forbade any contact between their citizens and foreigners and refused to let them enter Japanese territory, although they supplied the ship with fish, pigs, vegetables and water in abundance and all free of charge. Then on 10 September 1807, the *Eclipse* was wrecked at Sannack Island off Alaska. Only four of the twenty-nine men on board survived, Campbell being one of the fortunate ones. From September to March, during the depths of the Alaskan winter, Campbell was employed by the Russians salvaging the cargo, during which time he underwent many complex adventures and hardships – including another shipwreck – before eventually ending up at the main Russian settlement of Alexandria on Kodiak Island, badly frost-bitten. The loss of two fingers was to prove a comparatively minor matter. However, his feet were so badly affected that the only possibility of saving his life was to amputate them both. In an era before the use of anaesthetics that would have been a considerable ordeal even in a civilised hospital conducted by the most able surgeon: Campbell was in a trading post in primitive Alaska relying on the company doctor. The first operation was carried out on 15 March 1808. Undergoing one operation without anaesthetic must have been terrible and waiting a month while he recovered from the shock of the first before the process could be repeated must have caused immense mental stress. Although he owed his life to the Russian doctor the amputations were never a complete success; for the rest of his life the stumps were subject to ulcers and sores.

Interestingly, the Russians treated this common seaman, the lives of whose peers were deemed cheap and expendable on virtually every commercial voyage, with great consideration. Having cured him to the best of their ability, they collected money to see him on his way, and on 11 December 1808 they gave him free passage on the *Neva*, under Captain Hagemeister, to the Hawaiian Islands where he hoped to find a ship for home.

When the *Neva* arrived the king himself came on board smartly dressed in a European-style blue coat and grey pantaloons and Campbell was introduced as a weaver and sail-maker. Always alert to any new skill which might benefit his people, the king invited Campbell to stay to make a loom and demonstrate weaving to his people with the idea of introducing the manufacture of cloth to Hawaii. This was not popular with many of the white traders because woven cloth was a major item of trade for the Europeans and they feared domestic competition. But the king was trying to remain independent and realised that the less he relied on foreign business the more likely he was to retain Hawaiian independence. He adopted western techniques whenever the opportunity arose and by now had a navy of European-style ships which still proudly flew the British flag. These ships could mount a battery of the sixteen cannons he had acquired, and it was through these that he could keep control of the different islands.

The king's wife, Queen Tamena, took pity on Campbell's condition and brought him to live in her house. She would have fed him but warned him that if he ever ate with women he would never be allowed to eat with the men. He chose to preserve his status as a man by continuing to eat on board the *Neva* for the three months it was there loading a cargo of salt pork and dried taro root. When the ship left the king invited him to dine at his table. That the common people cared less for the Europeans than did their chiefs is hinted at by the fact that when the king was absent his attendants did not always bother to feed Campbell – so he went to live with Isaac Davies who by then had been resident for some twenty years.

Davies was now a high-ranking chief and had been given lands which were occupied and farmed by four to five hundred people, who, as his tenants, paid him rent in kind. Campbell lived with him for six months until the king granted him 60 acres of land at Pearl-water, 12 miles to the west of Hanaroora (modern Honolulu) with fifteen tenants to work it. Campbell claimed that at this time there were nearly sixty whites on the island of Oahu, of whom some six or eight were convicts who had escaped from the penal colony of New South Wales. He added that the king no longer actively encouraged men to desert their ships, but willingly employed any who wished to stay and who possessed a skill which might be of advantage to his people. On the other hand, he did not prevent anyone living there from leaving. Personal freedom was an essential part of Hawaiian culture; tenants were not tied to the land as were European peasantry, and even the king's servants could leave his service without notice. He also encouraged his men to sail in European ships so that they might see the foreigners in their homelands and learn their ways.

In spite of the generous grant of land and the care with which he was carried around, Campbell could not settle into his new life. After just over a year on the island he found passage on the English whaler *Duke of Portland* which was homeward bound with a cargo of 11,000 seal skins and 50 tons of seal oil. Before his departure the king demanded to see him and instructed him to convey his royal greetings and a message to King George III, finding it hard to believe Campbell when he said that a lowly subject like himself would not be admitted to the royal palace. He found it incredible too that Campbell, along with thousands of his fellow subjects, had never so much as seen his king. Nor could he understand how anyone could rule if he did not go around meeting his people. It was as well he carried no message for King George because Archibald Campbell was a long while reaching home, spending two years in Rio de Janeiro *en route* before ending his days making a living with a barrel organ as a street musician in Edinburgh and later as a violinist entertaining passengers on the Clyde steamers. He had fulfilled his ambition of visiting one of the Pacific paradises in a most remarkable way, but getting there had cost him his feet; many a sailor paid with his life.

King Kamehameha had been a shrewd ruler. Not only had he retained the loyalty of his people, kept their society together under the impact of the Europeans and skilfully manipulated the latter to consolidate his rule over the entire island chain, but he had embraced European technology where it was advantageous and had won the respect of the traders and captains who met him. He welcomed to his islands white men who had skills he needed and gave them grants of land; he refused to sell land to anyone – it was always granted to them only for life. Although he preferred the British, while being obliged by their sheer weight of numbers to deal mainly with the Americans, he tried to keep an even hand in his dealings with all nations. In fact, one might suspect that his invitation to the Russians to trade with him was to provide a counterbalance to the growing dominance of the Americans. He built up the trade of the islands and, in so doing, secured power for himself. Nevertheless not all his actions benefited his people; the pace of change was sometimes misjudged. But it was beyond his powers to prevent the influx of foreign influence, which was bound to have an impact on the culture of the island.

The increase in trade meant an intensification of labour, and the old leisurely pattern of working to produce sufficient to support a simple lifestyle was being replaced by the need to produce more food to provision all the ships, while the new trade in sandalwood created previously unknown demands for labour; both of which were to raise the money to pay for the new imports. Perhaps unsurprisingly, their sudden entry into the world of commerce created social disruption among a people for whom the notion of commercial exchange had previously hardly existed:

Problems associated with the European presence in the Group became suddenly more acute in 1816. The sandalwood trade had swollen to enormous importance, and 1,000 tons had been shipped to China in 1812. The implications for the Hawaiian people were distinctly unfortunate. As soon as Kamehameha realized the commercial significance of sandalwood, he established a royal monopoly over the trade; undertook to pay for his requirements from foreigners by supplying them with quantities of sandalwood; and organized the Hawaiian people to abandon farming and fishing and concentrate their energies on cutting down their sandalwood groves to supply the foreign market. One predictable result was famine, which Kamehameha attempted to mitigate by periodically ordering both chiefs and commoners to turn to and produce food, just as he attempted to moderate the wholesale exploitation of the sandalwood reserves by placing *kapu* [taboo] on young trees.[1]

Thus the first substantial commercial trading links with the outside world, intended to increase the wealth of a country and its inhabitants, managed only to increase the amount of labour required while actually reducing their standard of living.

If this historical assessment is true in general it does not reflect the experience of one who was there at the time. Passing up the coast of Hawaii on 5 December 1815, Charles H. Barnard, who was taking passage with a Captain Bailey after having lived through a series of adventures and wrecks since leaving America in 1812, was aware of no such food shortages as canoes came out to trade with his ship. Captain Bailey let it be known that he was in search of a cargo of sandalwood. Two days later 'Mr Billy Pitt' with several other chiefs 'honoured us with a visit'[2] and informed them that the king was at Kirowan, 15 miles to the north. The king sent no less than three white men with instructions that the ship was to move to his location where he was welcomed aboard with a seven-gun salute. The king ensured that he took maximum advantage of the ships which sought to trade with him: he agreed to sell them sandalwood on condition that Captain Bailey first sail to one of the other islands with fifty Hawaiians to collect the tribute and taxes due to the king; only then would they be allowed to load sandalwood. This obligation to the king discharged, on 15 January 1816 they sailed to Toai Bay, home of the king's trusty John Young, who personally weighed all the cargo. According to Barnard, the islanders were still enjoying a fairly relaxed and easy life as they still would not work more than two or three hours a day.

On 16 February they sailed for Canton. As another service to the king Captain Bailey was persuaded to take on board an American and an Englishman who had been expelled for refusing to pay their taxes. These unwilling passengers were allowed to take with them two women and four men to labour for them as they intended to settle at Agregan, one of the Marianas Islands. Others expelled from Hawaii had settled there, making a living by raising supplies for ships which found them another convenient port of call on their way from Hawaii to China. Places where ships trading across the Pacific could be sure of finding fresh water and adequate supplies were slowly becoming established.

Chapter 10

THE BEAR AND THE EAGLE

[The King] . . . had established a system of appointing representatives or viceroys to enforce his rule over the various islands of the Group, apart from Kauai. Most were native-born chiefs. However, two of the most important viceroys were Europeans, John Young, who governed Hawaii between 1802 and 1812, and Oliver Holmes, who held office in Oahu.

Glen Barclay, A History of the Pacific . . .[1]

Kaumualii, paramount chief of the northern island of Kauai, reluctantly acknowledged that King Kamehameha had some claim to suzerainty, but nevertheless effectively ruled as an independent king, and was prepared to oppose Kamehameha the moment he felt he had any chance of success. Trade was the key to power and 'Each has offered sandal wood and other inducements to the Americans, for assistance in the invasion and conquest of the dominions of the other.'[2] The king tried to prevent civil wars and rebellions by keeping the paramount chiefs of other islands with him, but Kaumualii was strong enough to remain on his own island. One obvious advantage of giving positions of power to Europeans was that they could make no claim to be rulers in their own right as could the chiefs whose fathers had once ruled independently and who could still count on the traditional loyalties of their people. But above all the power of the king now came from Europeans and the services of mercenaries. In 1814 a trading ship driven ashore and wrecked on independent Kauai set in train a series of events which tempted the Russians to try to gain a foothold on the islands and ended in the latter's permanent and un-challengeable unification.

Sent from the Russian territory of Alaska the wrecked ship had been bound for Hawaii, and while the crew lived ashore protecting the cargo which had been salvaged their captain returned to report the loss. In Alaska, Governor Baranov could not have been pleased at the news, but with his cargo and crew ashore on Kauai, he sensed that his losses could be recovered and that the situation might even be turned to his nation's advantage. Either Chief Kaumualii would restore the cargo in order to win their friendship and trade away from the king, or King Kamehameha would be obliged to compensate them for the theft. Trade was mainly in the hands of the Americans who had used their influence with the king to exclude the Russians: Governor Baranov hoped that the incident might be manipulated to win greater concessions. He sent his representative, a German doctor, Georg Scheffer, on the mission to persuade Kamehameha to have their cargo returned or to recompense them for its value in sandalwood. Scheffer's presence on the island was resented by the existing traders who did not welcome a competitor and who urged the king not to trust the German. Their protestations were supported by the influential voice of John Young. And Scheffer was unsuccessful – until he was credited with curing the king of an illness.

In his gratitude the king overruled his advisors and granted concessions to the Russians, who were given permission to construct a trading station on the island of Oahu where the trade would be under the king's eyes and control. But Kamehameha declined to provoke his vassal king of Kauai and refused to issue an order for the return of the Russians' cargo. While Scheffer was engaged in these negotiations, Governor Baranov sent the *Otkrytie*, under the command of Lieutenant Podushkin, to recover the missing cargo by force. In May 1816, and having first collected Scheffer from Oahu, the *Otkrytie* arrived at Kauai only to find that the difficulty had been resolved and that most of the cargo had already been returned to Alaska, implying that the 'King' of Kauai had already decided to seek the goodwill of the Russians. Dr Scheffer's ambitions were greater than his friendship for King Kamehameha. He decided to back Chief Kaumualii in an outright rebellion against Kamehameha. Negotiations between Scheffer and the chief were concluded on 2 July 1816 when it was agreed that Chief Kaumualii would swear allegiance to Tsar Alexander I of Russia and also give the Russian-American Company the monopoly of trade on his island of Kauai. In return Scheffer recognised him as king of the island and promised him the armed protection of Russia. It was an amazing degree of political meddling for the lone agent of a minor governor to commit the Russian Empire to the military defence of an isolated island. But in those days of slow communications the men on the spot had to use their own judgement. Scheffer's diplomatic wisdom may have been fatally flawed but he did not lack drive and energy. In a remarkably short time, three forts were constructed to protect this new possession and in anticipation of new trade from Kauai to Alaska, Scheffer purchased two American vessels –

bought with the promise that Governor Baranov would pay for them when they arrived at Alaska.

Scheffer's ambitions, along with those of Kaumualii, extended beyond regaining the formal independence of Kauai Island from the suzerainty of Kamehameha. They planned to conquer the neighbouring island of Oahu; the Russians supplying arms and ammunition, Kaumualii the men. The island was to be divided equally between them on the successful conclusion of their plot. But Scheffer was impatient and overconfident. Once he felt sure that Kamehameha was unable to interfere with Russian actions on Kauai he also began to fortify the Russian-American Company's trading post at Honolulu in Oahu island in readiness for the implementation of the next part of their plan. This was too much for King Kamehameha to ignore: aided and encouraged by the Americans he ordered the Russians to be expelled. The Russians were forced to abandon Oahu and retire to Kauai. There the Russian flag did fly. But Scheffer had managed to turn everyone against himself save his ally the chief of Kauai: by securing a monopoly of trade there he had made enemies of all the other traders, and by supporting Kaumualii he had lost the friendship of Kamehameha. He desperately needed the backing of a Russian man-of-war.

It seemed that Scheffer was in luck. By an incredible coincidence, in November 1816 a Russian ship, the *Rurick*, was sighted, and since it was approaching from the south the vessel had to sail up the whole chain of islands before reaching Kauai and Scheffer. Expecting the worst, King Kamehameha stationed armed men along the coast. The Russian expedition was commanded by Lieutenant Otto von Kotzebue who was completely ignorant of the actions Scheffer had been taking in the name of the Russian government, for he had set sail long before news from the Pacific had reached Moscow. Despatches from Alaska had to be sent to the Siberian mainland, then overland by dog sledge from the Bering Straits or Kamchatka, a journey of some six months, before they arrived at the Russian capital. As soon as von Kotzebue learned what had been done in Russia's name he went ashore to assure King Kamehameha that the Russian government had absolutely no intention of annexing his islands. Not only did he refuse to involve Russia in a colonial escapade, but news came that Governor Baranov had also totally rejected Scheffer's adventurism, even refusing to buy the two American ships. As if to underline his absolute rejection of Scheffer's scheme to annex the Hawaiian Islands for the Russian Empire, von Kotzebue did not even visit the Russian enterprise at Kauai, but sailed direct to Alaska. The failure of a ship of the Russian Imperial Navy to support him spelt the end of Scheffer's career with the Russians, and the end of his time in Hawaii.

Realising that Scheffer was now a man of straw Kaumualii expelled him in a leaky boat which scarcely made it to Honolulu. There the hapless German was informed that if he landed he would be imprisoned, an option he rejected in spite of the condition of his boat. However, the situation was resolved when an American ship, whose captain had reason to be grateful to Scheffer for earlier medical treatment, offered to take him to Canton. It is illustrative of the slow communications of the day that 'The directors of the Russian-American Company in St Petersburg had not received Scheffer's first report until after he had been run out of the islands.'[3] The directors might have backed his ambitions more vigorously, but by the time they learnt of the opportunity, the moment had gone. For his part, having lost his ally and turned all the traders against him, Kuamaulii's ambitions of a larger and fully independent kingdom were ended. He was allowed to continue to rule as chief in his own lifetime but to avoid war and inevitable defeat he chose to submit absolutely to Kamehameha.

This was the end to challenges to the kingship, which now passed down the Kamehameha family line. The king had two wives: Queen Kaahumanu, a mature and impressive woman 6ft tall and weighing 30st, who exerted considerable influence in Hawaiian politics and was to rule as regent after his death; and an eleven-year-old in whose veins flowed the blood of all those chiefly families which also had legitimate claims to the throne on Kamehameha's death. This fusion of dynastic claims in marriages ensured that his son's right to the throne was never seriously contested.

Kamehameha had fulfilled his ambitions, but in doing so overreached himself and fell into the trap of accepting goods on credit. American commercial influence with the king and the chiefs became all-pervasive and traders advanced money and goods against promises of future supplies of island produce. It remained illegal for foreigners to own land in Hawaii but, to get money, the king and the chiefs started leasing it. American commercial houses leased thousands of acres to plant sugar, coffee, bananas and taro, thus introducing monoculture and labour for profit into the islands. The managers of these enterprises complained that labourers either did not arrive when wanted or were reluctant to work if they did. People had to be ordered to work for them by their chiefs, who apart from often gaining financial advantage through supplying labour, were straining the old loyalties which in the past had meant that the people were willing to work for their chiefs at necessary communal tasks. Jacques Arago, who was the official artist on board a French man-of-war which visited Hawaii in 1819, recorded his impression of the sandalwood trade.

> Commerce had attracted to this place [Oahu] some Americans, who, in the hope of speedily making their fortunes, established themselves here several years ago. I cannot say that they carry on any regular trade here, but rather contraband: they can obtain whatever they want at so cheap a rate! In the morning they take half a dozen [bottles] of wine to the Governor, and the good soul is soon stretched at their feet: they make presents of a few hatchets and muskets to the principal Chiefs; all the rest of the population are then quite at the disposal of these gentlemen. Some strong and active men are sent to the mountains; the forests are examined, and some sandal-wood trees cut down: those are conveyed to the water's edge at night by about twenty women, who are paid for either carrying or dragging them along, with a few ells of European cloth or linen; thence to be embarked on board a vessel that is always stationed in the harbour.[4]

This system of communal labour which the commoners owed to their chiefs had not been a burden before the arrival of international trade: then they had produced enough for their own consumption; now they were obliged to labour to accumulate capital for their masters. The one justification king and chiefs had had for this policy was the need to buy arms. And perhaps one should not be overcritical of this: without arms the islanders would always have been inferior to the seamen and traders who arrived off their shores, and the chief who did not buy arms while his neighbour did would soon cease to live as a chief – as Kamehameha's rise to power had proved. Nor was the problem confined to Hawaii and Tahiti, for the arms race affected some other islands even more deeply – to the extent that their chiefs would scarcely bother to trade for anything other than arms.

It would also be a mistake to assume, as did Arago, that there were always easy profits to be made. With the end of the Napoleonic Wars the French began to look for trading opportunities in the Pacific; and a good example of the difficulties encountered and the way the flag followed trade is inherent in the voyage of the *Bordelais*. A three-masted 200 ton ship, she was a French trader that sailed around the world between 1816 and 1819 under Camille de Roquefeuil in command of a complement of thirty-four officers and men – an exceptionally large crew for a small merchant ship. She sailed from

Pauillac (Bordeaux) on 19 October 1816 and arrived at Valparaiso on 5 February 1817, a comparatively fast voyage of three months seventeen days. She worked her way up the South American coast arriving at San Francisco on 3 August 1817 and from there traded for furs along the coast of present-day Canada. This was dangerous work as the Native American Indians were always liable to attack a ship and kill the crew should the opportunity arise. After three and a half months of trading the ship left San Francisco on 12 November, having lost nine crew through desertion and carrying many sick. In December they were at the Marquesas.

Here they proceeded with a great deal of caution as the Marquesans were warlike cannibals who would rather take a ship by force than trade with it. Indeed, Roquefeuil left some places without trading because the danger of attack was so evident. And with the ship's complement now down to twenty-five men, he needed to exercise extreme caution as to how many he had ashore or on board at any given time, and how many Marquesan men were allowed on board. Eventually he found a location where he felt secure enough to trade, starting, as was customary, with some bartering for food. For safety's sake he anchored well away from the shore, but nevertheless about fifty women swam out and in spite of efforts to repel them, insisted on boarding the ship. The Marquesans made it clear that there would be no trading until the women's wishes were met: 'In order to keep up a good understanding it had been necessary to admit some young girls, who had expressed a desire to become acquainted with our people.'[5] Once the crew had become acquainted to the satisfaction of the women, trading for sandalwood commenced, the islanders being interested only in muskets and powder as they too were engaged in an arms race, between clans and tribes competing for superiority on the island as well as in wars of conquest between islands. They were willing to trade food and artefacts for other goods with individuals in the crew, but to obtain food in any quantity the crew were obliged to trade in arms, exchanging three muskets for thirty hogs. Prices were up: 'a musket some time ago was worth a ton of wood. The following are the terms on which we concluded our bargains. For one musket, 500 lbs. of sandle wood; for two pounds and a quarter of powder, 200 lbs.; for a hatchet, 45 lbs.; a whale's tooth 200 lbs.'[6] Whales' teeth were a status symbol and obviously still very valuable, but only the largest and finest were given any value at all. Other trade goods they simply despised. Sandalwood on these islands was small inferior stuff and even that was becoming quite scarce.

From the Marquesas trade took the *Bordelais* up into the Russian territory of Alaska to take on more furs before heading to Canton with the cargo. The previous season the North American Indians had been difficult to deal with and otter skins scarce. This time a number of Eskimos were recruited and taken to the coast of America where they were to hunt the valuable sea-otter for the ship. If the North American Indians had given the French a difficult time the previous season, their temper was not improved by the spectacle of other hunters imported to collect their furs. Nineteen of the Eskimo hunters were attacked and slain. It had now taken over a year to collect a cargo for a small 200 ton ship, and with the sandalwood and furs they set course for Canton where those would be sold and Chinese goods loaded for the homeward journey. Commerce in the early years of its development in the north Pacific may not have been to the advantage of the native peoples, it may have returned large profits, but it was no sinecure either for those who pursued it.

Given that they were in North America and Alaska to collect furs it seems strange that the French had not gone to Hawaii, only half the distance from San Francisco as the Marquesas, to trade for sandalwood. Perhaps they felt that given the dominance of the Americans and English, they would not succeed in being granted a cargo. They may have gone to the Marquesas with the idea of establishing an area of French dominance through trade – and in due course the Marquesas did come under French control. And as French possessions increased in the Pacific so her citizens became more assertive in demanding equal rights with other nations to trade with Hawaii.

The impact of shipping on such islands was out of all proportion to the numbers: in the forty years following its discovery in 1778 Hawaii was visited by about a hundred ships. Some dozen of the British total of thirty-nine were men-of-war or ships bound on voyages of discovery – as were two early French visitors. The Russian interest was well marked with eleven visits. Thirty-one American ships were trading vessels, and another twelve whose nationality is not recorded were probably American: their dominance in trade was overwhelming. Regardless, however, of the nationality of those with whom they traded, Hawaiian debt continued to mount: 'The chiefs had for years been accumulating debts which they had undertaken to pay off with cargoes of sandalwood. The claims of the traders amounted to some $200,000 by 1826. Two American warships consequently arrived that year to compel Kaahumanu to acknowledge "the debts due to American citizens, to be Government debts".'[7] American entrepreneurs now enjoyed the advantage of trading with little or no risk. They could grant loans, sign contracts with any impecunious chief or person, and then demand payment from the Hawaiian government. The king himself had spent money on overpriced and pointless European luxury goods. The whole nation was to suffer as its people had to work harder and produce more for the profit of their masters, and those masters were increasingly Americans or chiefs controlled by American commercial interests. The British Lion may have refused to become involved, the Russian Bear may have been chased out, and the French Cockerel was still crowing beyond their horizon – but the American Eagle was casting an ever-growing shadow over traditional Hawaiian life and culture.

Chapter 11

HAWAII AND THE HAWAIIANS

Let us, therefore, leave these good people to their early habits and natural inclinations; why teach them desires and wants? If repose, comfort, tranquillity and pleasure constitute happiness, then they are happy; what more do they want? Would you propose to give them in exchange for these, interest, the love of glory, avarice, jealousy, and all the passions of which they are now ignorant, and which prevail in our wiser Europe? They will laugh at you, and, leaving you to your prejudices, return gaily to their own lowly huts.

　　Jacques Arago, Narrative of a Voyage Round the World . . . *(1823)[1]*

By the time Jacques Arago arrived at the Hawaiian Islands in August 1819 it was already too late to 'leave these good people to their early habits and natural inclinations', although he and many other observers felt that the islanders would have been far happier had their islands never been discovered by Europeans. Hawaii resembled Tahiti but was much larger, with Mount Mauna Kea rising to almost 14,000ft above sea level and although it had active volcanoes and parts of it were less fertile than Tahiti, much of it was covered in a similar lush vegetation. Like Tahiti and unlike so much of Africa, India and similar tropical and semi-tropical regions there were no poisonous reptiles or dangerous animals and endemic diseases were comparatively mild, so their inhabitants had little to fear from the natural world. This benevolent environment gave its inhabitants a benign view of nature and put them at ease with their surroundings in a way not possible in less safe regions of the world. As at Tahiti, they lived with an abundance of food which was raised and harvested with very little labour. It is small wonder that through their religion they saw their entire environment as holy.

Hawaiian creation myth reveals the islands to be the children of the gods, and their beliefs provide a significant link with Tahiti. The Mother of the Gods and the Father of Light (the parents of the gods) lived in the sky and when their first child was born it dropped into the sea and became the island of

Hawaii. Two subsequent children became the islands of Maui and Kahoolawe, after which the mother of the islands went to Tahiti. While she was away the God of Light had relations with two other women to produce two more Hawaiian Islands. When the Mother of the Gods returned to Hawaii she conceived the island of Oahu by another man in revenge for the God of Light's infidelity – after which they were reunited and produced the remaining islands. Thus the Hawaiian creation myth explains the eight major islands of the Hawaiian chain. This not only links Hawaii and Tahiti but involves both holy parents indulging in the multiple sexual relations which their worshippers accepted as part of normal life, the male god having relationships with three females and the female god with two males.

That the islands of Hawaii were effectively the children of the gods made all nature sacred. The Hawaiians preserved a deep sense of the sacredness of the natural world around them, and even to pluck and use a leaf called for thanks to the appropriate god. That the gods also enjoyed sexual relations legitimised the erotic aspects of human nature and its uninhibited enjoyment. While music and dance have been and still are included in religious ceremonies throughout the world, Hawaiian dances often incorporated and expressed sexual elements, although the hula dance, which Europeans came to associate with lines of bare-breasted women and condemned as too overtly erotic, had originally been exclusively male. Entering a hula school was not unlike entering a monastery as it involved a great deal of discipline and religious learning. In the late eighteenth century only men could perform the hula and only during temple worship services, but as traditional religion lost its power the hula gradually became mainly a female dance, albeit much changed and suppressed by Christian missionaries.

As is the case with other islands, the size of the Hawaiian population when first discovered by Europeans cannot be stated with any certainty. Captain Cook estimated the Hawaiian Islands to have a population of between 300,000 and 400,000. Modern research tends to reduce this figure to nearer 200,000, but it was about three times as great as that of Tahiti. This large and healthy population did not remain so for long. Captain Cook ordered that no man having any symptoms of venereal disease should lie with a woman, but his crew managed to infect the island with both syphilis and gonorrhoea: subsequent visitors added other common European diseases which were to reduce numbers to about 60,000 within eighty years of the island's discovery. Within sixty years Europeans had almost destroyed an entire population. Economic development played an important part, but much was due to the destruction of Hawaiian religion and culture. These two latter aspects were significantly disrupted wherever Europeans went in the Pacific, but the shock was particularly severe at Hawaii. The early European visitors to the islands – the naval personnel and men of science – were content to observe the local religion and culture rather than make any effort to change it. But the trauma of coming to appreciate that they were only one tiny fraction of an enormous world undermined the whole foundation of Hawaiian culture and destroyed their religious certainties.

Hawaiian gods were recognisably the same as Tahitian deities and elicited the same respect for the natural world. Kane, the foremost god, was the ancestor of all men and of sunlight, forests and fresh water, and did not accept human sacrifice. Lono was the god of fertility and agriculture, of clouds, wind and sea, who could assume dozens of different forms; he, too, eschewed human sacrifice. Of lesser or parallel status to these major gods, each craft had a minor guardian spirit which favoured it and was revered, much as trade guilds in Europe venerated their own particular saint. Unlike some Polynesians, the Hawaiians were not cannibals and the one great blot on Polynesian religion in the eyes of Europeans was human sacrifice. It seems likely that this practice increased in the later period just before the Europeans arrived, as it is little mentioned in earlier legends and oral sources. This was the period of more frequent wars and social unrest as the power of the chiefs was centralised and social distinctions became more pronounced, a process intensified by the European presence. On learning that human sacrifice was abhorred by the nations whose ships visited him, King Kamehameha promptly abolished the custom. Indeed, it was not an essential part of their beliefs. It was mainly Ku, the god of war, who required human sacrifice, although sacrifices would also be made to appease volcanic eruptions, eclipses of the sun and similar disturbing phenomena. Archibald Campbell, who lived on Hawaii for fifteen months commencing in 1809, was aware of only one execution during his stay. Arago, who arrived ten years after Campbell, discussed the death penalty with a Mr Marini, a long-time European resident on Hawaii: 'One thing of which Marini informed me is particularly worthy of remark; it is, that very few persons attend these executions, although they are of a very rare occurrence. Paris is a civilised place, Owhyee a savage island!'[2] The implied contrast between the revolutionary mobs of Paris enjoying the spectacle of the guillotine – or for that matter the crowds in London enjoying public executions – and the distaste of Hawaiians for witnessing such barbarity certainly justifies the exclamation mark.

According to Marshall Sahlins, 'The name of the political relationship in Hawaii is aloha. Aloha "love" is the people's consciousness of their servitude. It is how they describe their obligations and justify their loyalties to the chief. Reciprocally, the chief should have aloha for his people.'[3] In fact love, in all its forms, was the guiding principle of their society. Those sailors who refused the women's sexual invitations were mocked and derided by them.

Society was divided much as it was in Tahiti, although its chiefly class was more complicated with eleven grades so that they descended into quite small landowners. Commoners were granted land in return for services, and traditional rights entitled them to a share of the produce and other material necessities. They were not bound and if dissatisfied with the way in which their chief treated them, they could leave and enter the service of another. When they were too old to work the chief was obliged to keep them. As with Tahiti, the Hawaiian Islands were split into different divisions each headed by a chief, some of whom recognised a paramount chief or king. But it was alliances with and support from Europeans which ultimately enabled one chief to unify the whole island group under a single authority. The fact that authority rested on force was expressed every time tributes and taxes were collected. During November while the priests collected the taxes from the chiefs, the king was obliged to spend the whole month in religious ceremonies on the *marae*; but before the month started the king had three spears thrown at him as a symbol of resistance to his right to tax his people. He was obliged to catch the first and then ward off the other two. Archibald Campbell, who witnessed this event, wrote, 'This is not a mere formality. The spear is thrown with the utmost force; and should the king lose his life, there is no help for it',[4] although given the dual secular and sacred status of such chiefs or kings, one might be inclined to believe the first was thrown with little risk to life. Priestly functions and high religious office were inherited by those of upper rank, although commoners could enter the priesthood by serving an apprenticeship. Taboo (pronounced *kapu* in Hawaii) expressed sanctity as well as that which was prohibited. Individual sanctity prescribed different rituals: for example, in the presence of a paramount chief commoners were obliged to prostrate themselves fully, while a lesser chief need only kneel, since he too possessed some degree of taboo.

The respect paid to the king's person, to his house and even to his food, formed a remarkable contrast to the simplicity of his mode of living: 'whenever he passed, his subjects were obliged to uncover their heads and shoulders . . . When his food was carrying, from the cooking-house, each person within hearing of the call Noko, or, Sit down, given by the bearers, was obliged to uncover himself, and squat down on his hams';[5] even his water, carried from a stream 5 miles away, was shown the same respect. Although chiefs were so elevated above the rest of their people, Campbell tells us that the king's mode of living was virtually the same as that of his ordinary subjects. He breakfasted at eight, dined at noon, and supped at sunset. His principal chiefs being always about his person, there were generally twenty or thirty people present seated on mats spread on the floor. The breakfast and supper consisted of fish and sweet potatoes. For dinner a dish of poe, or taro pudding, was set before each of them, which they ate with their fingers, instead of spoons. This fare, together with salt fish and consecrated pork from the *marae*, formed the whole of the repast, no other food being permitted in the king's house. A plate, knife and fork, with boiled potatoes were, however, always set before Moxely (an American who acted as an interpreter) and Campbell, by his majesty's orders. The king concluded his meal by drinking half a glass of rum, but the bottle was immediately sent away, the liquor being tabooed, or interdicted to his guests. Away from the king's table, western alcohol was replacing the traditional kava '[which] is now giving way to the use of ardent spirits. I never saw it used, except as a medecine to prevent corpulency, and it is said to be an effective remedy. It causes a white scurf to strike out upon the skin, somewhat like the dry scurvy. The spirit distilled from tee-root now usurps its place, and I fear the consequences will be still more pernicious.'[6] Distilling had been introduced by one of Campbell's fellow Scots – William Stevenson, a convict who had escaped from the Australian penal colony – and its output was to become more widespread than the drinking of kava, which had been mainly consumed by the chiefs and on ritual occasions.

Away from the king's table, too, each chief had a separate eating house, with the lower ranks combining to have one such house for every six or seven families so eating was always a male social occasion. Women ate in their own houses. Taro pudding was the staple and was prepared by being baked in a pit and then mixed with cold water and mashed. Fish was eaten both raw and cooked. Most food was cooked in the usual Polynesian manner in a pit, although it was occasionally wrapped in leaves and placed directly in a fire. The islanders had few foodstuffs which could be stored for long such as wheat and similar grains or pulses, so they could hoard very little against possible crop failure and famine. Pork was preserved by boning then salting and drying, although meat formed a comparatively small part of their regular diet, and taro could be sliced and dried in the sun; but in general food was produced for immediate consumption.

As in Tahiti, the Europeans were struck by the cleanliness of both the people and their dwellings. Houses were oblong with low side walls and high thatched roofs and had one open room with neither tables nor seats. Much of life was lived out of doors and in public. Chiefs' houses were larger and carpeted with elaborately patterned woven mats, but apart from a few wooden dishes kept hanging on the walls and an occasional carved stool, they were of much the same pattern. The biggest difference was that they had a raised platform at one end where the family slept while their retainers slept at the other end. To one visitor in 1819 who had touched at several island groups in the Pacific,

> The huts at Owhyee appear to me the best that we have seen since we have been in these semi-barbarous regions. Almost the whole of them have only one apartment ornamented with mats, calabashes, and some country cloths. In that room fathers, mothers, boys, girls, and some times even hogs and dogs, all sleep together pele-mele: there the mothers offer their daughters to strangers; there the children learn, almost as soon as they are born, what they ought scarcely to know when they are grown-up; there the son forgets what he owes to the father, because the father forgets what is due to the son; there, in short, the head of the family has no authority, except what derives from his own strength, while his son is yet in the bounds of infancy.[7]

Arago's comments on the mixing of inhabitants in the houses could have been reproduced throughout Europe, from Ireland in the west to as far east as one cared to enquire – and most of such inhabitants would have been harder worked and underfed. As for his perception of lack of respect, he simply did not understand the social customs of the country and was quite wrong in believing that the head of the family had no authority; his mistake was to assume that the husband and father was head according to European practice, not the child.

Mourning was an important ritual and the public displays of grief and frenzy at the death of royalty exceeded anything that took place in Tahiti. In May 1809, Terremytee, the king's brother, died. 'The natives cut their hair, and went about completely naked. Many of them, particularly the women, disfigured themselves by knocking out their front teeth, and branding their faces with red hot stones . . . at the same time, a general, I believe I may say an universal, public prostitution of the women took place. The queens, and the widow of the deceased, were alone excepted.'[8] The queen kept the bones of her father wrapped in a cloth and slept with them at her side 'because she loved her father so dearly'.[9] This excessive emotion and hysteria coupled with the obligation that commoners prostrate themselves before a paramount chief (instead of merely kneeling, as in Tahiti) leaves the impression that Hawaiian society, although it had a great deal in common with Tahiti, was more authoritarian and its culture fiercer and more aggressive, even if the position of women in Hawaiian society was similar to that of their Tahitian counterparts.

To Europeans the cultural taboos appeared to place females in an inferior position to males, although it may have been a matter of different treatment for each gender rather than of superior or inferior treatment. Clearly, women in both island groups had a firmly entrenched set of rights and a great deal of freedom. Taboos were, however, quite complicated and Caroline Ralston makes the important point, often overlooked by historians, that religious obligations are not always followed in practice – one only has to think of Catholicism and its 'taboo' on contraception to realise just how large a proportion of those practising any religion ignore one or more of its tenets. This observation raises the perhaps now unanswerable question as to how often ordinary Hawaiians broke their taboos. Ralston[10] sensibly suggests that many of the taboos placed on women were ignored by the common people. For example, during her menses a woman was supposed to live in a separate hut, and also to have a separate house for childbirth, but from contemporary observations of the buildings it is doubtful if these facilities were available to the lower classes. It is claimed that women rarely had shelters during such times, but lived beneath the stars, simply retiring to the woods for ten days after childbirth and for three days a month, when they were supposed not to be seen by men. As is ever the case, in religion and culture there was a gap between the ideal and the real; and between the practices of the upper and lower classes, as only the chiefly classes had the economic resources to construct separate houses for these rituals.

Women were subject, too, to a strict taboo in terms of the types of food they were permitted to eat:

Articles of delicacy, such as pork, turtle, shark, cocoa-nuts, bananas or plantains, are also forbidden. Dog's flesh and fish were the only kinds of animal food lawful for them to eat; but since the introduction of sheep and goats, which are not tabooed, the ladies have less reason to complain. Notwithstanding the vigour with which these ceremonies are generally observed, the women seldom scruple to break them, when it can be done in secret; they often swim off to ships at night during the taboo; and I have known them eat of the forbidden delicacies of pork and shark's flesh.[11]

Campbell reports that he once saw the queen eating forbidden meat; she swore him to silence saying that her life was at stake, but he scarcely believed that the punishment would have been so draconian. Campbell also records that while the king was fulfilling his religious duties and was safely confined to the *marae* for two nights and a day every month, the queen always took the opportunity to get drunk.

The benign climate meant that dress was of little practical importance; women generally wore a piece of cloth 3ft by 9ft wrapped around their waist and reaching down to their calves, but went to great pains 'in ornamenting themselves, for which purpose every female is provided with a small mirror. All ranks pay the utmost attention to personal cleanliness.'[12] Their style was more contrived and artificial than that of Tahitian women. Hawaiian women combed their hair back off the forehead and bleached it almost white. Flowers were in constant use around the neck and were wound around the head two or three times and into the hair. The preferred blooms were purple, yellow and white which were woven together with 3 or 4ins of each colour in turn. Tapa cloth was dyed brown, green, blue, black and yellow; as it disintegrated when wet they held their clothes above their heads with one hand when swimming to a ship. Most Hawaiians, male and female, had well-fed athletic bodies somewhat larger than the average European. The French expedition's artist cast a professional eye on them:

Their mouths and lips are of the middle size, their teeth very beautiful; and we cannot do otherwise than pity them on account of the wretched superstition, which makes it a duty to extract some of those ornaments of the mouth at the death of a friend or benefactor . . . The women are not by any means as handsome as the men, and rather short than tall. The scars with which they cover their bodies, are much more tastefully finished than those of the men. They ornament in preference the most delicate parts, such as the cheeks and breasts. What guilty profanity! the bust of these females seems in general to rival anything the ancients have told us, of that part of Greek and Georgian beauties. Unconstrained by stays or bands, it attains the size and elasticity, intended by nature. It is neither too large nor too small, but firm and separated: the dignified breadth of this part in the young women, and their small feet and hands, are the principle beauties to which they are indebted for the voluntary homage paid them by strangers . . . They are extremely clean in their persons; . . . Their gestures are indecent, their allurements obscene, and their looks not expressive. The custom followed by many of them, of whitening the top of the head, and sometimes all the hair, with quick lime, completes their disfigurement, by giving them when young the appearance of age.[13]

A less flattering description than that furnished by most observers. The 'scars' he refers to are undoubtedly tattoos.

In defiance of all regulations, the commander of this French expedition had smuggled his young wife, Rose, on board. Her impression of Hawaiian visitors on board ship is possibly the first description of a Hawaiian woman by a European female:

We were still at table when to our great surprise Keohuna, wife of this prince, arrived with one of her friends. Her height astonished me as much as her presence on board; picture yourselves a woman of about thirty years old, 5 feet 10 inches tall, stout, not in, but out of proportion, in fact enormous. Besides, think what such corpulence is when it is entirely exposed. A piece of cloth covers her fully from the waist downwards, but from the waist up, almost nothing at all but flesh; sometimes she drapes a second wrap on one shoulder, but not always. Both wore earrings and necklaces of some pretty seeds from plants unknown to me and of varying shapes.[14]

The French artist with the expedition left his written impressions as well as his paintings. He also met the dowager queens and the king's wives, and he confirmed the general tendency of queens to become gross:

There were five of these Queens, and she of whom I speak, who weighed at least thirty stone, was the smallest. The others were rather shapeless masses of flesh than human figures . . . all of them were lying on their faces, and I have not seen a female here while lying singly on her mats, in the opposite position.[15]

In spite of these overweight queens, time and again European visitors remark on the sheer physical strength and athleticism of these island people. They were even more struck by the sexual licence by which women as well as men were free to indulge their appetites. Arago arrived off Owhyee on 6 August 1819:

On the 7th, a great number of handsome canoes from every part of the coast accompanied us in our route: there were women in the greater number of them, who did not wait to be presented to us. Their indecent gestures, and their motions still more indecent were intended to provoke desire, and make us ashamed of our self-command. They quarrelled for our attention, they solicited for a word, and seemed piqued at the continued but not very meritorious refusal of the crew. The chief of a small village came on board, and dined with the captain, while his wife, who remained close to the door of the cabin, went out at times and romped with the sailors. It was pardonable in a European, and particularly in a Frenchman, to suppose that the coquette profited by the absence of her husband to seek admirers; and that the caresses she bestowed on those who accosted her were unknown to her husband, whom we pitied sincerely for his good faith and confidence. But we were ere long convinced that the husbands of Owhyee, in general, only take one or more wives in order to make an offer of them to strangers, and set them an example of noble generosity . . . What a disgrace to European husbands is the conduct of these men, whom in our pride, we call savages.[16]

Quite clearly, the bantering tone of Arago's letter is intended to amuse a friend, but it underlines the open acceptance of sexual matters in Hawaii compared to the clandestine, or semi-clandestine, extra-marital affairs which were so widespread among the European aristocracy of the period. The attention from the women was unceasing; as the French came to their anchorage they were surrounded by canoes:

some were steered by women, slightly covered with a small piece of cloth round their waists, who eagerly solicited to be admitted on board. It was in vain to give orders that no communication should be allowed; several of them (excited, no doubt by the enticements of the crew) braved all the prohibitions, escaped the watchfulness of the officers on deck, and were welcomed below in a manner with which they appeared perfectly satisfied.[17]

Once ashore Arago found that it was easy to find a woman for sexual purposes: one simply went to any dwelling,

> You need not be afraid of a refusal, even if you address yourself to the husband or brother; they will immediately go out, and not attempt to return until you allow them. Here there is no rivalry or jealousy between the women: if you do not like her whom you first selected, she will go and find you another, who will please you better; she will lend you her mat; she will offer you the use of her cabin. The word licentiousness had no meaning here; every one runs after pleasure, and no one finds the least fault, I repeat, is there any fear that a Parisienne would ever come to settle here?[18]

That last remark is surely tongue in cheek.

Children, too, gratified their sexual urges as soon as they were aware of them. Once again girls were as valued as boys and the sex of both was celebrated from their first welcome into society:

> Songs and chants were specially composed to the genitalia of new born children, both male and female . . . Adolescents from the age of 11 and 12 enjoyed great sexual freedom, and offspring of those casual liaisons were easily assimilated into society . . . Two popular games, *kilo* and *ume*, played by chiefly and non-chiefly people respectively, culminated in sexual relations between couples not married to each [other] . . . Eroticism, the sense and appreciation of sexuality which permeated Hawaiian life and thought, was a basic motif of Hawaiian civilisation.[19]

The free sexuality found in Tahitian society had, in Hawaii, also been formalised into games. In one of the games mentioned above, 'men rolled little balls towards the outspread legs of women seated before them. If the pellet struck its target, the couple retired for sexual intercourse. The real point of interest in this and similar games is that the players were married persons.'[20]

In the early days of contact, having a western sailor as a lover was as much a matter of sexual curiosity as anything else: a matter of novelty which had the added advantage of enriching the women through the gifts they received. It just added spice to their overwhelming interest in all forms of sexual activity and variation of partners. As the kudos associated with intimacy with ordinary sailors diminished with the increased level of contact, the women began to demand payment. Then when traders and businessmen began to settle on the island, having a child by them could ensure prosperity. The power of women was thus enhanced by these white strangers. The chiefs used their traditional powers of taboo to control large-scale trade, but it was impossible to supervise and control the activities of the entire population of women. The whole system of taboo began to fall into disrepute because of the imperviousness of foreigners – and of the women who were intimate with them.

Sexual activity was seen as a leisure pursuit and although it was only one among many, it was the one which was of most interest. The amount of leisure the islanders enjoyed not only impressed Europeans, but seemed to make them uncomfortable. At this time European workers customarily worked ten or twelve hours a day, six days a week – the reward for such intensive labour for many no more than the ability barely to survive. No wonder people remarked on the good nature of these islanders. Arago contrasts the violence present whenever a group of French people gathered together to the good-natured behaviour of the Hawaiian crowds: 'Collect a certain number of the lower classes in our cities, towns, or fields, and let them indulge in any exercise whatever, let them be ever such good friends when they meet, it is ten to one that before the day closes disputes will arise among them, quarrels break out, and not infrequently blood shed. Here I have witnessed but one quarrel . . . at which the disputants themselves laughed when it was settled.'[21] Most afternoons were given up to games or indolence. The men flew huge kites which were so powerful that the line had to be belayed round trees to keep control of them. They gambled on sports: they would see who could stand on a greasy ball the longest, and there were the usual foot races, throwing stones and sticks at targets and for distance. Spear catching and wrestling were also popular. Dancing was one of the joys of both sexes, and swimming and surf-boarding were recreations for both sexes and all ages. Hawaiians were almost as at home in the sea as on land, and thought nothing of swimming several miles to be the first to board an incoming ship. Charles Barnard, who was in Hawaii in 1815, said of the people: 'They are of a lively disposition, friendly towards each other, open-hearted and generous; extremely superstitious, and not inclined to labour; seldom working more than two or three hours in the day, unless on some important occasion, or when at work for the king. In all their sports they are very active; and when at war impetuously brave, but not cruel.'[22]

Although Hawaiian society had evolved to a high level of organisation, their buildings were less impressive than the Tahitian *maraes*. Yet at some point in their history they had constructed stone breakwaters enclosing large areas of up to 200 hectares of the sea in a semi-natural form of fish farming. These breakwaters had finely woven grilles built into them through which small fry could pass into the enclosed water; once they grew slightly, however, they were trapped and remained confined until needed: a good system of natural fish farming which did not harm the environment.

The continuation of this culture, living in harmony with the environment, and its political independence were increasingly under threat from intrusion by outsiders. It was an attempt to neutralise that threat which would eventually impel the Hawaiian king to undertake the long journey to London in order to negotiate with King George III. However, his visit was preceded by a Tahitian islander.

Chapter 12

EUROPEAN INTERLUDE

The native of Otaheite, who voluntarily came over with Capt. Fonnereau [Furneaux], was presented to his Majesty on Sunday last, and is now with Mr Banks, the Gentleman who first projected the voyages to the South Seas for discoveries . . . He is a tall genteel well-made man, and having seen Mr Banks when in that Island, upon seeing him in England he immediately accosted him with the greatest seeming pleasure.

London Chronicle, *21 July 1774*

So a newspaper noticed the arrival of the first Tahitian to set foot in England. Although Omai was only a minor chief he was received by King George III, cared for by Joseph Banks and a number of other gentlemen, and became quite a social lion. He came originally from the island of Raiatea, but his father had been killed and his land taken in the course of a war with the island of Bora Bora. Omai, the rest of his family and a number of fellow islanders had fled to Tahiti where they had been given refuge. These refugees were fully accepted into that island's society and one, the defeated Chief Tupia, became the lover of Queen Obearea and was appointed chief priest of her family *marae*. Tupia had wanted to come to England with Captain Wallis but failed to appear at the last moment either due to a change of heart or because Obearea was not willing to let her lover go. Whatever the cause, he lost the opportunity to be the first Tahitian to sail for Europe.

That distinction was to go to Aoutourou who attached himself to the French expedition of Bougainville and embarked with him on the *Boudeuse* when the ship left the island in April 1768. He was to spend nearly a year in France, was feted by the Parisian *beau monde* and, although this may have been a momentary whim on the part of the aristocracy, there was also a genuine concern for his welfare and much thought and effort were expended to return him to his native land. He was to prove an expensive charge for Bougainville, who gave a large proportion of his wealth to finance the voyage of exploration which would also return Aoutourou to Tahiti.

It seems extraordinary that in an age when Europeans were transporting Africans across the Atlantic to work as slaves in their plantations, natives from the Pacific should have been so cared for, even lionised. This can be explained, at least in part, because Tahitians seemed to be living proof of the theories of Romanticism. The second half of the eighteenth century in Europe has been dubbed the Age of Enlightenment and that enlightenment – the advance of scientific knowledge and the concomitant re-evaluation of traditional assumptions about the nature of mankind – called into question the very truth and authority of the Christian religion, and through that, the basis of western morality. Romanticism was at the height of its appeal and the philosophy of Rousseau claimed that modern society corrupted natural man. The Christian religion taught that man was born in sin and must seek redemption; but Rousseau and others argued that man in his natural state was innately good, becoming corrupt only because European civilisation itself was artificial and depraved. Thus, the nearer mankind was to a state of nature and the more it indulged its natural inclinations, the better it was; this 'hedonistic psychology effected a drastic reorientation in moral ideas. It deprived revealed religion of any relevance to moral truth and by its denial of innate ideas opened the door to the questioning of all traditional morals . . . A whole library of eighteenth-century works upholding happiness, *bonheur*, or utility as the criterion for morality could be collected.'[1] The discovery of Tahiti and the hedonistic life of the population was just the example which critics of their own western society welcomed as endorsement of their theories. Denis Diderot, the instigator and principal editor of the first seventeen volumes of the French *Encyclopédie*, who had been imprisoned for his writings criticising religion and the State, welcomed and idealised Tahitian society in his *Supplement au voyage de Bougainville* published in 1772. Here, apparently, was an island people who had had no connection with corrupt civilisation, living in plenty, enjoying ample leisure and spending most of that in sensual enjoyment. This was in sharp contrast to European culture which condemned the bulk of the French population, taxed and oppressed by a corrupt and decadent ruling class, to endless labour rewarded only by a miserable life of hunger and deprivation. The Tahitians were good-natured, generous, affectionate and well-fed; their superiority to the embittered, mean, ragged and emaciated peasantry of France was self-evident. Everything the first voyagers wrote and related about Tahiti seemed to confirm Rousseau's philosophical speculations. This island paradise was used as the example with which to condemn the religion and the political economy of the country; a country so desperately exploited and misgoverned that twenty years later it would erupt in the French Revolution.

Aoutourou duly sailed from France but was never to see Tahiti again; he died of smallpox *en route*. It was a fate to which Tahitians were subject. Their island was a healthy one with very few endemic diseases so they had very little natural immunity to the common diseases of Europe or the rest of the world.

When the British again arrived in Matavai Bay, Tupia, by then replaced as the queen's lover by a younger man, renewed his efforts to be taken aboard the ship. Captain Cook refused – an understandable stance given that the Admiralty might hold him responsible for the cost of his care, upkeep and eventual return to Tahiti. Mr Banks was, however, an extremely wealthy man who could afford to indulge his whims and it was he who agreed to take him. Tupia was to prove his worth from the moment he stepped on board as he had a good deal of geographical knowledge and helped to identify some of the nearer islands as the ship cruised through the south Pacific to New Zealand. There the language was similar enough for him to converse with the Maoris. Polynesian must surely at that time have been the most widely dispersed language in the world, common to indigenous peoples ranging from Hawaii in the north to New Zealand in the south. That Tupia did not understand a word of the language of the aborigines whom they encountered as the ship worked its way up the Australian coast of modern-day Queensland heading for the Dutch port of Batavia, was confirmation that they were of different origin. But Tupia and his young servant boy were never to see Europe: both died of malaria in Batavia along with a number of the *Endeavour*'s crew.

Chief Tupia's failed attempt to reach England on Cook's first voyage and Omai's success on his second were not motivated by pure curiosity. Omai had been at Matavai Bay when Captain Wallis first arrived; he had been wounded by the British in an affray on Cook's first voyage; and he was well aware of the power of firearms. He wanted to enlist British help to repossess his family's lands in Raiatea. Since the visit of Captain Wallis he had moved from Tahiti to Huahine where he was hoping to gather a force to expel the Bora Bora islanders from Raiatea. Captain Cook recorded that the people there expressed their hatred for the men from Bora Bora and wanted to kill them. He had refused Omai's pleas for help because he did not want to take sides in local wars and also because Oree, the chief of Huahine, was opposed to the idea as the chief of Bora Bora was his friend. Cook took care not to let himself and his men be drawn into supporting either of the warring factions.

Captain Cook's sister ship the *Adventure* was under the command of Captain Tobias Furneaux, who had so distinguished himself during the difficult first days of Tahiti's discovery while second lieutenant on the *Dolphin*. Omai recognised Furneaux and set about ingratiating himself with him rather than with Cook and begged to be taken to Britain. Furneaux allowed himself to be persuaded. When they left Huahine, Omai was safely on board full of plans to enlist British aid once he arrived in England. Although in command of the expedition, Cook could not prevent another captain from having anyone he chose on his ship. Cook was, however, of a mind to keep a diplomatic balance. When they called briefly at Raiatea, Cook took aboard the *Resolution* a young man of eighteen named Oedidee, who came from Bora Bora and was related to an important chief, and so the enemy of Omai. Oedidee, however, decided to stay at home when Cook finally sailed for England.

The ships left Tahiti and cruised down through the south Pacific, discovering and charting islands, on course for New Zealand where they intended to take aboard water and supplies before embarking on another search in high latitudes for the elusive Southern Continent. Off the coast of New Zealand the two ships were separated by a storm and when the *Adventure* failed to appear at the rendezvous, Cook left a message for Captain Furneaux advising him to make his way home independently: meanwhile Cook and his men sailed on to spend another season searching the southern ocean. The *Adventure* duly arrived only to suffer a disaster when ten of its fittest and healthiest crew were killed and cooked ready to be eaten, before the proposed cannibal feast was broken up and the flesh and bones collected and buried. The remaining crew left New Zealand and made a fast passage to Cape Town, where Omai saw his first 'European' town and strange African animals; they sailed into Spithead on 14 July 1774, having left Plymouth just two years earlier. Omai was taken on to London.

Exotic visitors were no longer a novelty for Londoners; a number of North American Indians had been regular sights, as had South American Indians, and Eskimos together with their huskies. But none of these earlier visitors captured the British imagination to the same degree as Omai. This can hardly be ascribed to his command of the language and ability to communicate, for his English was always quite limited. The Tahitian language consisted mainly of vowels, and consonants were difficult for the Tahitians to master – 'Cook', for example was always pronounced 'Toot' because a hard 'c' and 'k' were totally foreign to them. Omai also lacked the fine physique of most of his countrymen and was even considered less handsome than most of them. There was a long article on Omai in the *General Evening Post*, 9–11 August 1774 stating that he came from the island of Ulatea (Raiatea) and discussing its wars with Bora Bora. The paper recorded that he had been living as an exile on Tahiti and after he was wounded was taken in training to be a priest: 'but it is said, that the flatness of his nose, which indicated a mixture of the negro breed in his family, and made him less respectable in those islands, where blood is considered in the highest degree, contributed to make him more ready to undertake this voyage, that he might gain personal consequence from it, to compensate for this family disadvantage.'[2] If that was his calculation, his gamble was a huge success, for he was taken up and generally admired and liked by London society. The main tenor of the complimentary remarks refers to his natural ease, politeness and good manners. The one famous dissenting voice was that of Dr Johnson, who, having dined with Omai, was not impressed; he could hardly have reacted differently given that Rousseau's theories of the noble savage were the very antithesis of Dr Johnson's belief in civilised rationality and urban living.

Rousseau's philosophy of the advantages of the 'noble savage' and the corrupting influence of modern civilisation were much talked about in England. Whatever the reason, Omai found supporters. Among the first people to welcome Captain Furneaux home when his ship docked were Joseph Banks, whom Omai recognised, and Dr Solander whom he knew from his voice alone, for all that he pronounced his name Tolander ('s's' were not part of the Tahitian sound system either). The Earl of Sandwich, First Lord of the Admiralty, took him under his protection and, along with Joseph Banks, was to see that Omai was properly looked after. Why should such important and busy men take such care of a seemingly unimportant native? Although Banks could claim that as a scientist he was interested in how an unsophisticated native would react in these new surroundings, that could hardly explain the interest of the First Lord.

Omai was taken into Joseph Banks's London house and taught how to bow in readiness for his first important social engagement – a meeting with King George III. 'The Native of Otaheite, who was at Court the other day, had received some instructions for his behaviour in addressing his Majesty, but so great was his embarrassment when his Majesty approached him, that he forgot every thing but that of kneeling, and when his conductors endeavoured to make him speak to the King, he could only stretch out his hand, and get out the familiar phrase of "How do ye do?" which, it seems, was the first English phrase that he learned . . . His Majesty very freely shook him by the hand.'[3] According to one account, at that first meeting he took the opportunity to ask the king for gunpowder to destroy all his enemies on Bora Bora. King George granted him an allowance while in England, and promised to return him to his home when a ship was available. Meanwhile, the social whirl continued. 'On Thursday the native of Otaheite dined with the Duke of Gloucester, accompanied by Messrs Banks and Solander . . . he . . . is to continue with Mr Banks during his stay in England, which it is presumed will be for some years.'[4] The king had shown his concern by ordering that Omai be inoculated as soon as possible to protect him from smallpox as this disease had proved fatal to other visitors from the New World.

Inoculation was still considered a risky procedure and Doctor Dimsdale, its most eminent practitioner at the time, was engaged for the purpose. Omai was obliged to go to him in Hertford where he would be required to stay as an in-patient for some days. It seems almost incredible that so important and busy a man as Joseph Banks should have gone to live with Omai while he was a patient, as did Dr Solander, and Mr Andrews who had served as surgeon aboard the *Adventure*. After the Tahitian's ordeal, Banks took Omai to stay at various seats of the aristocracy around the country and to the races. Lord Sandwich also played his part in entertaining Omai. Back in London, Omai was given 5 guineas a month, provided with lodgings and it was arranged that Dr Andrews would be his guardian.

In London he was taken to the theatre and to the State Opening of Parliament; he was shown off at the Royal Society, not as an exhibit, but as a guest who dined with the learned gentlemen. Banks arranged for Omai, wearing native tapa cloth, to have his portrait painted by none other than Sir Joshua Reynolds, and William Parry painted him with his patrons Joseph Banks and Dr Solander. Lord Sandwich took Omai on a tour of naval dockyards. No distinguished visitor could have been shown greater attention and consideration. After Omai had been a dinner guest at her home, Fanny Burney, the famous novelist and diarist, who sat next to him at table, wrote that 'he appears to be a perfectly rational and intelligent man, with an understanding far superior to the common race of us cultivated gentry. He could not else borne so well the way of Life into which he is thrown, without some practice';[5] and this led her to comment on the supposed superior advantage of being a child of nature rather than the recipient of a European education. What she and others failed to realise was that far from being 'natural' and 'untutored', Omai was the product of a very complex society in which protocol and correct manners were as important and as artificial as ever they were in eighteenth-century Europe. So solicitous for his welfare were his patrons that strings were pulled at the Admiralty and James Burney, Fanny's brother, was recalled from the American colonies so that he could be on the ship which returned Omai to Tahiti. Having served with Captain Cook on his second voyage, it was felt that James would be another familiar face to help Omai feel at home.

It was now that another expedition to the Pacific was planned. King George gave Omai a second audience, this time to inform him that he was being sent home, and Omai was presented to the queen and her daughters. Once Omai knew that he was soon to leave, he again tried to persuade Lord Sandwich to drive the Bora Bora conquerors from Raiatea. His pleas were rejected, but Sandwich did go so far as to promise him some firearms when he was put ashore. His friends did their best to send him back with sufficient goods to set him up in style. Much – such as a set of table cutlery – was inappropriate; nevertheless, having been to Britain and having a quantity of European goods could only serve to enhance his status among his compatriots. Cook was to have overall command again, sailing as captain of the *Resolution* with John Gore as his first lieutenant. Gore, too, was an old Pacific hand, having not only participated in the original discovery of Tahiti with Captain Wallis but having sailed there again aboard the *Endeavour*. The *Discovery* was captained by Charles Clerke and had James Burney as first lieutenant – so Omai was to sail among many familiar faces. One new member of the company, and one whose name would come to be forever associated with Tahiti and the Pacific, was William Bligh, sailing master of the *Resolution*.

On 8 July 1776 the *Resolution* left Plymouth. After the usual stops for provisions at the Canary Islands and Cape Town they dropped anchor near the site of modern Hobart, Tasmania, on 24 January 1777, anxious, no doubt, not only for fresh water for their own use, but to cut fodder for the livestock on board – cows, horses, sheep, goats, rabbits as well as turkeys and peacocks, not counting cats and dogs. They moved on to New Zealand where Omai wanted to take back to Tahiti one of the Maoris whom he had met on his earlier visit. In fact, when they sailed the ship's complement had been increased by two Maoris, Tayweherooa the son of a chief, and a young boy, Coco. They went to the Tongan Islands and, after presenting the chiefs of Tonga with a bull and cow, a stallion and mare, and a ram and ewe, the *Resolution* dropped anchor in Matavai Bay on 13 August 1777 – men and beasts having been cooped up together for a year and five weeks. At Tahiti, the feel of solid land must have been as welcome to the two remaining horses as it was to Omai. Perhaps disappointingly, although reports of his reception vary, most agree that he was largely ignored until, that is, he made presents of the invaluable red feathers and then even chiefs wanted to befriend him: in other words, he was welcomed for his wealth. But one of the journals relates the tears and love with which he was reunited with his sister.

Omai's subsequent life need not be examined in detail. He settled at Huahine where he was given a plot of land by the chiefs, as his wealth and arms would undoubtedly be an asset to them in the inter-island wars. The crew of the ships built Omai a house, cleared land and planted a garden for him. Omai was left with four firearms and some edged weapons and, most importantly, 20lb of gunpowder – after his experience on the grouse moors of Yorkshire he knew how to use them. Captain Cook continued to refuse Omai's incessant pleas for help to recover his lands in Raiatea by making war on Bora Bora. On 2 November 1777 the British ship sailed away, to his tearful farewells.

Eleven years later Captain Bligh, on Tahiti to collect breadfruit, heard that Omai had persuaded the chiefs to make war on Bora Bora and that his arms had proved decisive. However, he had not enjoyed his victory for long, as he died of an ague some two and a half years later. His two companions from New Zealand died at about the same time.

When, in 1783, William Cowper started his narrative poem 'The Task', which included a description of the Tahitian's experiences, Omai was already dead. The work contrasts the supposed innocent immorality of Tahiti with the conscious decadence and immorality of England, particularly that of her wealthy city-dwellers. This is of a piece with, if not quite a wholehearted endorsement of, the Romanticism of the 'noble' savage ethos of the period. It is, perhaps, more accurately an image of the 'ignorant' noble savage. For Cowper cannot help but feel that after having lived in 'civilised' England and seen at first hand all the great buildings and artefacts, scientific advances and entertainments of a European country, Omai could not but become discontented with his homeland. Cowper imagines Omai climbing each morning to the top of the mountain to search the horizon for the sight of a sail from England. The degree to which Omai regretted leaving England is beyond recall, but Cowper's general point is sound: there were no means by which the Polynesians who went into the wider world could return unchanged to the simplicity of their own culture.

Omai may have been the first Tahitian to reach Europe and return home. But after the discovery of Hawaii and the growth in whaling and commercial enterprises, ordinary Hawaiians very soon became as familiar with the world as any other seafaring race. Most of the ships were American from the shores of New England, for the west coast of what was to become the American state of California was then still a sparsely settled, wild territory lightly administered by Spain. American shipping in the Pacific came from the east coast and, like their European counterparts, had to make the long voyage down into the south Atlantic round Cape Horn and then north up through the Pacific. Hawaiians were often recruited to serve on American whalers to replace those crew members who died or deserted during the course of voyages which could keep a whaler away for three or four years. Not only did they prove to be in most ways superior mariners, they were also much cheaper to employ. The first Hawaiian islander in Boston had arrived aboard a whaler as early as 1790 and, as a chief, went ashore dressed in the dignity of his full regalia of red and yellow feathered cloak and helmet, to call upon Governor Hancock.

The Hawaiian Islands captured the American imagination much as Tahiti had the European: 'Several years later Hawaiians appeared in plays staged in Boston and New York depicting the tragedy of Captain Cook. The production in the latter city included a human sacrifice and ended with an earthquake and volcanic eruption.'[6] Thus the less commendable elements of Hawaiians' pagan religion became known to a wider audience, and their sexual mores deplored. Both appeared an affront and a challenge to Christian belief and practice.

The first party of missionaries bound for Hawaii in 1819 included three Hawaiians also trained as missionaries. One of them was a prince with wide experience of western ways. Having left Hawaii as a child, he attended an American school, served in the American Navy and had seen action in the Mediterranean against the pirates who preyed on American shipping. He had been wounded during the Anglo-American War of 1812. Clearly, not all the traffic in characters with strange histories was one way. From the very beginning Hawaiians sailed with the Europeans and returned home well able to tell their countrymen about the wider world. The Hawaiian world view and their appreciation of European rivalries were in no way inferior to that of the Europeans themselves.

King Kamehameha who had united the Hawaiian Islands under his rule died in 1819 and was succeeded by his son, Liholiho, who ruled as

Kamehameha II; although it might be truer to say that his mother Queen Kaahumanu controlled events, in one instance maintaining the unity of the islands by marrying both one potentially rebellious chief and his son. Internal affairs were still a cause for concern and civil war never far below the surface, but the main threat to the Hawaiian way of life and independence came from the Americans. American missionaries had now joined the influx of traders and whalers: America was exerting an intense influence which was hard to resist. In 1823 Kamehameha II decided that he must act to strengthen the British obligation to his kingdom for unlike the Americans they were not numerous enough to take commercial control of the island, and unlike the French they did not want it as a colony. But the Royal Navy was powerful enough to stop either the Americans or the French were it so minded. Before he died Kamehameha I had commissioned a Hawaiian national flag. It consisted of eight bars in red, white and blue, to represent the eight major islands, and the entire top left-hand quarter was the British Union Jack – a clearer statement of political preference would be hard to find. Future independence was so important that the new king decided that he would go to London in person and appeal directly to King George IV as one monarch to another.

Kamehameha II arranged to travel to London on the whaler *L'Aigle* accompanied by his wife Queen Kamamalu, Chief Boki governor of Oahu as chief advisor (who took his wife Liliha), and the son of his father's old and trusted advisor John Young. He had also intended to take the Reverend William Ellis, an English missionary, who worked for years in Tahiti giving the language an alphabet and transcribing it into written form, and who was then in Hawaii helping others do the same for the Hawaiian tongue. Ellis would have been the perfect interpreter, but Captain Starbuck of *L'Aigle* refused to accept him on his ship. It is not recorded why this was so, but there was no love lost between the missionaries, who were intent on eradicating alcohol and sexual licence from the islands, and the whalers, who liked the islands precisely because they supplied both items in abundance. As events turned out, however, it might have been part of a criminal conspiracy. When Ellis was refused passage Jean Rives (a Frenchman) was appointed interpreter in his place. On 27 November 1823, they set sail for England with Rives and Starbuck as the Europeans in charge. Part of the king's baggage consisted of locked chests containing $25,000 to pay the expenses of the party *en route* and while in England. But when the money was counted in order to be banked in England over half was found to be missing. It was widely believed that Captain Valentine Starbuck and Jean Rives had stolen the money, but as there was no proof no action was taken against them.

The arrival of King Kamehameha II and his retinue came as a complete surprise to the British government which, nevertheless, responded graciously to this unexpected visit. The Foreign Secretary, George Canning, gave them an official reception, allowing the government time to decide its policy. While arrangements were being made for the party's reception by King George IV, the Hawaiians visited London's famous buildings and were given the use of the royal box at the theatres. The two kings were destined never to meet. The Hawaiians, all staying at the Osborne Hotel, caught measles and as they had no immunity it proved a serious infection. King George IV sent his personal physician to attend them, and everyone seemed on the path to recovery except Queen Kamamalu. King Kamehameha II was deeply in love with her and insisted on sharing her bed to comfort her as she lay dying. She died on 8 July 1824 and it was said that so inconsolable was the king that he died of grief six days later.

Eventually the rest of the delegation was granted an audience with King George. Their plea to be taken under the protection of the British Crown was refused, however, and it was also made clear that Britain would take no role in their internal affairs. Nevertheless, they were assured that because of the history of the relationship between their two countries – Captain Cook had discovered them, and the late king's father had ceded the islands to Britain during Captain Vancouver's visit – Britain would permit no other nation to annex them.

That both the King and Queen of Hawaii should have died while in London was a tragic embarrassment and it was decided to make the best of events by returning their bodies with great pomp. The British government paid all the expenses of their stay and had the bodies placed in lead coffins enclosed in magnificent wooden caskets. They were shipped home on a large 46-gun frigate under the command of Captain Lord Byron who was familiar with the Hawaiian Islands. They were landed with great ceremony with a marine guard of honour and the ship's band playing appropriately solemn music. This ceremonious and official care of the Hawaiian royal dead was intended as a a public and diplomatic signal to other nations of British commitment to the Hawaiians and their independence. But the British promise was to prove hollow: in the long run Britain had no strategic interest in the fate of Hawaii.

PART THREE

CHRISTIANS AND COLONIES

Chapter 13

THE FIRST MISSIONARIES

Where the precepts of Christianity are diffused, idleness never fails to become disreputable.

Directors of the London Missionary Society, 1818

Had they known more of their European visitors' religion the thousands of happy and indolent pagans would have realised that their way of life could not be expected to continue undisturbed for long. The eighteenth century was a period of active missionary work in Britain, and even the much admired John Wesley believed that working children twelve hours or more a day, six days a week, in the strenuous and unhealthy cotton mills which deformed bodies and warped minds, was a good thing, for 'idle hands make mischief'. The missionaries believed in work, and it was quite clear from all reports that Tahitians were not doing enough of it. The missionaries considered that by some inexplicable oversight God had provided the islanders with all the necessities of life for little more than two or three hours' labour a day. They still inhabited a Garden of Eden and had not yet been expelled to 'earn their bread by the sweat of their brow', although from their behaviour they seemed to have had access to a whole orchard of sinful apples.

The London Missionary Society, which was to take upon itself the task of carrying the gospel to Tahiti and other Pacific islands, was established by John Eure who was founder and co-editor of the *Evangelical Magazine*. He drew together a number of Protestant churches and sects with the intention of spreading the evangelical message and energy at work in Britain throughout the world. The scope was wide as the indigenous populations of much of Africa, India and Asia were as yet untouched by Christianity – save for a few mainly Roman Catholic missions. Tahiti was selected as their first field of endeavour because of the supposed ease of starting a mission there. It was argued that it was impossible, or unwise, to attempt to set up missions in a country where government was absolute, where many languages were spoken, or in places such as Africa and India where climate, disease, poisonous reptiles and dangerous beasts made survival for Europeans difficult. Eure wrote that the least hardships were to be met in the South Seas – meaning especially Tahiti – as government was monarchical but benevolent and the missionaries were unlikely to be oppressed. The climate was healthy, food was plentiful and because the natives had much leisure time they were open to instruction. He was also under the impression that their language was easy to learn and that the populace had no religious prejudices. He was right on most counts, but wrong in that they proved to be firmly attached to their religion and that the few words of Tahitian which served to satisfy the appetites of the sailors were, on closer scrutiny, to prove only part of what was in fact a complex and sophisticated tongue: it was to be five years after they landed before any of the missionaries mastered enough of the language to address a public meeting.

By 1796 the enterprise had attracted sufficient funds and the whaling ship *Duff* was chartered to carry the first band of missionaries to Tahiti. Captain Wilson gave his services free of charge because of his sympathy with the mission's aims. He came out of retirement to command the *Duff* and, after landing the missionaries, was to proceed to Canton for a cargo of tea which would help defray the cost of the venture. In Canton the sober conduct of the crew he had hand-picked earned the ship the nickname *The Ten Commandments*. He was another of the many characters who were drawn to the Pacific for various motives. James Wilson had led an adventurous life. He fought at the Battle of Bunker Hill which opened the American War of Independence. In 1782 he was captured off Madras by the French, who handed him over to their Indian ally who marched him naked under the blazing sun for thirty days to his place of captivity: when released after a year he was one of only 35 survivors out of a group of 112. In the tradition of conversion statements, the captain acknowledged that he had been a sinner but had been fortunate late in life to come to God.

The *Duff* up-anchored at 6 a.m. on 10 August 1796 and left London to cheers from crowds on both banks of the river. After a rough passage to Portsmouth they were then wind bound, finally leaving Spithead on 24 September as part of a convoy of fifty-seven ships gathered for protection against the French for the first part of their voyage. The *Duff* carried a crew of twenty-two and was conveying thirty missionaries, six wives and three children. Only four of the missionaries were ordained, others often having been chosen for their useful skills: two blacksmiths, a bricklayer, a butcher, a cabinet maker, six carpenters, a cooper, a cotton manufacturer, a gardener, a harness maker, a hatter, a linen draper, a servant, two shoemakers, a shopkeeper, a surgeon, two tailors and two weavers. They had not been selected entirely for their occupational skills, for the mission was composed of many independent chapels and churches which had a tradition of lay preachers, and all were intended to work as missionaries as well as most having a useful trade to teach the natives. They deserve respect for their commitment to their beliefs and for their courage in launching themselves into the unknown; but their values were to leave them totally antipathetic to the society in which they were going to live:

> They were long on the Bible and the secular arts associated with production and trade, but they were short on anything we might call cultural understanding or anthropological insight. They had absolutely no understanding of the relativity of their own queer mixture of values, either in time or space, and therefore put on the same plane the absolutes of their supernatural religion and the values of the class from which they came. They believed with equal fervour in God, the Bible as divinely inspired law for personal and social salvation, diligence in secular work, the acquisition of wealth through trade, regular churchgoing, the wearing of the costumes of contemporary England . . . [hated] heathenism in all its protean mani-festations, and Roman Catholicism.[1]

Missionaries with a wider secular understanding might have achieved their ends without destroying all aspects of Tahitian culture and self-respect.

Tubuai in the Society Islands (where Fletcher Christian and the mutineers from the *Bounty* had once tried to settle) was the missionaries' first landfall near Tahiti, and then, on Sunday 5 March 1797, they sailed into Matavai Bay. There the usual scores of women clambered on board offering their now traditional welcome to these new arrivals, only to be amazed and bitterly offended that the men refused to copulate after their long months at sea. What is more, sailors were always desperate for the first fresh provisions after the monotony of shipboard diet and yet the Tahitians who arrived at the ship loaded with all manner of meat, vegetables and fruit were totally puzzled and somewhat chagrined that these people refused to buy, sell or exchange any goods because it was a Sunday. It was the Tahitians' first intimation that they were dealing with a different type of people from the sailors and traders who had preceded them.

The missionaries found that King Pomare had relinquished power to his son Otoo (also spelt Otu, and Tu) and it was claimed that he had now established himself king of all Tahiti and Mo'orea. The missionaries would have been hard put to explain themselves and their intentions had it not been for Peter, one of two Swedish seamen who had been living on the island for five years and could speak Tahitian. How complete was Peter's command of the religious dimension of the language and whether he managed to convey the reason for the advent of the missionaries might be doubted. But whatever the reason for their arrival, Pomare wanted this large group of white people in his territory; after all, it was due to the support of the British and their numerous visits that he had maintained his claim to control of the whole island against all contenders. He agreed to cede the land around Matavai Bay and gave them the 'British House' which Pomare had built for Captain Bligh who had (falsely) promised to return and live there. This was a huge, if somewhat stark rectangular structure 110ft long, 50ft wide and just over 16ft high. All this was handed over in a ceremony attended by the young King Otoo, who was about seventeen, and his queen. It would seem that she was not familiar with Europeans: 'The queen opened Mr Cover's shirt at the breast and sleeves, and seemed astonished at so clear a sight of the blue veins . . . for there could be but small difference between themselves and the dark complexions of the naked shipwrecked sailors who had lately taken refuge amongst them.'[2] The behaviour of the Tahitian royalty confused the missionaries. They noted that both Otoo and his queen were carried on the shoulders of their servants during the ceremony on shore, and knew from earlier reports that the king had the power of life and death over his subjects, but this awesome elevation was accompanied by very ordinary behaviour: 'After dinner Otoo and his wife came off, each in a small canoe, with only one man paddling; whilst they went several times round the ship, the queen was frequently baling her canoes with a cocoa-nut shell. This may help to form an idea of what a queen is in Otaheiti. They would not venture on board, because wheresoever they come is deemed sacred, none daring to enter there afterwards except their proper domestics.'[3] Leaving most of the party in Tahiti the ship was to take two of the missionaries on to Tongatabu in the Friendly Islands, some 1,200 miles distant to start a mission there – where once again they came upon two European sailors living quite securely and happily with the islanders. Having conveyed the two missionaries to the Friendly Islands, the *Duff* returned to Tahiti to make sure that the other missionaries had settled in. The surgeon had already decided that the missionary life was not for him and he returned home on the *Duff*, as did the more expendable hatter, who was ill. The *Duff* embarked its two passengers and finally sailed on 4 August 1797 leaving the missionaries to their task.

The zealous passengers of the *Duff* were not the first to seek to Christianise the Tahitians – Spain had already sent a Catholic mission. The Spanish government could view Wallis's discovery of Tahiti in 1767 and Cook's long sojourn there in 1769 only with concern: a permanent British base there would threaten their South and Central American colonies in time of war and endanger their communications across the Pacific. The French had also touched there and might return in force. That either of their European rivals should establish a base in Tahiti was thus an unwelcome possibility. By the standards of the slow communications of the day, and set against the alleged habitual procrastination of the Spanish, the latter moved with remarkable celerity. An expedition left Callao, Peru, on 26 September 1772 under the command of Captain Don Domingo de Boenechea on the frigate *Aguila*, and his orders were to verify the existence and location of Tahiti as reported by the British. The island was duly found and on 12 November the first boat was sent ashore and took possession in the name of the King of Spain.

Although the Spaniards landed on the other side of the island from where the British had twice stayed, westerners and the power of their firearms and cannon as originally demonstrated by Wallis were by now common knowledge among the inhabitants, as was the wealth in terms of metals and tools which the outsiders could bring to an area, none of which would have lost anything in the telling for those who had not witnessed such personages and events for themselves. The Spanish received a friendly, if somewhat muted, reception. They had landed in the jurisdiction of a different chief from either the English or the French but one whose people were as anxious as those of Matavai Bay to get possession of these rare goods. This first contact was part of a longer-term aim to colonise the islands, should they prove to be suitable for such a purpose. When the Spaniards left they took back with them four Tahitians in order to impress them with the cities, power and might of Spain. Their main function was to be Christianised, to learn Spanish and to serve as interpreters on their return to Tahiti.

The second expedition sailed on 20 September 1774 and disembarked on Tahiti on 15 November. Again it was welcomed. Like others the Spanish sailed with a variety of livestock and the *Aguila* landed bulls, asses, pigs, sheep and goats. The Spaniards were determined to maintain good relations and leave a mission behind them in a spirit of goodwill, and they seem to have succeeded. The frigate and its supply ship stayed for nine weeks negotiating a grant of land for the mission and the erection of a suitable building. During that time there were only two incidents leading to conflict – one due to the theft of some shirts; the other when a sailor took back the gift he had given a woman in return for her favours: a lack of incident which would have amazed the authorities of any European port playing host to a similar number of sailors.

The Tahitians were willing to give a grant of land for a house and provide the labour to build it. The chiefs supplied men to work with the Spaniards, building the house and clearing the land ready for cultivation. The only objections came when the Spaniards felled a great number of breadfruit trees, not just for their building but also to supply their ships with firewood. Like the Hawaiians, the Tahitians lived in close balance with their environment and knew how many breadfruit trees they needed to ensure their food supplies. But the ordinary people were overruled by the chiefs and the Spanish had their way. Finally, everything was ready for the two missionaries, Padre Narciso and Padre Geronimo, supported by the two Tahitians who had been converted in Peru (the two others had died), to start their mission. A marine named Rodriguez, who had served on the first voyage and proved adept at learning Tahitian, was the official interpreter and a seaman named Perez was to act as cook and general handyman. The Spanish were keen to force an agreement from the Tahitians which would make them responsible for the security and upkeep of the missionaries. Eventually both sides signed the Convention of Hatutira on 5 January 1775 which recognised the King of Spain as the island's *arii*, or overlord. This was approved by all the chief *arii*, notably chiefs Bexiatua and Hotu. But it is significant that the supreme chief, Otoo, the friend of the British, 'through being somewhat indisposed' was absent and did not sign – a diplomatic illness if ever there was one. Without his signature the treaty could always be repudiated. Nevertheless, the Convention gave the proposed mission some security as it promised to feed and protect the missionaries and effectively secured access to necessary materials and labour. However, the Convention had a purely internal application and reveals a degree of diplomatic sophistication on the Tahitian side: it did not, for instance, give an undertaking to protect the mission against other Europeans or from attacks from the island of Mo'orea, with which the Tahitians were frequently at war.

The Spanish missionaries were not a success, seemingly too timid to mix with the natives and keeping themselves very much to the mission building and gardens. A *Recital of Events* was written by the retiring Viceroy of Peru for his successor in March 1790, long after the attempt to bring Tahiti into the Spanish orbit had failed. He recorded that the *Aguila* had again set sail, on 27 September 1775, on a third expedition:

> She returned after 143 days, bringing back the two missionaries and the interpreter: the former without having effected any progress of an evangelical kind whatsoever, as it turned out that they did not possess at all that apostolic spirit which their holy vocation demands; for they lived in constant suspicion and fear of the Indians. The interpreter, on the contrary, roamed freely through the island and got to know every part of it. He learned that there was a good harbour named Matabay [Matavai] on the western side, where the English astronomers lay a long while at anchor.[4]

In fact, Matavai Bay is on the northernmost part of the island, but he was correct in that it lay on the other side from where the Spanish had tried to settle, and that the interpreter did travel around the island quite freely and without fear. This was confirmed by David Samwell, ship's surgeon during HMS *Discovery*'s second voyage. In August 1776, less than a year after the Spaniards had been evacuated, the Tahitians told him that one of the Spaniards, Rodriguez, had toured the whole island and that the Tahitian women in particular liked him. But no one liked the priests who kept themselves to themselves. While it would be unreasonable to criticise the Fathers for not sharing in the main recreation and interest of the islanders, according to Rodriguez, it seems that their self-enforced isolation was not due to their celibacy, but to fear.

Rodriguez's journal provides a source for some comment on the earlier English visits:

> 18th. day [February 1775] I went about mid-day to visit some of the *arii*, Otu's [Otoo] dependants, and as they asked me to give them some account of the lands our Sovereign possesses I complied. Next they brought up the subject of the English commander whom they call 'Otute' [Captain Cook]. They told me he was the owner of the district of Matabae [Matavai]; but I

undeceived them as to that, and gave them to believe that the said
commander would not put in an appearance again so long as we continued
in residence here. Notwithstanding this, however, they expect him within
the space of seventeen months, according to their account.[5]

It is an extraordinary coincidence that Captain Cook did return exactly
seventeen months from the date of that conversation – something neither
Cook nor the Tahitians could have known when he last left them. The fact
that the Tahitians named Captain James Cook as the *owner* of the Matavai
district might account for the willingness with which they later gave it to the
missionaries. Certainly, when James Morrison, one of the *Bounty* mutineers,
was living on the island in 1790 he witnessed a ceremony at Matavai Bay in
which Captain Cook was still proclaimed chief of everything from the beach
to the mountains, although it was then eleven years since he had been killed
in Hawaii.

By the time the British returned the Spanish had abandoned their
missionary effort. Their stay had no lasting impact on the Tahitians nor did
the Spanish ever again try to turn it into a colony.

The British missionaries who were left on the shore of Matavai Bay as the
Duff sailed away were rather more committed evangelists and more deeply
horrified by the paganism of the people. Even before the ship's departure the
mission's journal was recording events they could hardly believe:

April 8. – One of the arreoies, the tayo of brother Henry, came to us with
his wife: they were taking their leave of us in order, during their absence,
to destroy the infant son soon to be born, according to the ordinance of
that dreadful society . . . he acknowledged it a bloody act, pleading the
established custom, his loss of all privileges, and the dissolution of the
society if this should become general.

April 13. – Many *unnatural crimes*, which we dare not name, are committed
daily without the idea of shame or guilt. In various districts of the island
there are men who dress as women; work with them at the cloth; are
confined to the same provisions and rule of eating and dressing; may not
eat with the men, or of their food, but have separate plantations for their
peculiar use. It is remarkable that with all these horrid vices so
predominant, in our presence they never show an attitude or commit one

act unseemly; indeed, they profess hardly to know what we are, and suspect we are not Englishmen, or like any others they have seen who have ever visited their island.[6]

In spite of their shared nationality there is no doubt that the missionaries were as unlike the sailors and men of science in their demands upon the Tahitians as if they had come from another planet.

Pomare gained his first practical insight into the attitudes and values of the missionaries when the first ship to arrive since their installation anchored in early March 1798. When she sailed from Macao (China) the *Nautilus* had not the slightest intention of fetching up at Tahiti, but set course for the north-west coast of America (Canada) intending to seek a cargo of furs. But the vessel was driven so far south by a series of gales that she reshaped her course for South America where she again hoped to find a cargo of furs. Her captain pulled in to Tahiti for provisions. During her four-day stay the missionaries incurred the wrath of Pomare by persuading the captain of the ship not to sell him any arms or powder; they also incurred the hostility of the common people by 'discouraging immorality'. Two weeks after she sailed for South America the unfortunate *Nautilus* was back in the bay to repair storm damage. Once the ship was again seaworthy, her captain changed his plans once more, this time deciding to make for Sydney, Australia, in search of a profitable cargo. These mishaps to the *Nautilus* and the thousands of unprofitable miles sailed demonstrate just how vulnerable ships were to wind and current and how the captains of commercial vessels had to be adept traders and businessmen able eventually to find cargoes and profit wherever wind and fate blew them.

While the *Nautilus* was at Tahiti under repair two of the ship's crew deserted. In the eyes of the missionaries, these footloose sailors who 'went native' were one of the main reasons for their own lack of success, for they felt that the dissolute behaviour of these Europeans reflected badly on them all. A delegation of four missionaries went to Pomare to demand that he force the deserters back to their ship. Already angry because the missionaries had prevented him from obtaining arms from the ship, Pomare refused their demand. Taking Pomare's displeasure as licence, the people expressed their own dislike of the missionaries by stripping them of their clothes and administering a sound beating to all four.

This incident created mortal fear among the missionaries: they knew that if Pomare ever withdrew his favour they would undoubtedly be killed, since all the people were opposed to them. James Cover led the move to give up the mission and, after much debate and heart searching, eleven of the eighteen decided that they would sail for Sydney with the *Nautilus*. They took with them their share of the provisions and contents of the store room; and to purchase his goodwill and his permission to transship the goods, the rest was given to Pomare, leaving those who were to remain with nothing. These resolute souls also decided that they would not attempt to save their lives by force, hence all the muskets and powder were put aboard the ship so as not to fall into Pomare's hands. It was a courageous decision, but they could take some comfort from the number of beachcombers who lived alone, unarmed and in safety. Only one woman, Mrs Eyre, remained on the island. Those who stayed sent a letter to the London mission's directors recommending that as large numbers were not suitable for present needs, they should send out no more than six men at the utmost: a sensible letter from a brave and isolated band of people. It would take a good nine months, all being well, for the letter to reach London via Australia, and five or six more for a response. The *Nautilus* duly sailed and the six men and one woman withdrew to pray. They had placed their faith in God, but their lives were in Pomare's hands.

Pomare made his choice. He feared that if the missionaries were killed the British would come to take their revenge; having acquired power enough to become king of all Tahiti, thanks to British help, he dared not offend them. He signalled his subservience by punishing those who had stripped and beaten the missionaries, a highly unpopular act which precipitated a rebellion that cost many lives. It proved the beginning of what became a long period of conflict and civil war, as his subjects objected to the influence of the missionaries. While the civil war was rooted in part in the traditional warfare between clans endemic on the island since time immemorial, Pomare's acceptance of British influence in island affairs, now enshrined in his support of a permanent mission, earned him the enmity of those who wanted to preserve the traditional way of life, their customs and their own religion. Punishing those who had beaten the missionaries was seen by the mass of the population as a challenge to traditional life, and district after district rose to express their disaffection with Pomare's protection of these strangers.

Chapter 14

ALL AT SEA

They embarked in October [at London], and had an unpleasant passage to Portsmouth, where the vessel lay for several weeks, detained by contrary winds . . . Thursday, December 20, 1798, they moved from their native shores, possibly to revisit them no more.

Richard Lovett, History of the London Missionary Society[1]

Back in England the Mission was busily preparing the *Duff* for her second voyage which was intended to reinforce the first contingent. The staff and directors were ignorant of events in Tahiti and the letter pleading with them not to send more than six men still had not arrived. Perhaps precisely because of their ignorance of the fate of the first missionaries, the scale of preparations for this second voyage gives the impression that they intended to establish a permanent British colony. This time the *Duff* would carry even more people – thirty missionaries, ten wives and seven children. That they were on board ship from October to late December waiting for the right weather in order to leave port and clear the coast again underlines just how unpredictable sea travel was in the days of sail. Nor were adverse winds the only hazard of the sea. They had sailed as far as the coast of South America when they were captured by a French privateer and taken into Montevideo. There, according to naval custom of the time, the ship was sold as a prize, leaving the unfortunate missionaries and crew stranded.

In early May 1778 they managed to leave Montevideo by signing up as crew on a ship bound for Rio de Janeiro where they were more likely to find one for England. They duly set sail only to experience the most atrocious ill fortune. They were almost safe in Rio's harbour when their vessel was spotted, intercepted and all on board again taken as a prize, this time by a fleet of Portuguese men-of-war. They wrote of these disastrous experiences, apparently without irony:

How evidently did this day [of capture] speak the mind and will of God. We had been detained by contrary winds, fully three times longer than it was expected. Thrice we had arrived near the desired port, and twice been prevented from entering it. If we had been but one day sooner we should have reached the harbour without interruption, and if but one hour later the fleet would have been out of sight . . . This appeared to us so replete with sovereignty, and to speak so clearly the mind and will of God, that [we] were constrained to say 'It is the Lord's doing, and marvellous in our eyes'.[2]

They were conveyed as prisoners to Lisbon and the majority of them allowed to return to London in early November, having spent nearly twelve months isolated on board ship or as prisoners on land. Ill fortune continued to hound one of their number who, staying a little longer in Lisbon because his wife was dying, was again captured on his way home – this time by the French – but then recaptured by the Royal Navy. Such were the added risks of sea travel in wartime. The loss of the *Duff* and all her stores and the destruction of all their hopes, were, in the view of the Mission, signs of beneficent intervention by the Almighty. This 'seasonal interposition of Providence demands our gratitude' because they believed God had put all these disasters in their way in order to tell them that they were sending the wrong type of person.

The Mission did not have the early success anticipated considering the money, material and effort that were expended. Of the thirty missionaries who set out for Tahiti on the second voyage, twenty-three left the service of the Mission once safely back in England. The first voyage, although it had reached the islands without incident and the missionaries had been welcomed ashore, had also suffered similar defections: 'The history of the men whom the *Duff* carried to Tahiti in 1796 enforces similar lessons. By 1800, less than four years after sailing, twenty out of the thirty had proved either unequal or unfaithful to the work, while three had been killed in the mission service.'[3] Those killed died on other islands at the hands of islanders less tolerant than the Tahitians. In total, at the turn of the century the Mission had sent out sixty missionaries to have only nine effectively in place. The Tahitian way of life was not unattractive and the Mission lost one of its members to its charms: the missionaries excluded Thomas Lewis from their fellowship because he had decided to marry a Tahitian woman. The other missionaries were at pains to note that their actions were not in any way racist but were taken because his wife was, or had been, a heathen. She was not pure, and they thought that 'in all probability not one single female in the island over ten or twelve years of age had escaped pollution'.[4] That is to say that there were no virgins above that age and they felt convinced that she would continue with the customs of her upbringing so could never be a fitting wife for a missionary. But if they did not feel confident that they could change the life of one woman married to one of their number and living in their fellowship, it is difficult to imagine whom they thought they could convert. One suspects that the problem was that of Lewis turning Tahitian rather than of his wife remaining one.

On 24 August 1798 two whalers from London, the *Cornwall* and the *Sally*, arrived at Tahiti. They were there only two days to take on water and provisions but as they were *en route* for England they carried the missionaries' letters. One was a report disabusing the committee in London of their misconception that the language was easy to learn, and informing them that they were making only slow progress, and also that they were beginning to realise that the islanders' political culture was as complex and sophisticated as their own: 'They have their plots and court intrigues, their parties and partisans, as well here as in England; and they are as important in their way as the most refined court of Europe.'[5] They also began to realise that the natives did not want to imitate the Europeans in all aspects of their lives and that they did not wish to abandon their own way of life in which they took considerable pride. Journal entries reveal the confusion of the missionaries and the difficulties of accepting any one statement at face value, for on the same page as is recorded their complex politics the Tahitians are described as rude and uncultivated:

> The poor Otaheitians are deeply prejudiced in favour of their idolatrous worship, though they do not scruple frequently to say, *their gods are good for nothing*. Nor are they less attached to their manners and customs in civil life. Notwithstanding their rude and uncultivated state, they seem to hold themselves as civilised a people as any beneath the sun, and treat the arts and sciences, customs and manners of Europeans with great indifference and contempt.[6]

Such accounts illustrate that the missionaries were unworldly enough to have assumed that they would only have to carry the Christian message and immediately the nation would abandon the habits and customs of a lifetime, which were also those of their parents and grandparents. In their plaint, however, the missionaries did identify one aspect of the culture which was eventually to work to their advantage – the Tahitians' pragmatic approach to their gods. If one god failed to bestir himself on their behalf, they would simply direct their devotions to another. This pragmatism was to make it possible for them to change to the Europeans' god when they and their deity proved more powerful than their own chiefs and gods.

Lacking command of the language and possessing only limited imagination or empathy the missionaries were unable even to begin to understand Tahitian culture. Used as they were to the English control and discipline of children the missionaries were hard put to understand Tahitian family life in particular or authority in general: 'The authority of the parents appears to be but slightly regarded; of masters, not known. Children (the males), if they like not their situation, remove where they list, without any danger of suffering from want of food, covering, or shelter. Even the attendants of the chiefs remain no longer about their persons than they please.'[7] Well might the missionaries have felt confused. English children were flogged, jailed and even hanged for minor crimes. The Tahitians used none of these 'civilising' methods – a situation so different from anything they had experienced or of which they had dreamed. The missionaries believed all children were born in original sin, essentially wilful and disobedient, in need of constant control and correction. They did not realise that the Tahitian parents had no right to chastise children, and because it was an obligation upon everyone to share their food and raiment with whoever needed it, children were also fed and clothed by all and sundry. Perhaps it is not surprising that the missionaries took time to appreciate this point as very few Europeans of the period could visualise a society where parental authority was virtually non-existent. A similar freedom existed in the relationship between masters and men: the chiefs and king wielded enormous power, but there were no apprenticeships enforceable by law as in Europe, no men were press-ganged into years of unwilling sea service – if any person was not content with what he was doing, he stopped doing it. Given the great freedom experienced as a child, adult society could not suddenly become too authoritarian.

During the early years of their work the missionaries spent their time learning the language but making very little progress converting the Tahitians – and waiting daily for support and news from London. But it was not until the very end of December 1800 (some three and a half years after they had arrived) that the *Albion*, another whaler, finally brought them the news of the capture of the *Duff* and the knowledge that they would have to continue alone for a considerable time. This was bitter news, but there was a sign of hope and encouragement when the *Eliza* from Port Jackson, Australia, also arrived returning Mr and Mrs Henry and their daughter, who had been among those who had left Tahiti when it appeared that Pomare was withdrawing his protection. That they had rediscovered their courage and commitment was a considerable boost to morale. Mr and Mrs Henry's return was doubly fortunate because the mission had suffered the defection of another of their number: Mr Broomhall, the harness maker, announced that he no longer believed in the existence of the immortal soul, took a Tahitian wife and went to live on Raiatea.

However, the *Eliza*'s visit from the missionaries' point of view proved a mixed blessing, for the ship gave Pomare 'a carronade, two swivels, several muskets, and a great deal of ammunition';[8] in principle, the missionaries were opposed to arming the Tahitians. This time they did not dare to interfere as they now realised that Pomare needed European weapons to stay in power, and unless he was there to protect them the mission would not survive. Along with the weaponry, the *Eliza* also left behind 'four dissolute sailors who had deserted' whose behaviour they felt diminished the respect the Tahitians might have for Europeans; again, this time they made no complaint. On 10 July 1801 the missionaries finally received support from England: the *Royal Admiral* brought eight more missionaries. When it sailed it took Mr Broomhall and three of the runaway seamen.

The mission had survived; soon it would have reason to be grateful for the arms Pomare had acquired and to the dissolute sailors they so despised. Quite apart from the missionaries' presence and their growing influence over Pomare, traditional Tahitian life was being undermined by the ever greater frequency with which ships called at the island for the islanders were having to raise more crops and livestock than had been the custom when they fed only themselves. Such were the beginnings of the globalisation of commerce which would override the old easy ways of production for need and replace it with production for profit. Tahiti was now seen as a source of food for even the faraway convict colony of New South Wales and ships from there arrived to barter for hogs, which they salted down and carried to Port Jackson. Those Tahitians who valued traditional life were less and less happy with these changes and were prepared to fight in defence of their old customs. Their struggle was to take the form of a civil war between pagans and Christians.

Chapter 15

HOLY WAR

Friends, send also property and cloth for us, and we also will adopt English customs. Friends, send also plenty of muskets and powder, for wars are frequent in our country – should I be killed, you will have nothing in Tahete.
King Pomare II, Letter to the directors of the London Mission Society, 1806

The missionaries had survived until now through the protection of Pomare, but they had made little or no progress in propagating their religion. It was not until July 1801, well over four years after they landed, that they were able to give a sermon in public for the first time. It had taken them that long to learn the language sufficiently well to preach; before that they had struggled to convey their ideas through interpreters and half-understood face-to-face conversations. Their main effort had been directed at converting the king, as it was obvious that many of his people would follow his lead because of the traditional loyalty the people accorded their paramount chiefs. The king, in his turn, had learned that unless he retained the goodwill of the missionaries he would not remain king for long. Now that British ships were becoming more frequent visitors, the missionaries could influence who received European support. Pomare and the missionaries needed each other, but as time passed the missionaries grew more powerful: they could change their location and support one of Pomare's rivals; if they were killed by his people their deaths would be revenged by British ships. Pomare was obliged to make concessions.

All Europeans from Captain Cook onwards had expressed their disgust at human sacrifice and stopping it was one of the missionaries' main demands. Oro, the god of war, was the main recipient of human sacrifice, so Pomare judged that if he took action against his cult – something which no other chief would dare to do – he would retain the goodwill of the missionaries. It was also in Pomare's interest because the main *marae* of Oro was located outside his district, and as the presence of a *marae* enhanced power and prestige of the chief in whose territory it was located, he would thus also be weakening one of his envious rivals. Urged on by the missionaries, he invaded his neighbouring chief's district of Atahuru and stole the effigy from its guardians. The people of Atahuru were outraged and went to war. In this they were joined by the chiefs and people of other districts who also resented the growing influence of the missionaries.

In provoking civil war the missionaries were fortunate not to lose their own lives (a civil war had been the cause of the death of three missionaries at Tonga, as one side identified them as supporting the other), but the moment had been well chosen. They, and King Pomare, were well protected as there were seventeen shipwrecked sailors from the *Norfolk* ashore as well as the *Venus* lying at anchor in the bay. The sailors from these two ships, well equipped with firearms and cannon, fought on the side favoured by the missionaries and with their aid Pomare was able to defeat the rebels. The lands of those chiefs who had opposed him and the missionaries were devastated and the smaller part of Tahiti and the southern side of the larger part were left with 'scarcely a house left standing' according to the missionaries who, once the fighting was over, went on a preaching tour in the wake of the victorious army. If the sailors had brought European diseases, the missionaries deepened internal dissent. They were obliged to acknowledge their own unpopularity: 'The natives everywhere upbraid the English for the introduction of these disorders which they plainly see are dispeopling their country.'[1] European intervention was not exactly proving a blessing to these once happy islands. The small clan wars of the past were now being imbued with an ideological and religious fervour. But for the moment the missionaries and their ally King Pomare had crushed all overt opposition.

On 3 September 1803, Pomare I, the iron-fisted friend and sustainer of the missionaries, was paddling his canoe out to a ship in the bay when he suddenly collapsed and died from what was probably a heart attack. He had been a friend of the British since the time of Captain Cook, if only for selfish reasons, and for him the friendship had borne fruit. From being chief of a relatively minor district he had, first through the armed support of the mutineers from the *Bounty* at a crucial moment and then through the support of the missionaries, become king of Tahiti, even if his kingdom still had district chiefs capable of serious rebellion. While he had undoubtedly shielded the missionaries from death at the hands of the common people, he died unmourned by them. In their somewhat uncharitable assessment he was 'the most bigoted of Polynesian idolators . . . and several hundreds of his subjects he has, in his time, caused to be murdered, and presented as costly sacrifices to the powers of darkness'.[2] His son inherited his position under the title of Pomare II.

Pomare II had long before decided that his future lay in pleasing the British. He was of a more studious nature and more willing to enter into the mental world of the Europeans than his father or most of his contemporaries. By now the missionaries had realised that they would never produce enough fluent Tahitian speakers to preach the Word and they could not expect all Tahitians to learn English. As Tahitian was not a written language they set about creating a Tahitian alphabet and grammar. Pomare II lent his enthusiasm to the task and, with the help of a Hawaiian who had been to England, devoted himself to learning English and worked with the missionaries translating religious texts into Tahitian. Clearly, he viewed the written word and the ability to use it as the key to religious control, and given the force of religion in Tahitian life, he sought to keep that power for himself. At first he wanted to be the only Tahitian able to read and write. However, the missionaries overruled him, insisting that everyone should be able to read the Bible, whereupon he determined to be the most proficient of all his people at these new skills. In fact, he became proficient enough to write in person to the directors of the London Missionary Society promising to continue the work of his father in abolishing the god of war Oro, but making clear that in order to survive against the inevitable opposition these changes would provoke he needed more arms and goods.

Transcribing the language was arguably the missionaries' greatest achievement and service to the people of Tahiti and their most enduring monument. Above all, it was the achievement of Henry Nott, who arrived in 1797 with the first missionaries and was to prove the most dedicated. He set himself the task of learning Tahitian, created an alphabet, gave it grammatical form and then set about translating all the scriptures. It was a task which became his life's work, for as the years passed and he became increasingly proficient in the language and more aware of its complex subtleties, he was obliged to return to his earlier work to rewrite it more accurately: he finally laid down his pen in 1835 after nearly forty years of single-minded labour. Without Henry Nott it is doubtful that the mission would have survived more than a few months; it was his determination and commitment which held the mission together. He was not one of the ordained, but a bricklayer.

Pomare II's immersion in the new arts of reading and writing the Christian scriptures and his ever closer identification with the religion and customs of the foreigner did not endear him to his people. The danger of a new rebellion was growing when the brig *Perseverance* arrived on 25 October 1808 from Port Jackson, returning Mr Elder (one of those missionaries who had deserted the cause earlier) and his young bride. Two days later the captain shot himself out of 'a violent passion for Mr Elder's wife' which left her 'in a state of frenzy' for several months; it was a scandal that would normally have kept such an enclosed community buzzing with gossip for months had not graver matters intervened. Pomare II warned that a rebellion was imminent and that their lives were in danger. It was decided that they should keep the *Perseverance* at hand until the situation was clear. On 6 November, Taut, a high chief and Pomare II's prime minister, led the rebellion. Two of the missionaries tried to negotiate a peace; when this failed, and with their lives at serious risk, all but four men embarked on the ship and were taken to the island of Huahine. Fighting continued until, on 22 December, Pomare II, for all of his outward show of Christianity, reverted to his traditional ways and was advised by Metia the prophet of Oro, god of war, that it was an auspicious moment to give battle and that he would achieve a great victory. He attacked the rebels only to suffer a resounding defeat. Given the desecration that his father had inflicted on the *marae* of Oro, and Pomare II's continuation of that policy, it is surprising that Pomare put his trust in Oro's prophet.

After the defeat Pomare II, his court, his most faithful supporters and the missionaries were forced to flee to the island of Mo'orea where the king had powerful support. Matavai Bay district was, in its turn, devastated by the triumphant rebels and the mission buildings and gardens destroyed. The traditionalists had triumphed over the Christians. The missionaries were evacuated to Port Jackson, Australia, leaving only Mr Nott and Mr Hayward at Pomare II's side. Their decision to stay was to prove absolutely crucial to the ultimate outcome. Pomare II's faith in his native gods had been considerably weakened by his resounding defeat and the continued presence of two missionaries was an assurance that the European god, as well as European cannon, would stand by him. They were his main hope; had he been a traditional chief with powers confined only to Tahiti, he and the missionaries would have been killed and the war ended. But he had dynastic connections with the ruling chiefs of the island of Mo'orea; and he was married to Terito, a daughter of Tamato, chief of the island of Raiatea. These two islands were to form the base for his continued resistance.

The fortunes of war dragged back and forth. Pomare II was desperate to retain the support of the missionaries. They insisted that he needed to give better proofs of his abandonment of the old gods. To demonstrate his Christianity he ate food which, it was traditionally believed, would cause death to anyone not first offering it to the gods – he came to no harm. He had a Christian blessing recited at an important traditional ceremony and feast celebrating Tahitian gods – again he came to no harm. His example was followed most crucially by a priest in Mo'orea who converted to Christianity and publicly burned all the idols of the *marae* under his charge – he, too, came to no harm. Clearly, the native gods were powerless. Numerous others, including many influential chiefs and priests of Mo'orea followed the king's lead as he gradually broke the taboos which held the fabric of their society together. People were disoriented by the changes they were experiencing and weary of the endless civil war. Also loyalty to a chief was a strong element of their culture and more and more people in the two districts of Matavai and Pare, where Pomare was the traditional chief, wanted him back as their ruler, and were prepared to tolerate the missionaries in order that he should return. For their part, the rebels had split into three warring factions as districts which had been traditional enemies found it difficult to stay united once their common enemy had been expelled from the island. In Tahiti, Pomare's faction grew in strength. On 18 July 1812 Pomare II asked the missionaries to baptise him. They refused as they wanted to see a change in his lifestyle as incontrovertible evidence that his conversion was genuine, rather than mere lip service based on expediency. He was a heavy drinker and retained Tahitian sexual practices, both of which were anathema to the missionaries. By withholding baptism, their official acceptance, they also kept him anxious to win their approval.

Eventually, after seven years of war, Pomare II was able to return to his homeland on Sunday 12 November 1815. But because he returned with the missionaries very much the power behind the throne, the fires of resistance were rekindled and the traditionalists again plotted rebellion. Their plan was betrayed and Pomare II was warned that the pagans intended to attack the Christians while they were at worship. Giving no sign that they knew of the plot the congregation went to church as usual, but with concealed arms. Early in the ensuing battle, Chief Upufara, leader of the rebels, was killed and, as was customary in Tahitian warfare, with their chief dead his warriors fled. This was the last attempt by force of arms to reverse the spread of the new religion and European culture: it had been a forlorn hope for Pomare and his European supporters were now too powerful to be ousted by such means. But in the immediate aftermath of the victory the missionaries showed one beneficial aspect of their faith to good advantage. Pomare II would have followed the old rules of such internal wars, pursuing and slaughtering his enemies and laying waste their crops and homes. The missionaries insisted on a policy of clemency and reconciliation and in this the new religion showed a better side than did the old, and the victory without revenge helped ensure the supremacy of Pomare II and his Christian allies.

In 1816 Pomare offered his native household gods to the missionaries to do with as they wished; he was prepared to destroy them, but the missionaries sent them to London. The power of the missionaries as advisors had reached new political heights. The ability to read became the new mania and thousands of tracts were printed. The first gospel to be printed was St Luke's, and the missionaries decided that it was an opportune moment to place the mission on a sound commercial footing. They sold – rather than distributed – the gospel, taking cocoa-nut oil in payment. This had the additional advantage of obliging the islanders to work. The mission also built a small brig which was launched in December 1817 in order to collect cargoes of cocoa-nut oil and salt pork from around the various islands which would then be sent to New South Wales. By this time the missionaries were pushing ahead with the commercialisation of other island produce. They sent for a man to set up a sugar plantation and mill, but the enterprise was not a success: 'The experience Mr Gyles had had with negros did not fit him to deal with free natives like those of Tahiti'[3] – succinct expression of the world of difference between conditions on the slave plantations of the West Indies (or, for that matter, those of the wage slaves of England), and the freedom of the Tahitians. The islanders saw no reason why they should work just to profit other people: they had few needs which they could not satisfy with a morning's labour. Then, in 1819, the possibility arose of evacuating the population of Pitcairn Island as the growth in the number of descendants of the Tahitian women and *Bounty* mutineers who had settled there was exhausting the island's resources. One reporter saw them as a possible answer to the labour problem: 'We were thinking that they [the Pitcairners] would be a great acquisition at Opunuhu alongside of the sugar works, as they have been accustomed to labour, for the Taheitians will not labour for any payment.'[4] In the event, the Pitcairners voted to stay at home and risk the chances of a famine. In 1821 a scheme to spin and weave cotton failed for the same reason: no one was willing to devote their lives to endless toil.

The London Missionary Society expended a great deal of money and effort on machinery for these commercial enterprises in an effort to turn the Tahitians into labourers on the European model. As it was, the Europeans were increasing the amount of work forced on the common people. It was the custom that chiefs could call upon the people to labour at collective enterprises. In order to provision a ship, for example, the chief might demand a contribution of one pig, or its equivalent, from each of the landowners under him in order that he might purchase arms, powder or whatever else took his fancy. One major new collective enterprise ordered through the chiefs was the building of chapels. The greatest of these, built at Papaoa, in the district of Pare, was over 700ft long, 55ft wide and 35ft high, with the roof supported on thirty-six huge breadfruit tree trunks and the outer eaves on 280 lesser pillars. Building these constituted an enormous additional amount of toil for the leisure-loving Tahitians.

In spite of all that was done for them by his people, the missionaries continued to find fault with King Pomare II, for, although he had thrown out his household gods and asked to be baptised, they still refused him. Their negative attitude to the king who had done so much to promote their cause was due to his increasing homosexual activity which he no longer took pains to hide from them. If the missionaries' intransigence is understandable given that they were men with the prejudices of their time, it did little to help maintain the king's political and cultural authority. His quite minor deviations from western custom were also objected to, with complaints that, among other things, 'He supported the old practice that no woman should eat in any house that the king had honoured with his presence.'[5] It is, in fact, difficult to see why they should have taken exception to this customary taboo, particularly as women were by no means treated as the equals of men in England. In accepting Christianity and in trying to make it acceptable to his people, Pomare II needed to retain as many social customs as possible, otherwise there was a danger of provoking yet another rebellion. The early Christians in Europe had shown considerable diplomacy in bringing their religion to pagans, by including pagan elements in the festivals of Easter and Christmas and by turning pagan wells into holy ones, for example. These latter-day missionaries lacked that breadth of vision. Had they allowed the king and his subjects time to adapt their culture to the new religion, the people would have been spared the almost total demoralisation which followed from the rejection of all they had previously valued and respected.

Chapter 16

THE INSPECTORS

Before Christianity found them, the principal part of their time was spent in eating, sleeping, and profligacy; but now their hours are generally employed in honest and profitable labour.

Revd D. Tyerman and G. Bennet, Journal of Voyages and Travels *(1831)*

The London Missionary Society had gone from strength to strength, sending missionaries to China, India, the East Indies and Madagascar as well as to the Pacific islands. In 1821, the Revd Daniel Tyerman and George Bennet, were deputed by the Society to visit and report on the progress and activities of missions around the world. They decided to start their inspection in Tahiti. The two deputies and three married couples going to join the missionaries were given free passage to Tahiti on the *Tuscon*, a South Sea whaler of 360 tons captained by Francis Stavers with a crew of thirty-five. They left London and dropped down to Gravesend on 5 May 1821, reaching Portsmouth on the 12th, where they were detained by contrary winds until the 19th: they arrived off Tahiti on 25 September, a comparatively fast crossing of five months.

There, Mr Nott and Mr Wilson, resident missionaries, came aboard to greet them. For the first time the work of the mission was to be inspected and reported on by outsiders: work which the missionaries had, with enviable application, recorded in their journals. These journals are an invaluable quarry of historical information. Without their labours the world would know much less about the Tahitian people, their history and culture. A permanent presence, the missionaries witnessed the daily life of the people they wished to convert. Invaluable as these first-hand accounts are, one must appreciate that, like any other historical source, they reflect their own biases. The missionaries who had been working in Tahiti since the early days of 1797 wrote their journals, reports and letters in the knowledge that their work in the field would be discussed and evaluated by the Society in London. They would have been less than human had they understated the magnitude of their efforts or the problems which had made the winning of converts so difficult. Moreover, the very nature of their undertaking meant that they were not there to consider and expound upon any of the positive aspects of the pagan culture which surrounded them. Nor were they there as neutral observers, to record as objectively as possible; they were not anthropologists: their job was to condemn and eradicate paganism. In order to counter this bias, it is frequently advisable to read their words from a critical perspective. The two deputies were in Tahiti to act as the eyes of the London Society, and in reading their accounts it is important to distinguish what they *saw* for themselves from what they were *told* by the missionaries they were inspecting.

For example, the open practice of infanticide is featured in the visitors' journals almost immediately after their arrival:

He assured us, that three-fourths of the children born were wont to be murdered as soon as they were born, by one or other of the unnatural parents, or by some person employed for that purpose – wretches being found who might be called infant-assassins by trade. He mentioned having met a woman, soon after the abolition of the diabolical practice, to whom he said, 'How many children have you?' 'This one in my arms,' was her answer. 'And how many did you kill?' She replied, 'Eight!'

Another woman to whom the same questions were put, confessed that she had destroyed seventeen! Nor were these solitary cases. Sin was so effectually doing its work in these dark places of the earth, that, full as they were of the habitations of cruelty and wickedness, war, profligacy, and murder, were literally exterminating a people unworthy to live; and soon would the 'cities have been wasted without inhabitants, the houses without men, and the land been utterly desolate'. But the gospel stepped in, and the plague was stopped.[1]

The 'He' who informed them of this was the resident missionary Mr Nott, a man disinclined to underestimate the forces of darkness against which he and his companions had been working. Whatever one's opinion of abortion and infanticide or, for that matter, of 'war, profligacy, and murder' the conclusions they drew are not sustainable. Infanticide and war had been endemic ever since the islands had first been inhabited, and yet they had sustained high levels of population. While all the sources agree that the population of the islands declined after the arrival of the Europeans, had the native wars been so bloody – with the alleged massacre of the defeated – and had they really killed three-quarters of their offspring, they would never have been as populous as they were when the Europeans arrived. Given all that is said of their treatment of children, of their generous and amicable social relations, it is equally doubtful that their society would have evolved so agreeably had they lived under a reign of fear from chiefs and priests who constantly and arbitrarily culled them for human sacrifice.

Not that the missionaries objected to executions carried out by those Christian chiefs whom they favoured. The inspectors wrote that

A few weeks before our arrival, some dissatisfaction had arisen in a district of Tahi in consequence of the king's particularity in distributing his property among his chiefs. An individual had sent Pomare a large hog, for which he humbly asked a black-lead pencil in return. This being refused, he and some others who had taken offence for similar causes formed a conspiracy to destroy the king, and to effect a revolution in the government. The plot being discovered, the two ringleaders were apprehended, tried, and condemned. Tahitians seldom deny crime of which they have been guilty, when charged with it and those two culprits frankly acknowledged theirs. They were sentenced to death, and hanged upon a tree in the presence of multitudes, who witnessed the execution with indescribable horror, as a scene equally new and terrible; justice not having been wont to be administered with such solemnity, of old, when the most summary and cruel punishments were inflicted on offenders without any legal forms. Mr Crook attended on the spot, and while they were hanging (which they did for an hour) earnestly addressed the spectators, and 'reasoned with them of righteousness, temperance, and a judgement to come'.[2]

Clearly, this was presented as an example of the good work the missionaries were doing in the islands. The image of a man standing by two strangled men and haranguing a horrified crowd is barbaric. Previously the most common method of execution was by a single blow from a club, quicker and cleaner than hanging. And as executions had not been public displays, it is no wonder the crowd was horrified. That the Tahitians were appalled at the death of two men by hanging indicates that they were not hardened to scenes of suffering – one recalls their distress when Captain Cook summoned them to witness the flogging of a sailor.

That it did not horrify the British must be put down to the fact that in Britain hangings were not only public, but almost festive occasions which drew huge crowds to enjoy the spectacle of some poor wretch taking time to be strangled at the end of a rope. One might accept that the State had a right to punish treason and to execute traitors and that the two Tahitians were justly doomed. But in England an account of a public execution from 1746 describes in detail a traitor being hanged, drawn and quartered after which his head was displayed on Temple Bar. One trusts that the cultivated citizens going about their daily business in eighteenth-century London were not disturbed by the presence of the severed head under which they passed daily. English children fared little better at the hands of the law: 'In 1748 Chief Justice Willis postponed the execution of a boy of ten, sentenced to death for murder, in order to consult his fellow judges as to whether it was proper to hang a child so young. The judges were unanimous in thinking that the punishment should be carried out.'³ Lawyers were hard put to count the number of capital offences in England, but there were at least a hundred and fifty and the following extract from the *Gentleman's Magazine* shows that they were actively enforced: 'Executed at Tyburn, July 6 [1750], Elizabeth Banks, for stripping a child; Catherine Conway, for forging a seaman's ticket; and Margeret Harvey for robbing her master. They were all drunk.'⁴ Some writers claim that Tahitian and Hawaiian women could be executed for breaking taboos, but this author has found no contemporary account which describes such an event. No doubt hundreds witnessed the execution of those three unfortunate women whose minor offences were probably caused by hunger and poverty.

Captain Cook has sometimes been criticised for his treatment of Polynesian thieves, but compared to the customs of his own culture he was both mild and humane. Indeed, the respect accorded to the islanders by sailors and men of science who sailed with them shows them in a much more humane light than those who administered their laws at home or the missionaries who took their culture abroad. In recording the actions of the missionaries overseas, however, one must allow for the fact that they came from a cruel and repressive society and that their inability to step outside their own preconceptions compromises their interpretation of events. That a missionary could glory in preaching to a crowd of 'pagans' horrified by the strangled cadavers above him attests to his failure to see and understand either his own culture or theirs.

On 8 December the deputies visited Queen Pomare Vahine of Huahine, the sister of Pomare II's queen. There they found that

Huahine was subject to the same devastating system of superstition and licentiousness as the other islands. There was not, indeed, comparatively, so much war, human sacrifice, and pestilent disease, but infanticide was awfully frequent. An old chief informs us, that his father told him this was a modern practice, resorted to by the women to prolong a youthful and attractive appearance, which they supposed would be less, if they suckled their offspring; and the innovation was sanctioned by the chiefs, in regard to their own children, the fruit of unequal marriages, to preserve a pure and legitimate lineage of aristocracy. The Areois destroyed their children, because they would not been cumbered with them in pursuing their migratory habits; and girls were more especially made away with than boys, because it was very troublesome to rear them – the abominable proscription of the female sex requiring that their food should be dressed in separate ovens from that of their fathers, and brothers, their husbands and male kindred.[5]

If one assumes that the information is accurate, this extract is worth some analysis. The comparative lack of 'war, human sacrifice and pestilent disease' was almost certainly due to the fact that Huahine had had less contact with Europeans. The admission that there was also less human sacrifice supports the view that sacrifices became more widespread after the Europeans' arrival. If it is taken at face value, one might conclude that infanticide was particularly high because the lack of war left that as the only practical method of controlling the population. This would also account for the greater propensity to destroy female babies. Others have accepted the *arioris'* account of why they had no children. One thing which sits uneasily with the other comments is that the practice of infanticide was introduced by the women for no greater motive than vanity. All other observations claim that women, constrained by taboos, were very much inferior to the men in terms of political, social and religious authority. That such a powerless section of the population could introduce such a fundamental cultural change seems most unlikely.

But the inspectors confirmed the enormous decline in population from the evidence of their own eyes. They saw the great *marae* of Oro on Huahine and stood in awe at the amount of labour this had taken. They counted another nine *maraes*; such large-scale building had required a large population with time and energy to spare. Continuing their tour they met an old man who told them 'that, when he was a boy, the whole of this hill was covered with dwellings and gardens. Now there are but three houses standing upon it which one only is inhabited. Similar evidence of decay and devastation meet our eyes every where on this tour. So fatal, indeed, were the effects of war, licentiousness, infanticide, and idolatry, towards the close of the reign, that the population of Huahine, in the course of a few years, was reduced from at least ten, some say twenty, thousand, to little more than as many hundred.'[6] Given that in spite of all the native practices which took life – infanticide, war, human sacrifice – these islands had supported huge populations of well-fed people before the white man arrived, native pagan culture can hardly have been the cause of this catastrophic decline. Native culture had sustained thousands, where the inspectors found only hundreds. Such a demoralising collapse, and such a failure of indigenous culture to resist it, accounts for the Europeans' ability to denigrate and replace native culture: native power – economic, social and political – was not strong enough to defeat the incomers. With capitulation came the loss of cultural and religious life; the people were left disoriented and psychologically deracinated, despite still inhabiting their native soil. Their whole way of life as well as their gods had failed them.

There is one observation which implies that, in fact, the gods themselves did not approve of infanticide, for the missionaries recorded that 'A woman, intending to effect abortion during pregnancy (which was atrociously common), or to murder her offspring as soon as it should be born, presented herself, if possible, a day before the time, at the *marae*, with a *rou maraire* – a sprig of sweet-scented fern – in her hand, which she threw down upon the sacred stones, saying, "I intend to give you a man tomorrow; do not be angry with me".'[7] That it was deemed necessary to ask the gods not to be angry at an abortion suggests that the practice had not started as a religious obligation or as something to please the gods, but rather had evolved as a secular necessity. People who dwell on small islands with finite resources cannot afford to let the population grow to unsustainable numbers.

The inspectors' observations on childbirth are informative. While visiting the smaller Tahitian islands they were present when King Mahines' daughter-in-law was about to give birth to a child who was to carry on the royal succession in Tahiti:

> We were surprised to find this great lady, on whom the hopes of the nation are placed, in a small shed, about seven feet square, separated from a larger dwelling, for her special convenience on the august occasion of giving birth

to a prince. She was reposing on grass spread over the floor, and there was no other furniture in the apartment but a lamp made of a cocoa-nut shell . . . The queen of the island, Hautia, and Hautia Vahine, the father and mother, with another female, were her attendants. The shed stood within a few paces of the sea, and had been purposely chosen, according to the approved custom, for the benefit of free air, and to afford her an opportunity, as soon as she should be delivered, to plunge into the sea, and there sit in the water for an half an hour. This strange, and we might deem perilous practice, to a woman in such delicate circumstances, is common here; and we are assured that, in most instances, it is the means of restoring strength and animation to the exhausted mother, who frequently goes about her ordinary household business an hour of two after she has come out of the purifying flood.[8]

That the heir to the Tahitian kingdom should be born in such a simple setting was part of the custom which decreed that women would give birth in a specially constructed and separate dwelling. Her daughter was duly born on 23 February 1822, weight unrecorded. Her birthright might be thought to have been that semi-naked, free and happy Tahitian childhood so appropriate to the location and climate, but her traditional Tahitian start in life was soon to be enveloped in European trappings: 'The wife of one of the Missionaries was sent for immediately, to dress the babe in the English fashion, as it has been determined, on every occasion, to conform as nearly as possible to the manners and customs of the nation which has sent them spiritual fathers and instructions in righteousness.'[9] When the king received the deputies the queen and all her ladies were in European dress, even wearing stockings and shoes, although the queen did constantly breast-feed her son throughout the audience. So, as yet, not everything natural and normal had been suppressed.

The behaviour of royalty and the chiefs was, at this date, a mixture of their adoption of Christianity, symbolised by the use of western clothes and uniforms, and the traditional relationship with their people. When anything requiring a communal effort was undertaken, 'The kings, queens, and chiefs of both sexes, take the lead, and love to excel in all sorts of work. Though they have many persons at their command, and ready to execute all their wishes, they are not ashamed to labour with their own hands, both for examples sake, and for the delight they take in doing everything well – yea, better than others.'[10] They even laboured for the missionaries: 'Mr Platt [a missionary], wishing to have a piece of ground adjacent to his house planted with taro . . . The ground for the cultivation of this root is low and wet, and here it was covered with rank and coarse vegetation . . . On the occasion, sundry chiefs headed their vassals, and toiled with their own hands as hard as any of them. This is always the case when any public service is to be done, the principal men deeming it their honour to be the ablest and busiest of the multitude'.[11] Nowhere does the inspector record a similar unbending of the missionaries, who were not prepared to assist in the labour which they commanded. Coming from Europe where manual work was deemed beneath the dignity of men such as himself, let alone the aristocracy and royalty, it was worthy of note – although not of emulation.

The advantages of long hours of work were never far from the missionaries' thoughts and the visitors' report enlarged upon the failure to establish a sugar plantation and sugar mill: 'The sugar scheme failed here, in consequence of the king's jealousy, excited by false alarms insinuating into his mind, by foreigners, that slavery and the culture of the cane were necessarily associated; as though the Europeans would presently come and possess themselves of the islands, when they found that sugar was produced in them.'[12] The king's fears were not so foolish; many natives had lost their lands and freedom to one or other of the nations of Europe on lesser pretexts than that. And in the longer term his fears proved justified when Tahiti became yet another colony producing tropical goods for European consumers. Once land could supply commodities for the European market it acquired monetary value and the exploitation of the local inhabitants as a labour force soon followed. Mr Armitage, who had arrived at Tahiti in the *Tuscon*, had been sent specifically to start a cotton mill. The king was not enthusiastic, but gave reluctant permission for the scheme to go ahead. One can hardly deny that the king had good reason, whether from knowledge or intuition, for his misgivings. In 1821, the cotton mills of Merrie England were hardly temples of joy and freedom. If the children toiled no more than ten hours a day, six days a week, year in and year out, they were the more fortunate. John Moss, who was in charge of apprentices at a Lancashire cotton factory during 1814, testified to a parliamentary inquiry that boys and girls as young as seven years of age were taken from London to Lancashire to undertake this continuous and tiring labour. And the coal mines were no better than the mills: 'Children are taken into these mines to work as early as four years of age, sometimes five, . . . while from eight to nine is the ordinary age at which employment in these mines commences.'[13] Similar accounts can be had for a whole variety of other contemporary British industries. When the lives of

British children are compared to the free, healthy and open lives of Tahitian children and the loving care with which their whole community surrounded them, there can be little doubt who deserved to be called savages for working children so relentlessly.

Although the missionaries' schemes to profit from a sugar plantation and mill were rejected by the king, they benefited from being treated as chiefs and priests in terms of being the recipients of tribute: 'The contributions from the Missionary Association of the island [Huahine] in the present year, has been twelve balls of arrow-root, and six thousand three hundred and forty-nine bamboos of cocoa-nut oil.'[14] The process of obtaining cocoa-nut oil was a laborious one in which the meat of the nut was shaved into thin flakes and the flakes then left to drain. Whether the Tahitians needed or wanted these new labour-intensive methods is a moot point. 'The people of Tahiti are not of various trades and occupations, every man, even the chiefs, with few exceptions, being able to build his house, construct his canoe, manufacture his fishing tackle, etc., and when we consider with how few and simple tools he contrives to do all this, his skill and dexterity are admirable.'[15] The missionaries' desire to set up sugar production, cotton mills and other commercial enterprises was not only motivated by a desire for profit. They genuinely believed that the Tahitians enjoyed far too much leisure and that if they had to labour long hours they would have less time and inclination to sin. It is reported that at least one of the missionaries enjoyed having breadfruit trees cut down for church building as it removed a work-free source of food and obliged the Tahitians to plant alternative crops.

The Tahitians did not take kindly to working for accumulation rather than immediate need, and the old ways of sharing were slow to disappear. As the deputies recorded:

It is an ancient custom to give a friend whatever he asks for, whether food or raiment, and however much the owner may want it himself. To refuse a request of this kind would be deemed such a breach of hospitality as to bring upon the person the reproach of being a churl, a character held in abhorrence by these people, who, in some respects, live as if they were all one family, and had every thing in common. It was formerly so imperative to divide their morsel one with another that when a man killed a hog it was baked whole, and all his neighbours who chose came to partake of it; he himself having only as much as he could eat, and the entire carcass being devoured at a meal. Customs of this kind, which suited the lazy and the sensual, are now fast falling, as they ought, into decline; while Christian charity, the principle of the purest benevolence, makes them ready to communicate of their good things to those that are in need, without reckless waste or unnecessary impoverishment of themselves for worthless vagabonds, of whom, formerly, there were multitudes consuming the fruits of the soil, and the produce of industry, without cultivating the one or contributing to the other.[16]

This is an extraordinary attempt to denigrate the open, generous Tahitian charity while claiming that Christian charity was superior. To pontificate on charity to a society where no individual went hungry or without clothing or lacked any other necessary support, when the missionaries themselves came from a country where thousands of unfortunates went hungry and shivered on the streets for want of charity, is little short of wilful blindness.

From a practical point of view, if a pig were killed, how long did they think that pork would remain edible in the tropical heat? It made sense to take turns in killing a pig and in dining at each other's table on those occasions, if for no other reason than to prevent the waste of good food. Given the number of times gifts to them of meat, fish, fowl, fruit and vegetables of all kinds are recorded, it ill became them to criticise those who ate from the labour of others.

Chapter 17

THE LAST PAGANS

It was found that they had tatooed themselves, which, though harmless in itself, is now contrary to law, as associated with obsolete abominations; by then it was used as a symbol of their dissatisfactions with the better order of things, and a signal for revolt against the existing government . . . It is remarkable that, about the same time, there were similar insurrections in Tahiti and Raiatea, but in both these islands the projects of the factions were detected and frustrated.

James Montgomery writing of events in 1821[1]

The destruction of the old taboos which gave force of law to customary practices meant that many old obligations were no longer enforced. The missionaries, at the urging of the king, drew up a new code of laws. They used the opportunity to suppress many aspects of the traditional way of life; for example, because some tattoos were given to those who had observed certain pagan religious rites, tattooing was criminalised and severely punished. This too radical suppression of the traditional culture led to renewed anti-Christian uprisings in May 1821, only four months before the inspectors arrived. The revolt started on Huahine, an island whose people had had much less contact with Europeans, and where a hundred young men were determined to live in the traditional way. They objected to the anti-hedonistic dimension of Christian discipline and hoped that others – namely, the chiefs – would join them in overthrowing the king and his Christian mentors. The chiefs did not join them and when faced with the king's forces they surrendered without a fight. Such outbreaks were a predictable reaction from people whose indigenous culture was being suppressed by powerful incomers. Tattooing had significant social and aesthetic as well as religious dimensions, and a less fanatical approach to Tahitian ways could have made the transition from paganism less of an imposition.

The missionaries also insisted on challenging and breaking food taboos. Sometimes this may have been justified from their perspective, as when King

Pomare II broke the taboo against eating a turtle before it had been offered to the gods. He had to screw up his courage to do so, and no one else at his table would follow his example, but when nothing happened to him as a result he decided to become a Christian. This may have demonstrated the ineffectiveness of the pagan gods in pagan eyes, but the missionaries caused unnecessary resentment when they tried to eradicate those customs which controlled who could dine with whom, which could have been viewed as habitual social custom rather than a religious obligation. It was not that they did not recognise the intertwining of religion and the customary dimensions of life. It was precisely because the old religion intermingled the functions of kings, chiefs and priests that the missionaries would not let chiefs become deacons in the missions. They feared that any repeat of continual authority would be seen by the commoners as a confirmation of the old system and would reinforce the power of the chiefs. Also, to allow the king and chiefs to take over religious leadership would smack of a step towards a State Church, something abhorred by Nonconformist chapels and sects. But in undermining the respect given to chiefs it had the effect of weakening the traditional social fabric and fragmenting even further the Tahitian world and sense of self-worth. This did, however, set most of the chiefs and priests against the missionaries and made it more difficult for them to make influential converts: if their principled inflexibility did much to make conversions more difficult, one should perhaps respect them for not taking the easiest route to their desired ends.

In common with earlier commentators the visitors in 1821 saw that the traditional priests still had a multiplicity of functions in society:

> The priests of these islands were not confined to the exercise of their devotional functions; they were also warriors and statesmen, who accompanied kings both at the council-board and in the field – by sea as well as by land . . . This sacred canoe always led the van of the rest, and the priests were accustomed to fight to the most desperate extremity in defence of their palladium, for while this was uncaptured the conflict might be maintained, but, as soon as it was lost, the party to whom it belonged would fight no more. The moment the god fell into the adversary's hands, his divinity forsook him, and so did his adherents. Panic-struck, they fled in all directions.[2]

One thing the inspectors appear to have missed is the connection between the priesthood and the *ariori*: this might be because no one would invite them to

witness a pagan ceremony, or it is possible that paganism as an active force
no longer existed. Male *ariori* outnumbered females by about five to one since,
as has been mentioned, they were obliged to act as warriors as well as dance
and give dramatic performances. The missionaries described them as being
the most attractive and intelligent people of both sexes. They were a

> kind of strolling players, who went about the country, from one chief's
> district to another, reciting stories and singing songs for the entertainment
> of the people. The stories were called Aamu, and were dramatic in form, so
> that several speakers might take their distinct parts, and not merely recite
> but act them. These compositions, we are told, frequently did credit to the
> talents of the authors, while the accuracy and liveliness with which they
> were repeated showed considerable powers of memory as well as of
> imitation in the performances. But they were connected with unutterable
> abominations, and therefore have been entirely discontinued since purer
> manners have followed in the train of Christian principles.[3]

Thus they paid them a rather grudging compliment on their abilities, but
what was written is largely in the past tense as if the *ariori* belonged to an
earlier period. The implication is that by 1821 this enormous slice of Tahitian
cultural life had been suppressed.

There was one other serious charge of murder (besides infanticide) which
the inspectors placed against Tahitian culture:

> One of the monstrous practices of these islands before they embraced the
> gospel, was to bury their friends alive when, from their infirmities, they
> became bothersome to the young and vigorous. They would dig a hole in
> the sand on the sea-beach, then, under the pretext of taking their aged or
> sick relative to bathe, they would bear him on a litter to the spot, and
> tumble him into the grave which had been proposed, instantly heaping
> stones and earth upon him.[4]

There they trampled him to death. Alternatively, it was claimed, they
sometimes simply rushed into the person's abode and speared him to death.
Once again this is hearsay, and is not supported by other sources. In contrast,
however, there is some evidence that the Tahitians did care for their long-
term sick. Some suffered from a mild form of leprosy and their treatment was
reported on during Cook's first voyage: 'the people who were in that state

were secluded from society, living by themselves each in a small house built in some unfrequented place where they were daily supplyd with provisions; whither these had any hopes of relief or were doom'd in this manner to languish out a life of solitude we did not learn.'[5] If they were prepared to sustain such people for an indefinite period there seems little reason to assume that they would not sustain the elderly. The cruel practices the inspectors record were hearsay and may well have happened on other Polynesian islands rather than Tahiti.

During their stay the visitors found only two aspects worthy of respect or praise. One was the concern shown by the inhabitants for the dead:

> But often, as we have already mentioned, they did not bury at all the corpses of their favourite relations or friends; keeping them above ground till the bones were left bare from the decay of the flesh. They would then take the skulls, place them in conspicuous situations, near their abode, and deck them with flowers, stuck in the cavities or wreathed about the temples, and these they renew daily. However revolting their endurance of the previous process of corruption, within the cognizance of their senses, may be to our feelings of reverence for the dead, there is something indicative of tenderness and delicacy in this custom of adorning the saddest memorials of mortality, above ground, with the loveliest emblems of life above ground, poured, in perpetual succession, from the bosom of the earth.[6]

At last, the visitors appeared to comprehend the customs alien to their own. They did not, like so many, decry this keeping of skulls as barbaric, but rather appreciated the affection which impelled this action and the daily remembrance of the dead, which, as churchmen, they knew was less conscientiously observed in Britain. But this practice is hardly congruent with the elderly and disabled being casually interred on a beach. The only thing they commended, without any cavil, was the language: 'the allusions and similitudes of the natives are often exceedingly beautiful and appropriate; never redundant, nor verbose, but for the most part so condensed and perspicuous as to prove that they think with accuracy'.[7] They praise it as being musical and agreeable to the ear, and yet very precise, while being poetical in its use.

But for every two steps forward achieved by the missionaries the old ways took one step back. In the decade after the two inspectors left, the missionaries continued to be disliked by the people and for a short time their influence on the Tahitian royal family was again resisted. The male line of the Pomares had died out and the succession had gone to the female line with Queen Aimata reigning as Pomare Vahine IV. According to the missionaries, the queen was sinful, wilful and young and favoured the old religion or, perhaps, simply the old hedonistic customs and way of life.

The queen turned against the missionaries and their attempts to suppress all native customs. However, some of the Christian chiefs continued to support the missionaries, confident, no doubt, in the knowledge that just as the missionaries had made the fortunes of the house of Pomare, so they were equally likely to be able to make the fortunes of others. Civil war was again imminent and the two sides were once more facing each other under arms in May 1831, 'when two sail were announced in sight, which proved to be the *Comet*, a British man-of-war, and a transport, having on board all the inhabitants of Pitcairn's Island. The first could not have entered at a better moment, nor the latter at a worse . . . you have, of course, heard of these interesting islanders . . . The first moral lesson they received on their arrival, was to see about fifty women of Tahiti swim off to the ships in which they were, and commit in their presence, with the sailors, such acts of debauchery, that they instantly desired to return to their own island.'[8] The old form of welcome was still being practised and there was still opposition enough to the missionaries to provoke civil war. This time, however, as the queen was antagonistic towards the missionaries and as she commanded the royal arsenal as well as all the considerable loyalties accruing to the Pomare clan, it was a war which the missionaries and their Christian allies may well have lost. But again, the arrival of a British man-of-war strengthened the cause of the missionaries and ensured that they were, once more, the victors.

The queen's forces were no match for a British man-of-war and her stand against the missionaries' manipulation of political power collapsed. In 1834 the entire royal family was induced to sign the pledge and become teetotal. In the same year that the law prohibited the importation of spirits, it also made attendance at public worship compulsory. The latter was justified on the grounds that those who attended church were vulnerable to theft during services. Had the people meekly acquiesced in all that the missionaries required in terms of the end of leisure, sexual pleasure, popular entertainment and abstention from alcohol, one of the most hedonistic societies on earth would have become a miserable theocratic state. The missionaries were using their unprecedented authority to impose the regulations they would have promptly enforced in England had they enjoyed the same degree of power there.

But something new was entering into the Protestant missionaries' struggle against the pagan and the misguided – France and Roman Catholicism. The permanent residence of British missionaries inevitably brought Tahiti into the British orbit. Britain had already wrested Canada and India from the French, as well as other scattered islands; she had also beaten the French in claiming and settling Australia and New Zealand. The French were thus in no mood to see their influence entirely excluded from this corner of the globe. If Britain could back its missionaries, France could do the same. The London Missionary Society, with the aid of British muskets and cannon, had been certain, in the long run, to defeat the heathen, but their triumph was not to be absolute: they were about to be challenged by Roman Catholicism.

Chapter 18

HAWAIIAN ECLIPSE

Paul's injunctions are not observed on the Sandwich Islands. Women usurp
authority over the men & hold the reigns of government over large
districts.

M. *Jolly and M. Macintyre,* Family and Gender in the Pacific[1]

W hen early in 1819 King Kamehameha I fell ill the Hawaiian priests recommended a human sacrifice to effect a cure, but keeping to his earlier rejection of human sacrifice the king refused. As he lay dying, one of the last people to embrace him was the now elderly John Young, the sailor who had lived on Hawaii since 1790 and who had fought so valiantly in the king's wars, become his trusted advisor and sometime governor of Hawaii, whose granddaughter Emma was to become queen through her marriage to Kamahameha IV. On 8 May 1819 the king died. His son Liholiho was elected king as Kamehameha II in the traditional manner by all the chiefs assembled in their feathered robes and helmets and with the priests in charge of the ceremony. But if his feathered cloak symbolised traditional authority, the reality of the changing power relations was evident in the ornate British uniform he wore beneath it. There was no doubt that an era of Hawaiian history was coming to a close. One of the dead king's widows, Kaahumanu, 6ft tall and an acknowledged beauty, was also ambitious and demanded the right to be co-ruler with the new young king. Hers was the more forceful personality and she was duly proclaimed queen regent by the council of chiefs, who wanted a strong central leadership to maintain the unity of the kingdom.

The queen regent proved to be a strong force, too, in preserving the unity of the Hawaiian kingdom, but at the same time she embarked upon the most extraordinarily risky political action which led to a brief civil war. Within a year of Kamehameha I's death, she had instigated the official destruction of the traditional culture and religion of Hawaii and abolished virtually all the taboos which gave religious sanction to social custom. The queen regent strengthened the new king's will and, within months of his ascending the throne persuaded him to break one of the most fundamental taboos – he ate with the women. The courage to implement the policy had been strengthened once it became known that the King of Tahiti had recently broken food taboos and remained unharmed. This flagrant breach of custom not only undermined the power of the priests over the people, it also broke the power of the priests over the royal family itself, leaving them as the supreme traditional authority. For by being the medium through which gods spoke to man, and man appealed to the gods, the Hawaiian priesthood had hitherto exercised immense power over chiefs and royalty. The king, incited by the queen regent, followed up this defiance by ordering the destruction of the old gods and their places of worship. As in Tahiti, this provoked an armed rebellion fomented by the priests, chiefs and people who were loyal to the old religion and culture. The stand they made against the westernisation of their society was understandable, but as the royal family had the backing of all the American traders, who supplied its armoury, it was a forlorn and hopeless revolt. The royals emerged from the civil war stronger for having destroyed the power of the priests, but they were not to enjoy their new-found independence from religion for long.

The Americans lagged somewhat behind the British in sending missionaries into the Pacific. But early in the nineteenth century an interdenominational, though mainly Congregational, group set up a Board of Commissioners for Foreign Missions and resolved to establish missions in Hawaii as the British had done at Tahiti. Accordingly, on 19 October 1819, the *Thaddeus* sailed from Boston, Massachusetts, with a party of missionaries bound for Hawaii. Hiram Bingham and Asa Thurston were in charge and had five assistants – two teachers, plus a medical doctor, a printer and a mechanic – all trained to teach the gospel. All were married (a condition of employment) and the wives were to work alongside the men. Most were newly wed, although one couple had five children. With them were three Hawaiians who were also trained as missionaries. The American missionaries were more fortunate than their earlier British counterparts and enjoyed a tranquil and routine voyage via Cape Horn without any particular intervention from God, arriving at Hawaii after an average passage of five and a half months. Once ashore and having presented gifts to the king, they requested permission to teach Christianity. The king was reluctant and many of his advisors were apprehensive: they were worried that in accepting the Americans they might offend the British or French. Eventually, they granted permission for missions near Honolulu and at Kilua, where the king resided and who requested that the medical doctor be left at that station.

The missionaries could not have chosen a more auspicious time, arriving as they did just after the king had abolished the taboo system. Doubtless, the vast bulk of the population carried on living their lives as they had always done. But one suspects that the destruction of the old religion, which had been so omnipresent in all aspects, must have left a hunger for something to replace it. The missionaries certainly had a potentially rewarding field for their endeavours, but the Christianity of New England was a sober creed which offered few excitements in this world, especially to the pleasure-loving Hawaiians. The missionaries were nothing if not unbending, and they did not take the easy path to winning adherents. The king refused to convert as he was partial to rum and had five wives. To submit to the missionaries would entail having no drink and only one wife. Had the missionaries been willing to accept him as a nominal Christian, hundreds of his subjects might have chosen to follow his example. In the event, they laboured year after year to gain no more than a few dozen converts. But they insisted that conversion had to be visible in daily behaviour, not simply in a willingness to attend a service on Sunday.

When Kamehameha II died in London in 1824, he was succeeded by his younger brother who ruled as Kamehameha III. He was only eleven years old and the power to govern remained even more firmly in the hands of the queen regent, Kaahumanu. The queen regent had long been a westerniser, but the American Mission's breakthrough came only when she fell ill in April 1824 and was cured by Doctor Holman. She chose this as the occasion, some four years after the missionaries had landed, to publicly announce her adherence to Christianity. Prominent chiefs followed her example in order to curry favour with her, and their subordinates followed their lead. She also ordered commoners to attend church, and by the 1830s had promulgated laws against drunkenness, prostitution and lewdness, all of which reinforced the missionaries' message. While the Europeans stood apart from Hawaii by mutual agreement, 'Missionaries poured in from the United States, 100 women and 84 men in all, in twelve descents between 1820 and 1848 . . . [in 1820] . . . John C. Jones was officially appointed as United States Agent for Commerce and Seamen to represent American interests in the kingdom.'[2] Thus the missionaries were coming to represent commercial and political influence.

Unlike the British at Tahiti the Americans sent scores of female missionaries, and Hawaiian women became the focus of their efforts. They viewed the wife and mother as the 'angel in the home' and knew that if they could reform the morals and customs of the women they would change society; it was, after all, an American who said that 'the hand that rocks the cradle rules the world'. To leave the shores of New England to live among the Hawaiians was to be presented with an approach to life and leisure different enough to confuse the senses of these well-intentioned women. There was a strong thread of belief running through Christianity, and particularly among Protestants, that abstinence from pleasure is the path to righteousness which, although it is rarely expressed in a personal rejection of worldly goods, was obsessively imposed on sensual delights and particularly on sexual ones. Sex, even within marriage, was supposed to be limited only to procreation. The Hawaiians, on the other hand, were fairly indifferent to the acquisition of material wealth, but believed in packing into their lives as much sensual and sexual pleasure as they could. These New England women were horrified at the freedom and licentiousness of Hawaiian life: they could not believe their eyes. Hawaiian society was hedonistic to the core and women were free to indulge their appetites as freely as men, as were the children. 'What a place for American missionaries! One of them complained that Hawaiians had about twenty forms of what he considered illicit intercourse, with as many different names in the language; so that if any one term were selected to translate the Seventh Commandment, it was bound to leave the impression that the other nineteen activities were still permitted.'[3] The two cultures interacted like oil and water.

Missionary wives believed that God had created man and then woman as his helpmate. The only sexual activity they could sanction was procreative sex within a monogamous marriage: the only satisfactory family they could envisage was one where the man was head of the house, the breadwinner who left the home all day to go about the business of earning a living. They believed that the woman should stay at home and cook, clean and care for him and her children, the ideal of American family life based upon the nuclear family and the Bible. But Hawaiian women were much freer than their western counterparts and not subjected to much labour. In Britain, for example, many women had to toil in mill or mine, factory and field, as well as provide the greater part of domestic labour and, from lack of choice, give birth to large families. By contrast, Hawaiian women controlled family size and engaged in little productive or domestic labour. Men did most of what little heavy work there was to be done in the fields and also a share of cooking. Although the fear of divine retribution from the old gods had declined, the ordinary people still lived in the traditional way. That is to say that men and women still ate separately because these were habits of social life. The missionaries from New England actively campaigned to end these customs and to replace them with family life as they preferred it. They were always encouraging the women to perform more domestic duties, which, as children were looked after on a rather free basis from a very early age, and homes were simple, small, largely unfurnished thatched-roof structures, was not easy.

Turning the women into ideal Christian mothers was an area which the missionaries found particularly frustrating, because a child was not regarded as the possession of one woman: 'Sarah Lyman expressed the usual exasperation at this practise when, at a Maternal Association meeting at Hilo, she failed dismally to compile a neat list of mothers and children. Thirty women attended, but it proved impossible to discover exactly how many children they had as "their *real* mother, grandmother, aunt, nurse, and perhaps someone else would all claim the one child".'[4] This frustration, expressed in January 1837, was the result of the communal care for children and the great independence of Hawaiian children. They spent their time at play and would be fed and sheltered by virtually anyone: 'As one Hawaiian mother after another explained, if they were nasty to their children, the children simply rolled up their mats under their arms and moved to be welcomed by a related household.'[5] For adult Hawaiians the family of origin remained more important than the family of marriage, consequently women would often leave their husbands and children to return to care for one of their family members when need arose. The missionaries tried to instil into the women that it was wrong, indeed sinful, for them to leave their husband to go back to care for distant relatives, that they should put the domestic home before everything and be obedient to their husbands and always be available for their children. The missionaries were also constantly concerned with the failure of the natives to save and be provident; they could not see beyond their own society with its emphasis on material success and capital accumulation. In a letter dated 11 March 1830, one wrote, 'If we should give the natives in our family a whole hog or goat they would boil it up and share it with their friends and then perhaps go without any meat for 2 or 3 days.'[6] Such communal values were beyond the comprehension of individualistic westerners, and they seldom seemed inclined to reflect on the function or merit of such customs. They were convinced that the Hawaiians had everything to learn from them, and nothing to teach in return. But to have become practising Christians would have added to the subjection of Hawaiian women.

The American missionary effort was, however, about to be challenged by French-backed Catholicism. In 1827, the Congregation of the Sacred Hearts of Jesus and Mary landed a party of missionaries on Hawaii from two French ships. Queen Kaahumanu ordered them off the island, but the ships sailed before the missionaries could be re-embarked. The Catholics remained quietly enclosed for some months, sensibly learning the language. The queen saw in the Catholic ritual something of the rituals of the old pagan priesthood; she also feared that the two opposing Christian sects could become a rallying point for political dissent and renewed civil war. She had good reason to be wary. Those of her people who still supported the old ways, and the sailors and traders who liked the easy morals of the islanders, disliked the Protestant missionaries. Eventually Chief Boki, who had been Kamehamha II's chief advisor and who had travelled to London with him, had fallen out with the queen and her policies, saw the Catholics as possible allies against the Protestants and gave them a piece of land on which to build a church. The queen responded by first ordering Hawaiians not to attend Catholic service, and then by ordering the priests to stop preaching; they refused to obey. The queen then expelled them from the kingdom by transporting them to California. Over the next decade Catholic priests returned and made various attempts to re-establish their mission, and under the threat of punitive French action the Hawaiians were obliged to allow them to stay on the island, although they were accorded none of the privileges given to the American missionaries.

The presence of a mission invariably gave its country of origin an excuse to intervene in the country concerned: in this case the French claimed, quite correctly, that their citizens were treated less favourably than those from other countries. Finally the French government felt strong enough to take positive action and in July 1839 a frigate, L'Artémise, under the command of Captain Laplace arrived at the island. Captain Laplace had a list of demands: that Catholics were to enjoy equal rights with Protestants; that French citizens were to have equal rights with other foreign nationals; and that French commerce was to have equal access to Hawaiian markets. He anchored his ship off Honolulu and threatened to start hostilities – to bombard the town – unless the agreement was signed immediately. The Hawaiians had no choice but to concede.

This triggered a jockeying for power; although the British were not interested in acquiring another colony, they were not in favour of Hawaii becoming a French one. Lord George Paulet on HMS Carysfort was sent to investigate claims that it was British citizens who were now less favoured than the French. Paulet was not a good choice, being far too headstrong, and in February 1843, threatening armed force, he took the extreme action of coercing Kamehameha III to cede his country to Great Britain and take an oath of allegiance to its queen. Five months later the United States frigate *Constellation* under Commodore Kearny arrived to protest against the king's deed of concession and to assert the rights of American citizens. Hard on her heels arrived HMS *Dublin* under Rear-Admiral Thomas who had been sent urgently from Valparaiso with instructions from Lord Aberdeen, the British Foreign Secretary, to repudiate Lord George Paulet's action; although he refused to pay any compensation for Paulet's acts. The final outcome of these diplomatic exchanges and gunboat politics was a treaty which gave French and British citizens and commerce specific equal rights in Hawaii, and it might be thought that these rights needed to be specified. Under the old Hawaiian system chiefs and priests had enforced the taboos which maintained law and order. Clearly, many of these had never applied to Europeans, but now it was unclear who had the right to catch and punish criminals among this growing expatriate population or even what behaviour was considered criminal. The French and British wanted specified punishments and the right to trial by jury, rather than the arbitrary justice of a chief. They also insisted on specifying how a jury would be chosen to ensure that it included fellow expatriates whenever a French or British citizen stood trial. The Americans then claimed, with reason, that these privileges left their citizens less favoured than the Europeans, although they refused to join in signing the treaty.

The international western presence on the Hawaiian Islands was now so strong as to need a similarly constituted form of government. Internal reforms became part of a drive to be recognised as a 'state' and, therefore, rightfully independent as were all other states; and not merely treated as a group of 'unclaimed islands' whose indigenous peoples could be colonised by others. During the 1840s the Hawaiians sent a number of envoys around the world and signed treaties with most European countries as well as with Japan and Russia in an attempt to establish themselves as a nation state. This diplomatic activity did not, however, go unchallenged. The French were still ambitious to bring Hawaii within their sphere of influence, and sent a naval force under Admiral de Tromelin to coerce the Hawaiians, now claiming that the earlier treaty agreements favourable to France had not been fulfilled. This time military action took place, and on 25 August 1849 the French occupied government forts, offices, customs buildings and the king's yacht. The

Hawaiian king appointed Mr Judd to travel to the United States, London and Paris to resolve the matter. He had wide powers and, it was said, the right to cede Hawaii to either the British or the Americans if that proved the only way to dislodge the French. The visit to Europe resolved nothing: although Admiral de Tromelin had withdrawn his forces, the French still claimed the earlier rights. The Hawaiians then placed in the hands of the American government a deed of cession: America refused to act upon it, but as a result, on 14 July 1851, they instructed the American Navy to guarantee the independence of the Hawaiian Islands. Faced with the American naval shield, any French hopes of becoming the colonising power were ended.

Hawaii was now effectively recognised and protected as an independent State, but during these years of diplomatic activity life continued to change, not to say deteriorate, for her people. Here as elsewhere the missionaries blamed infanticide for the steep decline in population. But again this was clearly a total misunderstanding – even after the arrival of the missionaries and a decline in infanticide the population continued to fall. Here, too, this was often ascribed to the effect of venereal disease on the fertility of women and to imported European diseases. While these were undoubtedly important factors, the loss of their own culture and the discrediting of their traditional religion and way of life had a demoralising effect. In Hawaii the activities of the missionaries, important as they were, were less crucial to change than were their activities at Tahiti. In Hawaii, commerce grew much more rapidly; initially the export of sandalwood and provisioning of whaling ships increased the labour extracted from the Hawaiian people, which was then intensified with the growth of plantation agriculture stimulating an ever increasing demand for workers. The Hawaiians' reluctance to work simply to create capital was to lead, in the long run, to them becoming a minority in their own country, as indentured labour from overseas was imported to work in the commercial plantations. By 1900 the number of indigenous Polynesians had fallen to about forty thousand, little more than a quarter of the total population of the Hawaiian Islands. A people had been all but obliterated.

Not only had they become a minority in their own land, but they had lost title to the land itself. Traditionally land had been held through the authority of the paramount chiefs and kings and rights to it lasted only a lifetime: land was an inalienable sacred source to be preserved for the sustenance of the people. But by the 1840s, between 300 and 400 whaling ships a year were calling for fuel, water and provisions; by the 1850s, at the peak of the trade, their numbers had swelled to 500 annually. The leisurely life of the Hawaiians was increasingly being dislocated in support of the international whale oil industry. Other developments led to the establishment of coffee, banana and taro plantations. People were ordered to work under the old system of obligation to communal labour by their chiefs, who sometimes also drew their pay. Even so, the Hawaiians often failed to arrive and were loath to work if they did. This deformation of the traditional system of collective work for communal benefits was to further undermine Hawaiian social cohesion. Their situation was to worsen as land was cleared and appropriated to produce commodities for the (mainly) American market. Under Hawaiian law it had been illegal for foreigners to own land, but to obtain money chiefs and kings resorted to granting it away on long leases. Commerce was attractive to the missionaries because it provided those opportunities to labour which was so dear to their concept of a Christian life. The missionaries had an influential voice in who received these land grants and they, too, began to plant and work their own plantations. These forms of leasehold grants were replaced after 1844 with the start of massive legal reform whereby land passed into private ownership. As might have been predicted, most of the land ended up under the ownership of the foreign commercial interests and the combined land under native Hawaiian ownership was eventually reduced to about 1 per cent of the total acreage. Again the missionaries were very active in acquiring land – it has been said that the Hawaiians were taught to close their eyes in prayer, and when they opened them the land was gone. They had not only been dispossessed, their culture had been destroyed.

By the time Captain Henry B. Martin of the Royal Navy had his first view of Hawaii on 13 August 1849, the one-time sailors' paradise had been submerged beneath a blanket of narrow Christianity. Although the missionaries had not been personally responsible for the destruction of the old taboos, they had maintained a slow, sure and unremitting pressure on the leisure and hedonism of the Hawaiians. From the moment he landed, Captain Martin did not like much of what he saw; 16 August was a Sunday and all the grog shops were closed, no sailors were allowed ashore and no one was allowed out to the ships – 'Sunday is kept strictly here as in Glasgow',[7] was his disillusioned observation. He was one of the very few visitors who found the native-born Hawaiians ugly. In fact, he had an observant if rather jaundiced eye. He noticed that King Kamehameha III used a Bible inscribed to him by Elizabeth Fry, the English Quaker noted for her Evangelism and work for prison reform. He also met the king's ministers: Dr Judd (finance and prime minister) a surgeon, 'a sharp shrewd fellow'; Mr Wyllie (minister for foreign affairs), 'a clever, impudent Scotch attorney'; Mr Richards (minister for public instruction), a gentlemanly American missionary; and Mr Ricord, who 'is generally supposed to be a Canadian convict'[8] and not, one notes, a single Hawaiian among them. Herman Melville also met the king's ministers at this time and described Dr Judd rather more pointedly, as a sanctimonious apothecary-adventurer and the missionaries as a junta of ignorant and designing Methodist elders. Captain Martin complained that the place was overrun with Americans, and drew the conclusion that if the Americans continued to hold California they must gain Hawaii. Captain Martin's assessment was correct, although the process took rather longer than he may have suspected; nevertheless, by the mid-nineteenth century it was obvious that Hawaii's future lay in only one direction.

After a brief stay Captain Martin sailed for Tahiti on 29 August 1849 with, it would seem, few regrets.

In fact, the Hawaiian royal family remained on the throne of a nominally independent nation until it was deposed and a republic proclaimed in 1894. Becoming a republic was a preliminary to absorption by a larger one. On 12 August 1898 the islands were formally annexed by the United States of America, a step that had been demanded and forced by American commercial interests. Foreign sugar was about to be effectively excluded from the American market by an import tax. To protect their capital investment in Hawaii, the merchants and traders needed tax-free access to the American market, and the only way to achieve this was for Hawaii to become American. The nation's royal family and independence were sacrificed to profit.

Chapter 19

TAHITIANS DEFEATED

I suppose the missionaries have a certain influence over the people, and might be made useful; but like all churchmen of all nations and all ages, they aim at power and cannot be prevailed upon to play 2nd fiddle.

Captain H.B. Martin, The Polynesian Journal of Captain Henry Byam Martin RN[1]

Tahiti had become nominally Christian under Pomare II, who handed the education of his son and heir over to the missionaries. But the missionaries' ability to be the effective rulers of Tahiti through control of a child and his education was shattered when Pomare III died in 1817 aged only seven. According to the rules of succession, the heir was the daughter of Queen Teriitaria's younger sister. Aimata, the heir apparent, was young, pretty and, in the eyes of the missionaries, already depraved and dissolute. She had enjoyed a traditional Tahitian upbringing and the missionaries did not want a half-grown pagan as ruler. They tried to persuade Tati, a paramount chief of Tahiti, to take the throne, but he refused as did all the other chiefs. Influential as the missionaries were they could not persuade even the most ambitious chiefs to overturn traditional lines of inheritance: whatever religion they accepted on the surface they were still wedded to their own culture.

Aimata took the throne as Queen Pomare Vahine IV. Young and wilful, no longer a virgin and pagan she may have been, but as she was only fourteen years old when she inherited the throne she was unable to resist the influence of the missionaries. George Pritchard took control of her and, outwardly at least, she became a Christian. But her Christianity was forced upon her and at the age of twenty-eight she sided with those chiefs who rebelled in 1831, because they wanted to preserve many of the old customs which the missionaries were suppressing. Her defeat appears to have left her totally crushed. When HMS *Beagle*, commanded by Captain Fitzroy and carrying Charles Darwin on his trip around the world, arrived at Tahiti in October

1835 the queen was found living in a small dwelling with only a few female attendants. Captain Fitzroy invited her aboard with the pomp and ceremony due to a reigning monarch, but she remained withdrawn and depressed. Pritchard was by this time virtually prime minister and was advising her on all her dealings with foreigners, and reading and answering all her correspondence. The power and success of the London Missionary Society now appeared unchallenged. They had taken control of the rulers of the nation, and while it would take time for the bulk of the population to adapt their culture, the fact that they would change in the desired direction was not in question. The missionaries had given the Tahitians a written language and as they were the only printers, they controlled education; time would bring the younger generation to follow their ways.

To the credit of Pritchard's fellow Nonconformists, they disapproved of the Mission's becoming so directly involved in the business of the State: it was against their principles to have an Established Church in England and yet Pritchard was effectively turning them into the State Church in Tahiti. Some of their number felt that they should not allow themselves to play such an influential role in Tahitian political affairs. The last straw came in 1836 when Pritchard persuaded Lord Aberdeen, the British Foreign Secretary, to make him British Consul for Tahiti and the islands. He was forced to resign his position at the mission. Nevertheless, he continued at the queen's side as her chief advisor and his own Christian principles ensured that instilling Protestantism into the people remained the policy of the Court. At all events, the future appeared to be theirs; unfortunately for them, however, the British were not the only colonial power.

After the Napoleonic Wars the French set their hearts on re-establishing their position as a major power. To this end, in 1830, they invaded North Africa and began what would become a chain of conquests on that continent. They also maintained their ambitions in the south Pacific, despatching Captain Lavaud of the *Aube* to New Zealand in 1840 in order to claim it for France. They were too late – the British had signed a treaty with the Maoris a few months earlier. (Given that there was a large English presence in New Zealand and no French, their hopes of enforcing a claim were anyway pretty remote.) They were determined, however, to gain colonies and claimed the Marquesas Islands, New Caledonia and certain other minor islands, although these were by no means such attractive propositions as Tahiti or Hawaii.

International politics were to prove the undoing of the London Missionary Society's achievements in Tahiti as French opinion gradually determined on establishing a major colony in the Pacific. The British Protestant missionaries would have been hard put to decide which religion they hated and feared the most – paganism or Roman Catholicism. And if, from a common foundation in Christianity, they may by a small margin have hated paganism more, their fear of Roman Catholicism was in proportion to its greater power.

The French and Catholic interests at Tahiti were already present in the person of an influential and wealthy resident, Jacques Antoine Moerenhout, a Belgian by birth, who was a trader in pearls and nacre as well as a merchant supplying shipping with various necessities. He loathed the Protestant missionaries and their influence on the island and was very keen to promote and represent French interests. In 1836 two Roman Catholic missionaries of the Sacred Heart – Caret and Laval – had themselves secretly put ashore on Tahiti from a schooner which was *en route* to Valparaiso. Once on land they went to Papeete, the major commercial port of the island, and placed themselves under the protection of Moerenhout who was an accomplice in this plan to challenge the British Protestant monopoly. The intended *fait accompli* (there being no ship on which they could leave) was undone when the schooner, having sustained storm damage, was forced to return for repairs. When she left, Protestant influence had these Catholic priests forcibly put aboard and expelled from the island. George Pritchard would undoubtedly have persuaded the queen to exclude Moerenhout from the island had he been merely a foreign trader. But Moerenhout had extensive commercial dealings with American whaling ships and because he took good care of their crews, he had been appointed American Consul. His diplomatic status thus protected him from being expelled without a very grave cause.

The British had favoured Matavai Bay as their port of call; the French now favoured Papeete. Papeete proved to be much the better harbour and it developed as the main port of call for the ever increasing numbers of whalers and traders. Their business supported higher numbers of merchants ashore and Papeete was fast becoming the commercial centre of Tahiti; as home to a growing number of beachcombers and disorderly sailors, it was also gaining a well-merited reputation as a centre of vice and drunkenness. The old taboos which had served to maintain traditional law and order were weakening in a growing urban and cosmopolitan squalor and nothing had taken their place. Penniless white men were marrying native women and living on the work and charity of their family networks. The better-off traders and merchants were marrying higher up the social scale and were gaining control of land and political power through the loyalty still shown to chiefly clans. In an attempt to keep some economic and social power in Tahitian hands marriage between Tahitians and Europeans was made illegal in 1837, a policy rapidly brought into disrepute when one of the queen's favourites – Huruaata, a high-born princess – fell in love with and determined to marry a foreigner recently arrived at the island from California. He was Alexander Salmon, a member of a family of Jewish bankers who had fled to England during the French Revolution. Huruaata became pregnant by him and the queen suspended the marriage laws to enable them to marry. The influence of westerners continued to grow.

Papeete's reputation as the most sinful city in the Pacific was not helped when the French frigate *L'Artémise* was damaged and had to be beached and repaired. For six weeks nearly five hundred French sailors lived and rampaged ashore amid dissolute scenes which outdid all the lawlessness Papeete had previously known. The French had arrived in order to force the queen to give Roman Catholic priests and worshippers complete freedom of practice. The queen fled to Raiatea and George Pritchard returned to London to plead with his government to take over the island, a request promptly refused by the Foreign Office which had no desire to incur the additional costs of policing and protecting the islands. Since it took nearly a year for a message to be sent to Europe and a reply received, a country's *de facto* representative had to respond to unforeseen events largely on his own initiative and so create his government's foreign policy on the spot. In this instance, the senior French naval officer on the spot was Admiral Abel du Petit-Thouars, who firmly believed that his government was not following a sufficiently vigorous colonial policy. He was ambitious to make his name and while active in the Pacific exercised his powers and responsibility to the hilt.

French men-of-war increased the frequency of their visits to Tahiti to ensure that her citizens there and the Catholic religion were being accorded equal treatment. Moreover, the French were able to exploit traditional enmities between the chiefs and clans of Tahiti. The Pomares had always had their internal enemies and rebellion after rebellion had testified to the permanent existence of one disaffected faction or another on the island. Some of the disaffected were not averse to French control if it would rid them of the Protestant missionaries and would rule with a lighter hand. Whether this opposition could have been slowly nurtured to a majority by the French was never put to the test. Admiral du Petit-Thouars decided to take independent action and, anchoring his man-of-war in the harbour in September 1842, he sent the queen a letter demanding that French citizens – and missionaries –

should have equal rights with other nationals, and that she should pay compensation of $10,000 for the insult France had suffered through the ill-treatment of her citizens. He gave the queen until ten o'clock the next morning to concede to his demands, failing which he would bombard the town. This was to be followed by a declaration of war if she continued to refuse. (He offered all the resident Europeans refuge on his ship so they would not be injured by his punitive action.) The queen asked for time to consult her chiefs but was refused. Those chiefs who still opposed the Pomares invited the French to take Tahiti under their protection. Given a divided nation, the queen was obliged to concede all demands, to send a letter of apology, pay the indemnity, and allow the French to fly their flag in the harbour of Papeete which the Tahitian government was to salute. It was a serious coercion of a small island by a great power effected by the commander on the spot. The treaty also obliged the queen to accept Moerenhout as French Consul – thus giving the French the right to intervene on his behalf.

All this came at a bad moment for the queen, as after three earlier miscarriages she had just given birth to her first child, a boy Ariiave, vital for the succession. Admiral du Petit-Thouars tried to conciliate the queen but she steadfastly continued to show her disapproval by refusing to dine on the ship or to have anything other than enforced contact. When the French sailed away the queen ignored their officials and advisors who had been left behind as part of the 'protectorate' because the treaty had been signed under duress. Also left behind was Herman Melville, author of *Moby Dick*, who had been imprisoned for a while on the French ship, because he and fifteen of his shipmates had refused to continue to sail on an Australian whaling ship. Following that, and a few easy days in the so-called 'British Prison', he signed aboard an American whaler. He also happened to be in Hawaii in July 1843 when Rear Admiral Richard Thomas arrived with orders to haul down the British flag and restore Hawaiian independence.[2]

Missionary Pritchard had received no encouragement from the British Foreign Office, but when he returned to Tahiti on HMS *Vindictive* he urged the natives to resist the French, although when the *Vindictive* and another man-of-war promptly sailed away it was obvious that the British were not going to lend the Tahitians any material support. The British government's only action was to leave a tiny 100-ton ketch, the *Basilisk*, in harbour to provide a place of refuge for any British nationals who might need one. Eventually, rather than live in a French controlled town, the queen took refuge aboard the *Basilisk* for some months in Papeeete harbour before fleeing to the Pomare family's stronghold of Raiatea in 1844. The London missionaries were furious; they could see all the benefits of their efforts to plant Christianity being reaped by the Roman Catholics. Mr Pritchard's trip to London and his return as British Consul had split the Tahitian missionaries, as they felt he was sacrificing their principles to his personal political ambitions. In the face of the French there was no unity among the Tahitians or the missionaries: both were weakened by the indifference of the British government. Mr Pritchard, for all his dignity as British Consul, was arrested by the French and expelled from the island. As Britain took no action over that insult to her power, it was clear that as far as Britain was concerned the French had a clear path to occupation.

It was not unreasonable for the queen to ignore the officials Admiral du Petit-Thouars had left behind, as home governments did not always ratify what their headstrong commanders in the field had done or promised. Although the French government was anxious not to find itself in conflict with London over Tahiti, du Petit-Thouars's aggressive actions had proved so popular with the French public that it dared not repudiate him. The government in Paris confirmed the protectorate. Once his actions had been approved, Admiral du Petit-Thouars was not the man to permit his officials to be ignored, and a year later he returned with the clear intention of fomenting another incident. He claimed that the French flag flying at Papeete was an insult as it had been changed from the one flown at his orders (a crown of coconut fronds had been added). He threatened to depose the queen and take full possession of the island for France – he landed his troops, tore down her flag and raised the tricolour. The reaction of the Tahitians was mixed, but the vast majority supported the queen who continued to refuse to submit to his demands. Admiral du Petit-Thouars crystallised the issue by deposing Queen Pomare, confiscating all her property and claiming Tahiti as a colony of France. While this declaration of sovereignty was disavowed by the French government when news of his action eventually reached them, the legal and political distinction between being a protectorate or a colony made little or no difference to events on the ground. Du Petit-Thouars's actions started a war which was to end only when Tahiti became a French colony in all but name.

The French had gained some support through the vigorous policies of M. Bruat, formerly governor of the Marquesas, who had been sent to Tahiti to supervise its subjugation. He ordered all the chiefs to come to him and submit to French authority: those who refused either to submit or attend were outlawed and their property confiscated. A minority of chiefs submitted because they feared losing their positions, others because of their dislike of the Pomare dynasty and the British missionaries, or because they foresaw ultimate French victory. The majority, however, withdrew further from the French enclave around Papeete up into the wild interior. This led to a three-year war: a complicated war with the queen's army of 9,000 warriors fighting the French who were supported by 2,000 Tahitian warriors from the client chiefs. At first, each side simply withdrew, producing a stalemate during which provisions become very short for the French garrison. Inevitably there was an armed clash, and on 20 February 1844 some French sailors were wounded. The following month French soldiers were killed and the fighting intensified. Having received reinforcements from the Marquesas, Bruat sent his ships to force the other Society Islands of Raiatea and Bora Bora to submit to him, since they were part of the kingdom ruled from Tahiti. However, these islanders claimed to be independent and not bound by any agreement made between the French and any Tahitian authority, and put up a stiff resistance.

The scale of the Tahitian resistance and the destructiveness of the French occupation moved opinion in Britain and with it her government. With the prior knowledge and agreement of the French government, Sir George Seymour was sent to negotiate with Governor Bruat for a withdrawal from these smaller islands until it was established whether they were in fact part of Pomare's dominions. But Bruat was determined to push ahead with his conquest, and given the distance from Paris and the support of his commander-in-chief Admiral du Petit-Thouars, in the short term there was little the French government could do to rein him in. Bruat and Seymour could not agree a joint policy, and Sir George left Papeete on his own to inform those islands that in his view they were independent until such time as the British government decided otherwise. This move served to encourage the resistance to the French, although Sir George Seymour left without giving or promising the Tahitians any practical aid. The men of Bora Bora lived up to their reputation as fearsome warriors by inflicting several hundred casualties on the French troops, forcing them to abandon the island. The French withdrew only after burning villages, destroying the breadfruit trees and causing as much material damage as they could in retaliation. By April 1846, Governor Bruat was forced to acknowledge defeat and withdraw from all these outer islands to Tahiti where the queen's forces also appeared to be gaining the upper hand. The French held the town of

Papeete but little else, and with their supplies cut off their situation was becoming untenable.

Captain Henry Byam Martin left Hawaii without regret and shaped course for Tahiti, sailing into Papeete Harbour on 28 September 1846. HMS *Grampus* could not have been much of a counterweight to the influence of the French flotilla of seven ships lying in the harbour. The *Grampus* was more dangerous to those who sailed in her than to a potential enemy. She was sixty-five years old and had started life as a 74-gun ship of the line; due to be scrapped, she had instead been cut down to a 50-gun frigate. Although she offered Martin his first opportunity to command, initially he refused on the grounds that she was unseaworthy; but nearly five years ashore on half pay convinced him that he had little choice but to accept. In spite of their obvious naval superiority, the French were not pleased to see the *Grampus* arrive, because they knew that the queen and her supporters would interpret her arrival as a sign of British encouragement.

It is worth noting that one of the French flotilla was a steamship; a development which was to strengthen the maritime powers' impetus for colonies, however small, scattered around the globe. Sailing ships could operate independently away from home and stay at sea for months or even years; but steamships, especially the early ones, used a great deal of water and fuel and needed secure and permanent bases where coal could be stockpiled, and where engineering facilities and repair yards could be constructed.

Unable to force the surrender of the Tahitians, Bruat was obliged to concentrate on preserving Papeete Harbour behind a chain of forts. Captain Martin observed:

On my arrival here [Papeete] I find that after a French occupation of 3 years they occupy a straggling village and the ground for ½ a mile in the rear of it; and so much of the sea board as is commanded by their blockhouses & ships. At each extremity of Papeete there is a work sufficiently strong for its purpose and another by the government house. The village is intersected by barricades of casks filled with earth – the guards many & strong & the troops in a state of constant qui vive. Thus it would seem that up to the present time the protectors have enough to do to protect themselves.[3]

The French were within a hair's-breadth of losing the war and the islands.

Captain Martin met M. Bruat and, while trying to keep out of politics, agreed to sail to Raiatea with Bruat's latest conciliatory offer to the queen: if she would return to live under the French, Bruat offered to pay her 25,000 francs a year in recompense for the harbour dues which he was taking for France. But he also insisted that if she accepted she must be seen to return in a French ship. Martin sailed to Raiatea and on 23 October wrote, 'Though there may be a certain quantity of romance in Pomare's story when told at a distance of 17000 miles; a good deal of it vanished when reality stands revealed in the form of a fat oily woman without a particle of clothing but a cotton shirt.'[4] This was neither a kind nor a gentlemanly observation, since he might have given her some credit for instantly refusing to accept a bribe, which would have left her a very wealthy woman. But Captain Martin liked neither the islanders nor the missionaries, writing with disapproval that no man, woman or child neglects the chance to get drunk, and that chastity is unknown; but also criticising the missionaries for forbidding the native women to wear flowers on Sundays while forcing them to wear approved bonnets, 'one of the most hideous of human inventions'.[5] Even he, however, acknowledged that the Tahitians were the most good-natured people on earth; a rare tribute from him. Indeed, he also doubted how committed the ordinary people were to the war they had been waging for years. He was certain, however, that in spite of their public protestations of wanting peace, the majority of islanders wanted the struggle to continue until the French were forced to leave.

The Tahitians fought well, and in spite of French superior arms and the support of the ship's cannon, French casualties were often equal to or even greater than those suffered by the Tahitians in any battle. The French would have incurred even heavier losses and had less success had the Tahitians been more ruthless. But they fought according to traditional Tahitian ideas of warfare: for example, when a French infantry patrol of a lieutenant and six men got lost in the mountains and stumbled tired and exhausted on a camp of some two to three hundred Tahitian warriors, instead of being taken prisoner or being slaughtered, they were fed, rested and sent back to the French lines, the Tahitians not deigning to take advantage of such a small and demoralised group. The war reached an impasse. The French could call on a seemingly endless supply of munitions, and with the firepower of their ships they could hold Papeete; the queen's forces could control the interior of the island but while the war dragged on the Tahitians could not return to their relaxed and carefree lifestyle.

Back in England a section of the London Missionary Society membership was furious with the government for allowing the French to occupy Tahiti and to abuse the inhabitants, but, if anything, they were even more outraged with the directors of the Missionary Society for having failed to raise an effective national protest and for having publicly expressed themselves satisfied with government policy and action.

Satisfied, indeed! Why, if on the instant of it being distinctly known that France was sending forth, 500 troops, with ordnance stores, to subdue the island, the Directors had done their duty by the question, there had been such a cry come up from our churches and the land, as might have given hope for the redemption of a doomed, and innocent, and brave, and pious people! . . . They should have secured the independence of these islands years ago, and did not – yet they are satisfied.[6]

So wrote Andrew Reed from Hackney in London on 25 January 1847. He continued: 'Tahiti – the beautiful and the free – is wasted, desolate, in bonds, and bleeding. Her homes and churches forsaken. Her men struggling as though they were Englishmen, for life and liberty against oppressors who come to them in the disguise of friends; while, by those who *should befriend* her, she is rather abandoned than succoured or assisted. Woe is the day!'[7] His attempt to stir up public opinion to aid the Tahitians came far too late.

The Tahitians held out with dogged persistence and fought with great bravery, but the end was predictable. A fortnight after Andrew Reed published his heartfelt outcry against the course of events, on 9 February 1847, Queen Pomare finally had no choice but to sign a Treaty of Protection and be returned to Papeete as a trophy aboard a French ship. The Tahitians were no longer an independent nation.

Chapter 20

REFLECTIONS

How beautiful our realm was when nothing was sold there! All the year
through the people sang . . . To sing always, always to give.
Paul Gauguin, Tahiti, 1891, relating the words of Princess Vaitua[1]

The subjection of Tahiti and Hawaii to outside political power and
commercial interests undoubtedly changed the lifestyle of the
islanders, but their romantic image continued to attract adventurers,
writers and painters throughout the nineteenth and into the twentieth
centuries – Herman Melville went to both islands on whaling ships; Robert
Louis Stevenson did the same in the 1890s by chartered yacht; Jack London
followed his voyage in 1906. The painter Paul Gauguin, who arrived in Tahiti
in 1891, has left the most memorable images of the island, and his use of
light and colour enticed Henri Matisse to visit in 1930. Much is made of the
myth of unspoiled paradises, but it is arguable that the Polynesians preserved
enough of their traditional ways to give an inner core of reality to an
increasingly tourist-based travesty of their beliefs and culture.

Paul Gauguin arrived at Tahiti just in time to witness the funeral of the
last Polynesian king, Pomare V, whom the French had forced to abdicate
eleven years earlier in 1880: but he was also in time to experience the
customs of giving and singing. Princess Vaitua, the dead king's niece, came to
visit and care for Gauguin when he was ill in bed. She was a large, wide-
shouldered woman, bare-footed, who wore a simple black dress, her only
adornment a flower in her hair. At first he found her big and ugly, but soon
began to appreciate her poise and calm and saw beauty in her dignity. Her
words quoted above express nostalgia for a past world, a sense of longing and
loss with which Gauguin imbues his images of calm, monumental Tahitian
women. He too felt a sense of loss when he first arrived, finding Papeete, the
main town, too Europeanised, full of 'colonial snobbism . . . [and the] . . .
absurdities of civilisation'.[2] Quickly he left for the countryside, where he
discovered remnants of traditional Tahitian culture. He found that he had

moved to a place with no shops from which to buy food. His nearest Tahitian neighbours, however, realising that his supplies were exhausted, invited him with traditional hospitality to their table to share their food; when he initially refused, being ashamed to accept 'charity' – his neighbours simply sent the food to him.

In the countryside Gauguin heard the traditional singing. His neighbours would gather together, then

> [a] woman begins. Her voice rises like the flight of a bird, and from the first note reaches even to the highest of the scale; then by strong modulations it lowers again and remounts and finally soars, the while the voices of the other women about her, so to speak, take flight in their turn, and faithfully follow and accompany her. Finally all the men in a single guttural and barbarous cry close the song in a tonic chord.[3]

Quite clearly, at the end of the nineteenth century much of the Tahitian way of life was still intact in the country areas where commerce was not over-dominant. Indeed, Gauguin's account of his stay suggests that there was still more joy in Tahitian lives than the unsmiling figures in his pictures might imply. Native Tahitians were never submerged under mass immigration as were the Hawaiians: Europeans and other incomers remained a minority and as late as the 1988 population census native Polynesians still comprised 83 per cent of the population, Europeans were the next largest group at 11.5 per cent, the rest being of mixed race or of Asian descent. The Tahitian majority, much of which would have been little affected by Europeans who were located mainly in the few towns, had continued to live by slowly changing customary practices in common with undisturbed rural areas throughout the world.

Although apparently replaced by European religions, commerce and political control Polynesian culture proved to be very resilient; from New Zealand through the Tongan Islands and Samoa to far Hawaii the people continued to believe in the merits of their old communal ways. Robert Louis Stevenson, who was at Tahiti the year before Gauguin, had a similar experience of living in a rural area where his supplies ran out and he and his party were freely fed by the local chief and his people.

Throughout the twentieth century Hawaii and Tahiti remained the major focus of a romanticised view of the Polynesian Pacific which has been constantly celebrated in paintings, books and films: why they should have so captured the European Romantic imagination is less clear. One can point to the excellent climate, the warmth of the seas, the dramatic contours of the islands, the lack of venomous reptiles or predatory beasts and the natural bounty of the land. But other islands – such as some of the West Indies – have enjoyed similar advantages without attracting the same degree of admiration. But if the physical attributes of the Polynesian 'Paradises' cannot fully account for their place in the Romantic imagination, then one must look to the people and culture for illumination.

As a people they were immediately admired for their physical appearance and athleticism. They were never looked at with disdain as Europeans viewed Negroes and so many other dark-skinned people around the globe. In part they owed this to their late discovery, at a time when European attitudes to slavery were changing: Polynesians were not viewed as a resource to be bought or sold and used to produce wealth for their owners. This meant that their image was not shaped and coloured by centuries of slavery, a mindset which continued to affect the European view of Africans. Culturally, Tahitian and Hawaiian societies were comparatively indifferent to accumulating wealth or working more than was necessary to sustain life. This, together with the amount of time they devoted to sensual pleasures, conveyed an impression of enviable relaxation, good-humoured leisure and plenty. And given such values and lifestyle, the people have not prospered in a world dominated by market relationships and individual accumulation for the market. Their belief in communal support and respect for their natural surroundings persisted. The Tahitians and Hawaiians would rarely work simply to gain wages. In spite of the best efforts of some of their chiefs, especially in Hawaii, to use the custom of collective work for the communal good to hire them out as plantation labour, employers found them too unwilling and found it necessary to import workers from abroad. The Polynesians in Hawaii became something of a poor underprivileged minority in an American-owned plantation economy, whereas in Tahiti they remained the major ethnic group living under a fairly lax foreign administration.

Although Tahiti did become part of the modern world, when a French Protectorate, if not before, and underwent a degree of commercial development producing vanilla, cotton and copra for export, it was not geographically large enough (at less than 400 square miles), or near enough to a larger market, to become a significant economic centre. Tahiti remained something of a tropical backwater of the type described in the works of Robert Louis Stevenson and in Somerset Maugham's novel *The Moon and*

Sixpence, which he based loosely on Gauguin's life. The First World War was to provide a brief moment of excitement when on 21 September 1914 the German battle cruisers *Scharnhorst* and *Gneisenau* dropped anchor at Bora Bora before going on two days later to shell Papeete and its French fort. These ships were part of the German East Asia fleet which was attempting to inflict the maximum damage on British and French shipping and commerce while making its way back to Germany. The following month the fleet was to win a complete victory over an outdated British squadron at the Battle of Coronel, only to be annihilated some five weeks later by a more modern British fleet in the Battle of the Falklands. In fact, before the development of large-scale tourism, European and American wars and security interests accounted for most of Tahiti's involvement with the outside world.

During the Second World War American troops were stationed on Bora Bora to forestall any attempt by the Japanese to invade. During the Cold War, from 1963, the islands became the centre for testing French nuclear weapons. The group of islands which early discoverers called the Society Islands had traditionally been divided into the Windward Islands (which included Tahiti) and the Leeward Islands (five small islands which included Bora Bora). Under the French these two areas were grouped with the Tuamotu, Gambier, Austral and Marquesian archipelagos under one administration – French Polynesia. The actual test sites were two small atolls, Moruroa and Fanfataufa, in the Tuamato Islands some 600 miles to the south-east of Tahiti. Nuclear testing in the region was initially accepted by the Tahitian islanders as giving a boost to the weak local economy and testing continued for twenty years until growing international pressure and local riots in Papeete against the ever-growing nuclear contamination ended them in 1995. The campaign against nuclear testing helped to politicise the local inhabitants as they joined with and intensified a small pro-independence movement. Calls for independence from France have not, as yet, become powerful enough to threaten French sovereignty, with which many islanders seem content, but it has resulted in France giving a Territorial Assembly considerable internal political independence.

In spite of its enforced connection with Europeans for more than two hundred years, Tahiti undoubtedly remains a Polynesian island in reality as well as in myth: given that Tahiti's population was under 140,000 at the end of the twentieth century and the islands are only lightly populated, much must have remained unspoiled. Undoubtedly much of what is presented to tourists is a commercialised, stage version of the ancient culture.

But reflecting on the history of that culture might lead one to the conclusion that instead of considering the degree to which Polynesians have become westernised, it might be salutary to consider how far westeners have adopted many aspects of Polynesian culture.

The experience of the Tahitians and Hawaiians in the centuries before they were chanced upon by British ships in the late eighteenth century had been one of successful self-sufficiency. At a time when Polynesians were well-fed and no one was left without food or clothing, the vast mass of Europe's population, whether living in the temperate food-producing areas of the north or in the Mediterranean south, lived squalid lives overburdened by work and with scarcely enough food to suppress hunger. From Ireland in the west to Russia in the east famine was an all too common experience. Such deprivations were to fuel the French Revolution only decades after Tahiti had been discovered. Polynesians' bountiful lives were ascribed – superficially – to the natural advantages they enjoyed through climate, fertility of the terrain and to the abundance of nature. There is no doubt that while these were agreeable advantages, human activities can degrade any environment. The Native American Indians of Canada and America, for example, also lived a life of self-sufficiency in a far more hostile climate.

Social organisation, cultural and political forms all bear on how a society treats the environment. In Polynesian society taboos were applied to prevent the over-exploitation of a particular area or resource. Self-imposed limits were placed on the degree to which the natural world could be exploited. It is self-evident that the world, or any one part of it, can support only a given number of people, and many so-called primitive peoples evolved cultural as well as physical means of controlling population. The Polynesians practised abortion and infanticide, at the time excoriated by the missionaries as an abomination; at the beginning of the twenty-first century, in Britain alone legal abortion disposes of about two hundred thousand foetuses a year. In the eighteenth century Polynesians openly did what Europeans achieved by other means such as overwork, poverty, slums and overcrowding, which ensured that infant mortality took an immense toll of the new born – not that abortion and infanticide were uncommon.[4]

Whatever the variations between western countries or within them, the system of reproduction was based on the nuclear family. The ideal and moral form of sexual expression was held to be an exclusive relationship between two people, male and female, united by a religious, civil or customary

ceremony and undertaken for the reproduction of the species. It was largely
the Judeo-Christian view of how people should live and love within society.
The discovery of the wider world, which started with the sailing ship voyages
in the fifteenth century but became more frequent in the seventeenth and
eighteenth centuries, provided the sometimes outraged, but always fascinated,
voyagers with examples of how other societies regulated relationships and the
sexual activities upon which these were based. These were frequently
perceived by Europeans as degenerate and dissolute practices which should
be eradicated.

One of the most widely remarked aspects of the lives of the Tahitian and
Hawaiian islanders was the open manner in which they enjoyed a full sexual
life. This was greatly condemned at the time and for decades afterwards, and
it is only relatively recently that much of Europe has followed their example.
For example, Tahitians accepted that either partner in a marriage had the
right to end it at will, also that sexual behaviour was a matter of personal
choice: divorce and homosexuality are now accepted in most legal codes in
the west. We have now accepted much of Polynesian culture as advances in
personal choice and freedom. When the way in which Polynesians cared for
children is compared to western society it is clear which ill-treated and cruelly
exploited its children. Once again, recent legislation in England finally
outlawing physical punishment of schoolchildren means that, over two
hundred years later, we are slowly moving towards those more enlightened
practices of the Polynesians.[5]

Hawaii's fate in the modern period was very different from that of Tahiti. Its
islands are much bigger than Tahiti, having 11,000 square miles of land
surface and, with the ever-growing population and economy of California a
convenient market, the production and export of agricultural produce was an
obvious development. But by the 1870s the Hawaiian population had dropped
to about fifty thousand from the estimated two hundred thousand when first
discovered, so employers turned to importing labourers from China and
Japan. The latest census of 2000 revealed that less than 10 per cent of the
population were ethnic Hawaiians or other Polynesians; people of European
descent now make up a quarter of the population. Asians – of whom the
majority are of Japanese origin – are the largest ethnic group comprising over
40 per cent of the population: most are descendants of labourers imported to
work in plantation agriculture. The Hawaiians, as well as their culture, were
overwhelmed by incomers. Given the tiny minority of Polynesians, it is

surprising to find that traditional Hawaiian culture, or at least the tourist version of it, continues to be so vigorous, for there can be no doubt that the historical and cultural image projected by Hawaiian institutions is dominated by their Polynesian roots.

Much of this continuity can be ascribed to the Polynesian sense of loyalty to their culture and chiefs, which provided a core of resistance to the blatant grasping of economic and political power by white – mainly American – businessmen. King Kalakaua came to the throne in 1871, and although self-indulgent and grossly extravagant, he encouraged a revival of traditional Polynesian ways. However, the business community saw him as a danger to its commercial position. In 1887 armed force was used to impose a new constitution on the king which curtailed his powers and limited the vote to the wealthy, thus disenfranchising most Hawaiians and leaving political control in the hands of the white community. When the king died in 1891 he was succeeded by his sister Queen Liliuokalani. She continued her brother's championing of Hawaiian independence until she was overthrown in January 1893 by the same white faction that had opposed Kalakaua, aided by American troops from a warship. Stanford B. Dole, the son of an American missionary, became the first president of the new republic. The islands then officially became part of America as a United States Territory in 1900.

After it was absorbed into the United States the idyllic area of Honolulu and Pearl Harbor, where Isaac Davies had had his lands and where Archibald Campbell lived in 1809, developed into a major base for American naval and military power in the Pacific. The surprise Japanese attack on 7 December 1941, which brought America into the Second World War, was noted in a Congressional report as the greatest military disaster in American history: it has influenced American military thinking and strategic planning ever since. Reconstruction after the attack and further development during the Cold War has led to the military replacing agriculture as the major employer, and the military and tourism are now the mainstays of the Hawaiian economy. But whatever the political or economic events which culminated in Hawaii being granted full statehood in 1959, ethnic Hawaiians have remained a dis-advantaged minority in terms of income, health and educational achievement. Yet a bland version of their traditional song, dance and costume continued to be the public face of Hawaii and, increasingly with statehood and air travel, the image which attracted tourists. In spite of Hawaiians being outnumbered, their indigenous culture – whether as myth or history – was never supplanted by that of the more numerous incomers.

Since statehood they have used American federal legislation to provide the means with which to assert their traditional culture. Schools and universities now devote much of their resources to the study of the history and culture of the Polynesian Pacific, re-examining a story previously written only from outside. The Hawaiians had themselves designated as 'Native Americans' which enabled them to gain access to federal funds intended to improve the lot of indigenous American Indians who suffered similar disadvantages. On 23 November 1993 Bill Clinton, President of the United States, signed an 'Apology Resolution' passed by Congress which accepted that the United States was party to the illegal overthrow of the Hawaiian monarchy. It acknowledged that prior to the European incursion 'Hawaiian people lived in a highly organized, self-sufficient, subsistent, social system based on communal land tenure with a sophisticated language, culture, and religion . . . [and that] . . . the health and well-being of the Native Hawaiian people is intrinsically tied to their deep feeling and attachment to the land',[6] and stated its intention of providing foundations for reconciliation. Federal funds have since been allocated to compensate for common land lost by Hawaiians in the nineteenth century.

The population of the islands is now around 1¼ million, but as over 90 per cent of these live in urban areas, mostly in Honolulu, much of the land must be empty and unspoilt, road access to the mountainous areas being still very limited. The ethnic Polynesian population has more than doubled from its low point, and although there are still tensions between ethnic groups there is a great deal of intermarriage, which draws many of those of immigrant descent into supporting ethnic Hawaiian political power. President Clinton's Congressional apology acknowledges that 'Native Hawaiian people are determined to preserve, develop and transmit to future generations their ancestral territory, and their cultural identity in accordance with their own spiritual and traditional beliefs, customs, practices, language, and social institutions.'[7]

Many elements of the country, climate and culture of Polynesia gave rise to romanticised myths in the past and to tourist images in the present. But the Hawaiians have not forgotten that these myths are based on their historical practices. And if 'Paradises' never existed, even on agreeable Pacific islands, from the moment they landed on Tahiti, its European discoverers were convinced that these were as close to an earthly paradise as they could come.

NOTES

CHAPTER 1

1. Public Record Office (PRO) Adm 51/4539, Journal of George Robertson, Master of HMS *Dolphin*. The spelling and grammar in this and subsequent quotations have been left as in the original.
2. *Ibid.*
3. *Ibid.*
4. John Hawkesworth, *An Account of Voyages Undertaken by the Order of His Present Majesty for Making Discoveries in the Southern Hemisphere*, London, W. Strahan & T. Cadell, 1773, pp. 438–9.
5. *Ibid.*, p. 440.
6. *Ibid.*, pp. 443–4.
7. PRO Adm 51/4539, Journal of George Robertson.
8. Hawkesworth, *An Account of Voyages*, p. 450.
9. *Ibid.*, p. 455.
10. *Ibid.*, p. 457.
11. *Ibid.*, p. 458.
12. PRO Adm 51/4538, Log of Charles Clerke, Lieutenant of HMS *Dolphin*.
13. Hawkesworth, *An Account of Voyages*, pp. 458–9.
14. *Ibid.*, p. 460.
15. *Ibid.*, p. 461.
16. *Ibid.*, p. 467.
17. *Ibid.*, pp. 467–8.
18. *Ibid.*, p. 461.
19. *Ibid.*, pp. 463–4.
20. *Ibid.*, p. 469.
21. PRO Adm 51/4539, Journal of George Robertson.
22. Hawkesworth, *An Account of Voyages*, p. 479.
23. Louis-Antoine de Bougainville, *A Voyage Round the World*, tr. John Reinhold Forster, London, J. Nourse & T. Davies, 1772.
24. *Ibid.*, p. 228.

CHAPTER 2

1. Glen Barclay, *A History of the Pacific from the Stone Age to the Present Day*, London, Sidgwick & Jackson, 1978, p. 13.
2. I. Goldman, *Ancient Polynesian Society*, Chicago, University of Chicago Press, 1970, p. 202.

3. Peter Bellwood, *The Polynesians: Prehistory of an Island People*, ed. Glyn Daniel, London, Thames & Hudson, 1987, Vol. 92 in the series *Ancient Peoples and Places*, p. 44.

4. Taro, with breadfruit, was a basic part of the Tahitian and Hawaiian diet. It was valued mainly for its potato-like tubers, which were much more nutritious than potatoes. Its leaves, which could grow to a height of 6ft, were eaten as a green vegetable.

5. A.H. Carrington, 'A Note by Captain James Cook of the Tahitian Creation Myth', *Journal of the Polynesian Society*, no. 1, vol. 48 (March 1939), p. 30.

6. Bellwood, *The Polynesians*, p. 39.

7. Barclay, *A History of the Pacific*, p. 11.

8. Bellwood, *The Polynesians*, p. 14.

9. See Richard H. Grove, *Green Imperialism: Colonial Expansion, Tropical Island Edens and the Origins of Environmentalism, 1600–1860*, Cambridge, Cambridge University Press, 1997. Anyone interested in early environmental thought should read Grove's detailed study, which also highlights the role played by the naturalists who accompanied Cook's expedition and those of the French.

10. See Trevor Lummis, *Life and Death in Eden*, London, Phoenix, 2000.

CHAPTER 3

1. S. Passfield Oliver, *The Life of Philibert Commerson*, London, John Murray, 1909, pp. 124–5.

2. H. Murray (ed.), *Constable's Miscellany Vol. IV, British Seamen*, Edinburgh, Constable & Co., 1827, pp. 2–3.

3. *Ibid.*, p. 323.

4. *Ibid.*, p. 324.

CHAPTER 4

1. George Hamilton, *A Voyage Round the World in His Majesty's Frigate* Pandora . . . *1790–2*, Berwick, W. Phorson, 1793.

2. J.C. Beaglehole (ed.), *The Journals of Captain James Cook*, Hakluyt Society, Cambridge, Cambridge University Press, 1974, p. 150.

3. *Ibid.*, p. 60.

4. *Ibid.*, p. 171.

CHAPTER 5

1. Alan Moorehead, *The Fatal Impact: the Brutal and Tragic Story of How the South Pacific was 'Civilised' 1767–1840*, Harmondsworth, Penguin, 1987, pp. 19–20.

2. J.C. Beaglehole (ed.), *The Endeavour Journal of Joseph Banks 1768–1771*, Sydney, Angus & Robertson, 1962, p. 286.

3. *Ibid.*, p. 325.

4. *Ibid.*, p. 254.

5. Hawkesworth, *An Account of Voyages*, p. 489.

6. Beaglehole, *Endeavour Journal*, p. 261.

7. Just how savage were the civil and inter-island wars is difficult to assess with any confidence. Some accounts claim that in the aftermath of victory women and children were also slain; others state that battles were fierce but brief between

opposing warriors. Because of these discrepancies these events cannot be quantified with any confidence from contemporary European documents. Even in modern times events which pass into popular memory are often wildly inaccurate. For example, 15 September was chosen as 'Battle of Britain Day' because official figures arrived at by debriefing pilots after each sortie claimed 185 German aircraft had been destroyed that day: the true figure (from postwar documents) was sixty. See Richard Hough and Denis Richards, *The Battle of Britain*, London, Coronet, 1990, pp. 310–11.

8. Beaglehole, *Endeavour Journal*, p. 344.
9. *Ibid.*, p. 266.
10. Hawkesworth, *An Account of Voyages*, p. 257.
11. *Ibid.*, p. 268.

CHAPTER 6

1. Edwin N. Ferdon, *Early Tahiti, as the Explorers Saw It, 1767–1797*, Tucson, University of Arizona Press, 1981, p. 50.
2. J. Morrison, *The Journal of James Morrison*, intro. Owen Rutter, London, Golden Cockerel Press, 1935, p. 117.
3. Ferdon, *Early Tahiti*, p. 145.
4. Morrison, *Journal of James Morrison*, p. 187.
5. *Ibid.*, p. 236.
6. *Ibid.*, p. 235.
7. *Ibid.*, p. 22.
8. Goldman, *Ancient Polynesian Society*, p. 192.
9. W. Bligh, *The Log of H.M.S.* Bounty *1787–1789*, Guildford, Genesis Publications, 1975, p. 197.
10. Hamilton, *A Voyage Round the World*, pp. 36–7.
11. Ferdon, *Early Tahiti*, p. 86.
12. Morrison, *Journal of James Morrison*, p. 165

CHAPTER 7

1. Goldman, *Ancient Polynesian Society*, p. 518.
2. Gannath Obeyesekere, *The Apotheosis of Captain Cook: European Mythmaking in the Pacific*, Princeton, Princeton University Press, 1992, p. 126.
3. Marshall Sahlins, *Islands of History*, London, Tavistock Publications, 1987.
4. See Obeyesekere, *The Apotheosis of Captain Cook*, for a detailed exposition of the debate.
5. Edward Joesting, *Hawaii: An Uncommon History*, London, Robert Hale, 1974, p. 31.
6. *Ibid.*, p. 38, citing the journal of Lieutenant King of HMS *Resolution*.
7. *Ibid.*, p. 74.

CHAPTER 8

1. Barclay, *A History of the Pacific*, p. 54.
2. See Nathaniel Portlock, *A Voyage Round the World, 1785–1788*, London, John Stockdale, 1789.

3. Joesting, *Hawaii: An Uncommon History*, p. 45.

4. Polynesian names are rendered into English in many different spellings; Tamaammaah is another common form of the king's name.

5. Charles H. Barnard, *A Narrative of the Suffering and Adventures of Captain Charles H. Barnard in a Voyage Round the World during the Years 1812, 1813, 1814, 1815 & 1816*, New York, J. Lindon, 1829, p. 225.

CHAPTER 9

1. Barclay, *A History of the Pacific*, p. 68.

2. Barnard, *A Narrative*, p. 217.

CHAPTER 10

1. Barclay, *A History of the Pacific*, p. 68.

2. Barnard, *A Narrative*, p. 287.

3. Joesting, *Hawaii: An Uncommon History*, p. 64.

4. Jacques Arago, *Narrative of a Voyage Round the World in the* Uranie *and* Physicienne *Corvettes Commanded by Captain Freycinet during the years 1817, 1818, 1819, and 1820; on a scientific exploration undertaken by order of the French Government. In a series of letters to a friend*, London, Treutte and Wurtz, 1823, p. 125.

5. Camille de Roquefeuil, *A Voyage Round the World Between the Years 1816–1819 by Camille de Roquefeuil, in the ship* Bordelais, London, Sir Richard Phillips & Co., 1823, p. 43.

6. *Ibid.*, p. 53.

7. Barclay, *A History of the Pacific*, p. 79. Kaahumanu is an alternative spelling of Kamehameha.

CHAPTER 11

1. Arago, *Narrative of a Voyage Round the World*, pp. 120–1.

2. *Ibid.*, p. 138.

3. Sahlins, *Islands of History*, p. 17.

4. Archibald Campbell, *A Voyage Round the World 1806–12*, Edinburgh, Archibald Constable & Co., 1816, p. 179.

5. *Ibid.*, pp. 131–2.

6. *Ibid.*, p. 185.

7. Arago, *Narrative of a Voyage Round the World*, pp. 64–5.

8. Campbell, *A Voyage Round the World*, pp. 142–3.

9. *Ibid.*, p. 207.

10. See Caroline Ralston, 'Changes in the Lives of Ordinary Women in Early Post-Contact Hawaii', in M. Jolly and M. Macintyre (eds), *Family and Gender in the Pacific: Domestic Contradictions and the Colonial Input*, Cambridge, Cambridge University Press, 1989.

11. Campbell, *A Voyage Round the World*, pp. 187–8.

12. *Ibid.*, p. 192.

13. Arago, *Narrative of a Voyage Round the World*, pp. 75–7.

14. Marnie Bassett, *Realms and Islands: The World Voyage of Louis and Rose de Freycinet in the Corvette* Uranie, *1817–1824*, ed. John Barrow and intro. Simon Marshall, London, Oxford University Press, 1962, p. 154.
15. Arago, *Narrative of a Voyage*, p. 92.
16. *Ibid.*, pp. 60–1.
17. *Ibid.*, p. 62.
18. *Ibid.*, pp. 145–6
19. Ralston, 'Changes in the Lives of Ordinary Women', pp. 53–4.
20. Goldman, *Ancient Polynesian Society*, p. 566.
21. Arago, *Narrative of a Voyage*, p. 131.
22. Barnard, *A Narrative*, p. 238.

CHAPTER 12

1. A. Cobban, 'The Enlightenment', in J.O. Lindsay (ed.), *The New Cambridge Modern History*, Vol. VII, Cambridge, Cambridge University Press, 1963, p. 97.
2. *General Evening Post*, 19–21 July 1774.
3. *London Chronicle*, 19–21 July 1774.
4. *Ibid.*
5. Michael Alexander, *Omai 'Noble Savage'*, London, Collins & Harvill Press, 1977, p. 90.
6. Joesting, *Hawaii: An Uncommon History*, p. 28.

CHAPTER 13

1. C. Hartley Gratton, *The South-western Pacific to 1900*, Michigan, University of Michigan Press, 1963, p. 197.
2. Richard Lovett, *The History of the London Missionary Society 1795–1895*, London, Henry Froude, 1899, p. 138.
3. *Ibid.*, p. 139.
4. Bolton Glanvil Corney (tr. and intro.), *Quest and Occupation of Tahiti by Emissaries of Spain in 1772–1776*, Hakluyt Society, Series 11, Vol. 36, London, 1915, pp. 425–6.
5. *Ibid.*, p. 67.
6. Lovett, *History of the London Missionary Society*, pp. 141–2.

CHAPTER 14

1. Lovett, *History of the London Missionary Society*, p. 59.
2. *Ibid.*, p. 61.
3. *Ibid.*, p. 64.
4. *Ibid.*, p. 154.
5. *Ibid.*, p. 158.
6. *Ibid.*, p. 158.
7. *Ibid.*, p. 161.
8. *Ibid.*, p. 161.

CHAPTER 15

1. Lovett, *History of the London Missionary Society*, p. 180.
2. *Ibid.*, p. 180.
3. *Ibid.*, p. 218.
4. *Sydney Gazette*, 17 July 1819.
5. Lovett, *History of the London Missionary Society*, p. 321.

CHAPTER 16

1. James Montgomery, *Journal of Voyages and Travels by the Rev. Daniel Tyerman and George Bennet, Esq . . . between the Years 1821 and 1829*, London, Frederick Westley & A.H. Davis, 1831, pp. 71–2.
2. *Ibid.*, pp. 77–8.
3. Anthony Babington, *The Power to Silence: A History of Punishment in Britain*, London, Robert Maxwell, 1968, pp. 45–6.
4. Cited in Christopher Hibbert, *The Roots of Evil: A Social History of Crime and Punishment*, Harmondsworth, Penguin, 1966.
5. Montgomery, *Journal of Voyages*, p. 196.
6. *Ibid.*, pp. 282–4.
7. *Ibid.*, p. 332.
8. *Ibid.*, pp. 351–2.
9. *Ibid.*, p. 358.
10. *Ibid.*, p. 219.
11. *Ibid.*, pp. 178–9.
12. *Ibid.*, p. 108.
13. Cited in E. Royston Pike, *Human Documents of the Industrial Revolution in Britain*, London, George Allen & Unwin, 1966.
14. Montgomery, *Journal of Voyages*, p. 197. A bamboo of oil was a section of bamboo plugged at both ends containing between 3 and 4 quarts – a quart being 2 pints. The weight of a 'ball' is not recorded.
15. *Ibid.*, p. 89.
16. *Ibid.*, p. 177.

CHAPTER 17

1. Montgomery, *Journal of Voyages*, pp. 219–20.
2. *Ibid.*, pp. 33–4.
3. *Ibid.*, p. 94.
4. *Ibid.*, p. 328.
5. Beaglehole, *Journals of Captain James Cook*, p. 374.
6. Montgomery, *Journals of Voyages*, p. 332.
7. *Ibid.*, p. 305.
8. *United Services Journal 1832* (1), pp. 99–100.

CHAPTER 18

1. Ralston, 'Changes in the Lives of Ordinary Women', p. 60. Citing a letter from missionary L. Lyons.
2. Barclay, *A History of the Pacific*, p. 77.
3. Sahlins, *Islands of History*, p. 10.
4. Patricia Grimshaw, 'New England missionary wives, Hawaiian women and "the cult of womanhood"', in M. Jolly & M. Macintyre (eds), *Family and Gender in the Pacific: Domestic Contradictions and the Colonial Input*, Cambridge, Cambridge University Press, 1989, p. 38.
5. *Ibid.*, p. 38.
6. *Ibid.*, p. 34.
7. Captain Henry Byam Martin RN, *The Polynesian Journal of Captain Henry Byam Martin RN*, Canberra, Australian National University Press, 1981, p. 15.
8. *Ibid.*, pp. 23–4.

CHAPTER 19

1. Martin, *Polynesian Journal*, p. 33.
2. See Gay Wilson Allen, *Melville and His World*, London, Thames & Hudson, 1971, for an account of Melville in the Pacific.
3. Martin, *Polynesian Journal*, pp. 43–4.
4. *Ibid.*, p. 56.
5. *Ibid.*, p. 58.
6. Andrew Reed, *The Case of Tahiti: An Appeal to the Constituents of the London Missionary Society*, London, Ward & Co., 1847, p. 15.
7. *Ibid.*, p. 19.

CHAPTER 20

1. Paul Gauguin, *Noa Noa*, tr. O.F. Theis and intro. A. Warner, New York, Noonday Press, 1961, p. 17.
2. *Ibid.*, p. 7.
3. *Ibid.*, p. 37.
4. In England, before 1803 abortion was not illegal under common law provided the termination took place before the foetus moved. It was made a criminal offence in 1803 with severe penalties culminating in life imprisonment. Since it was legalised in 1967 some 5 million legal abortions have been carried out in England and Wales. Abortion was legalised in USA in 1973 and the number of abortions carried out there since then is estimated at 40 million.
5. The United Kingdom prohibited corporal punishment in all state schools in 1986; this legislation was widened to include English private schools in 1998. Corporal punishment is, however, still legal in all the States and Territories of the USA save in (Polynesian) American Samoa.
6. Internet. Hawaiian Independence Home Page 'Apology Resolution', p. 1.
7. *Ibid.*, p. 2.

BIBLIOGRAPHY

BOOKS AND ARTICLES

Account, *Circumnavigation of the Globe: from the voyage of Magellan to Cook*, Edinburgh, Oliver & Boyd, 1836

Alexander, Michael, *Omai 'Noble Savage'*, London, Collins & Harvill Press, 1977

Allen, Gay Wilson, *Melville and His World*, London, Thames & Hudson, 1971

Arago, Jacques, *Narrative of a Voyage Round the World in the* Uranie *and* Physicienne *Corvettes Commanded by Captain Freycinet during the Years 1817, 1818, 1819, and 1820; on a scientific exploration undertaken by order of the French Government. In a series of letters to a friend*, London, Treutte and Wurtz, 1823

Babington, Anthony, *The Power to Silence: a History of Punishment in Britain*, London, Robert Maxwell, 1968

Barclay, Glen, *A History of the Pacific from the Stone Age to the Present Day*, London, Sidgwick & Jackson, 1978

Barnard, Charles H., *A Narrative of the Suffering and Adventures of Captain Charles H. Barnard in a Voyage Round the World during the Years 1812, 1813, 1814, 1815 & 1816*, New York, J. Lindon, 1829

Barratt, Glynn, *The Russian Discovery of Hawaii*, Honolulu, Editions Ltd, 1987

Barrow, John (ed.), *The Voyages of Captain Cook*, Wordsworth Classics of World Literature, Ware, Wordsworth Editions, 1999

Bassett, Marnie, *Realms and Islands: The World Voyage of Louis and Rose de Freycinet in the Corvette* Uranie, *1817–1824*, ed. John Barrow and intro. Simon Marshall, London, Oxford University Press, 1962

Beaglehole, J.C. *The Exploration of the Pacific*, London, Adam & Charles Black, 1947

—— (ed.), *The Endeavour Journal of Joseph Banks 1768–1771*, Sydney, Angus & Robertson,1962

——, *The Journals of Captain James Cook*, Hakluyt Society, Cambridge, Cambridge University Press, 1974

Bechervaise J., *Thirty-Six Years of Seafaring Life*, London, Longman & Co., 1836

Bellwood, Peter, *The Polynesians: Prehistory of an Island People*, ed. Glyn Daniel, *Ancient Peoples and Places*, Vol. 92, London, Thames & Hudson, 1987

Bennett, Frederick, D., *Narrative of a Whaling Voyage 1833–1836*, London, Richard Bentley, 1840

Bingham, Hiram, *Residence of Twenty-one Years in the Sandwich Islands*, Hartford CT, Hezekiah Huntingdon, 1849

Bligh, W., *The Log of H.M.S.* Bounty *1787–1789*, Guildford, Genesis Publications, 1975

Bougainville, Louis-Antoine de, *A Voyage Round the World*, tr. John Reinhold Forster, London, J. Nourse & T. Davies, 1772

Campbell, Archibald, *A Voyage Round the World 1806–12*, Edinburgh, Archibald Constable & Co., 1816

Campbell, John, *Maritime Discovery and Christian Missions*, London, John Snow, 1840

Carrington, A.H., 'A Note by Captain James Cook of the Tahitian Creation Myth', *Journal of the Polynesian Society*, No. 1, Vol. 48 (March 1939), pp. 30–1

Carrington, Hugh (ed.), *The Discovery of Tahiti*, London, Hakluyt Society, 1948

Cobbe, Hugh (ed.), *Cook's Voyages and the Peoples of the Pacific*, London, British Museum Publications, 1979

Corney, Bolton Glanvil (tr. and intro.) *Quest and Occupation of Tahiti by Emissaries of Spain in 1772–1776*, Hakluyt Society, Series 11, Vol. 36, London, 1915

Cuzent, Gilbert, *Tahiti*, Rochfort, Ch. Theze, 1860

Danielsson, B.E., *Love in the South Seas*, tr. F.H. Lyon, London, George Allen & Unwin, 1956

Darwin, Charles, *The Voyage of a Naturalist Round the World in HMS* Beagle, *1832–1836*, London, George Routledge, 1905

Davies, John, *History of the Tahitian Mission*, ed. C.W. Newbury, Cambridge, Cambridge University Press, 1961

Delano, Amaso, *A Narrative of Voyages and Travels*, Boston, privately printed, 1817

Directors (The), *Narrative of the Mission at Otaheiti, and other Islands in the South Seas; Commenced by the London Missionary Society in the Year 1797; with a Map, and a Geographical Description of the Islands*, London, Williams & Co., 1818

Dodd, Edward, *The Ring of Fire: Vol. IV, The Rape of Tahiti*, New York, Dodd, New York, 1983

Dunmore, John (tr. and ed.), *Journal of Jean-Francois de Galaup de la Perouse 1785–1788*, Vol. 11, London, Hakluyt Society, 1995

Ellis, William, *A Vindication of South-sea Missions*, London, Frederick Westley and A.H. Davies, 1831

——, *The History of the London Missionary Society*, London, John Snow, 1844

Ferdon, Edwin N., *Early Tahiti, as the Explorers Saw It, 1767–1797*, Tucson, University of Arizona Press, 1981

Forster, George, *A Voyage Round the World 1772–75*, London, B. White, J. Robson & P. Elmsly, 1777

Gauguin, Paul, *Noa Noa*, tr. O.F. Theis and intro. A. Warner, New York, Noonday Press, 1961

Goldman, I., *Ancient Polynesian Society*, Chicago, University of Chicago Press, 1970

Gratton, C. Hartley, *The South-western Pacific to 1900*, Michigan, University of Michigan Press, 1963

Grimshaw, Patricia, 'New England missionary wives, Hawaiian women and "the cult of womanhood"', in M. Jolly & M. Macintyre (eds) *Family and Gender in the Pacific: Domestic Contradictions and the Colonial Input*, Cambridge, Cambridge University Press, 1989

Grove, Richard H., *Green Imperialism: Colonial Expansion, Tropical Island Edens and the Origins of Environmentalism, 1600–1860*, Cambridge, Cambridge University Press, 1997

Hamilton, George, *A Voyage Round the World in His Majesty's Frigate* Pandora . . . *1790–92*, Berwick, W. Phorson, 1793

Handy, E.S. Craighill, *History and Culture in the Society Islands*, Honolulu, Bernice P. Bishop Museum, No. 79, 1930

Hawkesworth, John, *An Account of Voyages Undertaken by the Order of His Present Majesty for Making Discoveries in the Southern Hemisphere*, London, W. Strahan & T. Cadell, 1773

Henry, T., *Ancient Tahiti*, Honolulu, Bernice P. Bishop Museum, 1928

Heyerdahl, Thor, *The Kon-Tiki*, Harmondsworth, Penguin, 1974

Hibbert, Christopher, *The Roots of Evil: A Social History of Crime and Punishment*, Harmondsworth, Penguin, 1966

Hoefer, H.J., Lueras, L. and Chung, N., *Hawaii*, Honolulu, Insight Guides, Apa Productions (HK), 1980

Joesting, Edward, *Hawaii: An Uncommon History*, London, Robert Hale, 1974

Jolly, M., and Macintyre, M. (eds), *Family and Gender in the Pacific: Domestic Contradictions and the Colonial Imput*, Cambridge, Cambridge University Press, 1989

Kennedy, Gavin, *The Death of Captain Cook*, London, Duckworth, 1987

Kuykendall, Ralph S., *The Hawaiian Kingdom 1778–1854*, Honolulu, University of Hawaii Press, 1938

Lewis, David, *We the Navigators: the Ancient Art of Landfinding in the Pacific*, Canberra, Australian National University Press, 1972

Lindsay, J.O. (ed.), *The New Cambridge Modern History*, Vol. VII, Cambridge, Cambridge University Press, 1963

Lloyd, Christopher, *Captain Cook*, London, Faber & Faber, 1952

Lovett, Richard, *The History of the London Missionary Society 1795–1895*, London, Henry Froude, 1899

Lummis, Trevor, *Life and Death in Eden*, London, Phoenix, 2000

Martin, Henry Byam, Captain, RN, *The Polynesian Journal of Captain Henry Byam Martin R.N.*, Canberra, Australian National University Press, 1981

Montgomery, James, *Journal of Voyages and Travels by the Rev. Daniel Tyerman and George Bennet, Esq . . . between the years 1821 and 1829*, London, Frederick Westley & A.H. Davis, 1831

Moorehead, Alan, *The Fatal Impact: the Brutal and Tragic Story of How the South Pacific was 'Civilised' 1767–1840*, Harmondsworth, Penguin, 1987

Morrison, J. (intro. Owen Rutter), *The Journal of James Morrison*, London, Golden Cockerel Press, 1935

Murray, H. (ed.), *Constable's Miscellany Vol. IV, British Seamen*, Edinburgh, Constable & Co., 1827

Obeyesekere, Gannath, *The Apotheosis of Captain Cook: European Mythmaking in the Pacific*, Princeton, Princeton University Press, 1992

Oliver, Douglas, *Return to Tahiti, Bligh's Second Breadfruit Voyage*, Carlton, Victoria, Melbourne University Press, 1988

Oliver, S. Passfield, *The Life of Philibert Commerson*, London, John Murray, 1909

Pierce, Richard A., *Russia's Hawaiian Adventure 1815–1817*, Kingston, Ontario, Limestone Press, 1976

Pike, E. Royston, *Human Documents of the Industrial Revolution in Britain*, London, George Allen & Unwin, 1966

Portlock, Nathaniel, *A Voyage Round the World, 1785–1788*, London, John Stockdale, 1789

Ralston, Caroline, 'Changes in the Lives of Ordinary Women in Early Post-Contact Hawaii', in M. Jolly & M. Macintyre (eds) *Family and Gender in the Pacific: Domestic Contradictions and the Colonial Imput*, Cambridge, Cambridge University Press, 1989

Reed, Andrew, *The Case of Tahiti: an Appeal to the Constituents of the London Missionary Society*, London, Ward & Co., 1847

Robertson, Jillian, *The Captain Cook Myth*, London, Angus & Robertson, 1981

Roquefeuil, Camille de, *A Voyage Round the World Between the Years 1816–1819 by Camille de Roquefeuil, in the Ship* Bordelais, London, Sir Richard Phillips & Co., 1823

Sahlins, Marshall, *Islands of History*, London, Tavistock Publications, 1987

Villiers, Captain Alan, *Captain Cook, the Seaman's Seaman*, Aylesbury, Penguin, 1969

ARCHIVE SOURCES

London 111 [British Library Ref: 4745 bbb 23] *Mission at Otaheite 1797*,1818

London 111 [British Library Ref: Ac 6172/156] *Tahitian Mission 1799–1830*, ed. W. Newberry, 1961

TAHITI [British Library. 116785 a 6] *Laws. A Translation of Part of the Law on Aliens*, 1843

TAHITI [British Library. 4767 c 30] *Tahitian Mission. A Report on the Windward Division*, 1824

NEWSPAPERS

General Evening Post [London], 19–21 July and 9–11 August 1774

London Chronicle, 19–23 July 1774

Sydney Gazette, 17 July 1819

United Services Journal 1832 (1), pp. 99–100

PUBLIC RECORD OFFICE

Adm 51/4539, Journal of George Robertson, Master of HMS *Dolphin*

Adm 51/4538, Log of Charles Clerke, Lieutenant of HMS *Dolphin*

INTERNET

Various sources were consulted to check facts and biographies but notably:

The American National Biography

United States of America Congressional Documents: (Hawaiian Islands) Hawaiian Kingdom

Hawaiian Independence Home Page

La Croix, Sumner J., *The Economic History of Hawai'i: A Short Introduction*, Working Paper No.02. 3 January 2002. Encarta Online Encyclopedia, Microsoft Corporation, 2004

Merlin, Mark D., and Fuchs, Lawrence H., *Hawaii (State)*, Encarta Online Encyclopedia, Microsoft Corporation, 2004

INDEX

abortion, *see* infanticide

Adventure, HMS 118, 120

Africa 35, 88, 102, 116, 118, 129–30, 178, 194

African negroes 34, 37, 119, 149, 189

Aguila 133, 134, 135

Aigle, L' 124

Aimata, Queen 177

Albion 142

Aleutian Islands 67, 87

Alexander I, Tsar 95

American Congress 23, 193, 194

Andrews, Dr 120

Antarctic 49, 65

Antelope 26

Aoutourou 25, 115, 117

Apology Resolution 194

Arago, Jacques 98–9, 102, 103, 107, 111–13

Ariori 48–9, 58–60, 64, 155, 162–3

Artemise, L' 172, 180

Asia 15, 79, 129, 188, 190, 192

Aube 178

Australia 15, 20, 106, 117, 137, 138, 143, 147, 166 181

Banks, Joseph (later Sir Joseph)
  London home 115, 119–20
  scientist 22, 24, 117
  Tahitian life 42–5, 46, 48–9, 55, 57, 59

Baranov, Alexander 88, 94–6

Barclay, Glen 15, 18, 77, 94

Baré, Jeanne 25

Barnard, Charles 87, 92, 113

Basilisk 181–2

Batavia 19, 117

Beagle, HMS 177

Bellwood, Peter 16

Bering Straits 67, 96

Bexiatua, Chief 134

Billy Pitt, Chief (nickname) 84, 92

birth control, *see* infanticide

births 27, 48, 56, 108, 156–7, 170, 181

Bligh, Captain William 38, 50, 59, 62, 74, 121, 122, 132

Boenechea, Captain Don Domingo de 133

Boki, Chief 124

Bordelais 98–100

Bora Bora 46, 51, 115, 117, 118, 119, 120, 121, 122, 183, 190

Boudeuse, La 13, 24, 115

Bougainville, Count Louis de 13, 22–5, 32, 43, 115–16

Bounty, HMS 21, 50, 53, 57, 60, 74, 131, 136, 145, 149

Boyd 27

British House 132

British Museum 24

Bruat, Governor 182–4, 185

Bowman, William 10

Burney, Fanny 120

Burney, James 121

Byron, Captain Lord 79, 125

Callao 133

Campbell, Archibald 88–91, 104, 105, 106, 109

Canada 32, 65, 66, 79, 85–6, 87, 99, 137, 166, 191

canoes
  armed 6, 72, 83, 86, 162
  construction 7, 47 63, 159
  journeys 16–19, 51

use 3, 4, 45–6, 62, 67, 84, 92, 111, 132, 145
Canary Islands 15, 16, 20, 121
cannibalism 27–8, 68, 99, 104, 118
Canning, George 125
Canton 80, 81, 84, 87, 93, 97, 100, 130
Cape Horn 37, 49, 51, 79, 123, 168
Cape of Good Hope 20, 85, 88
Carysfort, HMS 172
Charlotte, Queen 24
Chatham 85
childhood
    British 121, 154, 158–9, 192
    Polynesian 56–7, 58, 60, 107, 112, 140–1, 142, 157, 170, 171, 185
China 15, 19, 26, 115, 137
Christian, Fletcher 131
Churchill, Charles 57
Clerke, Charles 10, 70, 74, 121
climate
    danger 65–6
    effects 44, 109, 189
    ideal 14, 19, 49, 130
Clinton, President Bill 194
clothing 25, 60, 70, 89, 109, 123, 136, 137, 157, 167, 187
Cobbett, William 24
Columbus, Christopher 16, 18, 20, 22
Commerson, Dr Philibert 22, 24–5
Cowper, William 122
commerce
    development 87, 92, 97, 124, 143, 174, 179, 190
    missionaries 149–50, 159, 169, 175
    opportunities 30, 79–80, 88, 172–3
    risks 82–3, 89, 99, 100, 137, 193
    social and political effects 91, 92, 94, 97, 98, 123, 176, 187, 188, 189
conservation 20–2, 54, 62, 102–3, 114, 134, 156
    livestock transported 12, 17, 19, 20, 62, 121–2
Constellation 173
consuls 178, 179, 181, 182
Convention of Hatutira 134–5
Cook, Captain James 22, 41, 52, 59, 117–18, 133, 135–6, 144
    career 31–3, 121
    death 17, 31, 46, 68, 73–4, 75–6, 80
    discoveries 46, 49–50, 66, 71, 77, 78, 79, 103, 118, 121, 125
    disease 19, 36, 37–8
    divinity 68–9
    drunkenness 36–7
    family 34
    funeral 76
    Northwest Passage 65, 66, 67, 71
    punishment 37–8, 41, 44, 153
    reputation 23–4, 38, 42, 65, 72–3, 123, 154
Cook Islands 15
Cornwall 141
court 119, 141, 147, 178
crime 27, 35, 134, 153, 161
    on ship 124–5
    sex 57, 136
    Tahiti 47, 55–6
    see also punishment
culture 28, 189, 191, 192, 193, 194

Darwin, Charles 177
Davies, Isaac 83, 84–5, 90, 193
Diana, HMS 88
Diderot, Denis 116, 123
Dimsdale, Dr 120
Discovery, HMS
    Cook's voyages 65, 70, 72, 73, 79, 121, 135
    Vancouver's voyage 85
disease, 19, 26, 41, 49, 53, 102, 103, 117, 120, 130, 145, 155, 163–4, 174
    scurvy 4, 9, 28–9, 36–7, 106
    venereal disease 43, 103, 174
dissolute behaviour
    Queen Aimata 177
    sailors 143, 180
    Tahitians 57–8, 192
Dixon, Captain 79, 81
Douglas, Captain William 81–2
Dole, Stanford 193
Dolphin, HMS 3, 4, 12
drink
    Britain 54, 175

Hawaii 106, 124, 169, 175
  kava 47–8, 106
  on ship 36
  Tahiti 7, 41, 48, 124, 165–6, 185
Duke of Portland 90
Duff 130, 132–3, 136, 139, 140, 142

Easter Island 15, 16, 20
Eclipse 89
Eden, Garden of 17, 29, 129
Eleanora 82–4
Eliza 143
Endeavour, HMS 33, 36, 41, 43, 48, 51,
      117, 121
Enlightenment, The 23, 116
environment, *see* conservation
Étoile, L' 13
executions, *see* human sacrifice

Fair American 82, 83
firearms
  cannon 4, 6, 8–9, 25, 64, 72–3,
      81–3, 85, 90, 133, 145, 147,
      166, 185
  muskets 6, 8, 25, 57, 64, 70, 81–4, 86,
      98–9, 137, 143–4, 166
Fitzroy, Captain 177–8
flogging, *see* punishments
food
  Hawaii 71, 90, 97, 102, 106–7, 108–9,
      171
  sailors 17, 19, 20–1, 28, 29, 36–8, 42,
      67, 76, 95
  Tahiti 4–5, 8, 9, 13, 42, 45, 47–8, 50,
      54, 56, 61–2, 131, 134, 143,
      159–60
Forster, George 22, 47, 52
Forster, Johann Reinhold 22
Franklin, Benjamin 23
Friendly Islands 132
French
  as privateers 139, 140, 166, 168,
      172–3, 174
  effect of 83
  foreign influence 80, 81–2, 84–5, 86,
      105, 173, 194
  French War 172, 173–4
  Hawaiian wars, alliances 78–9

  in Canada 32
  in New Zealand 178–9, 180–5, 186,
      187, 189, 190, 191
  missionary influence 167–8, 172
  Russian ambition and 96–7
Furneaux, Tobias 7, 115, 118, 119

Gauguin, Paul 187–8
George III, King 30, 91, 114, 115, 119–20,
      121
George IV, King 124, 125
Gloucester, Duke of 120
Goldman, I. 16, 17, 65
Grampus, HMS 184
Green, Mr 34
Grove, Richard H. 20, 21
Gore, John 41, 79, 121

hedonism 116, 161, 165, 170, 175
Heyerdahl, Thor 19
homosexuality 61, 136, 150, 192
Honolulu 90, 96, 97, 169, 172, 193, 194
Hotu Chief 134
Huahine 51, 117, 118, 122, 147, 154–6,
      159, 161
human sacrifice
  England 154
  Hawaii 104, 167
  Tahiti 55–6, 144, 153, 155–6
hunger 47, 62, 84, 116, 154, 160, 191

immigration 188, 194
India 20, 102, 129, 130, 151, 166
infanticide
  European 191
  Hawaiian 170, 174
  Tahitian 48, 58, 136, 152–3, 155–6
independence 186, 190, 193, *see also*
      rebellions
industrial conditions 158–9, 170
international cooperation 23–4
  occupations 86, 176, 180–1, 186, 193
  responsibility 31–2, 35, 124, 186
  rivalry 85, 87, 101, 124–5, 133, 166,
      172–4, 178–9
Isabella 88

Japan 15, 79, 89, 173, 190, 192, 193

Jefferson, Kearney, Commodore 173–4
Jefferson, President Thomas 87
Johnson, Dr Samuel 119
Judd, Dr 174

Kaahumanu, Queen 97, 124
Kahekili, King 86
Kaiana 80–1, 85
Kalakaua, King 193
Kalaniopuu, King 72, 86
Kamahameha I 82, 86, 91–2, 94–7, 98,
        104, 123, 124, 167
Kamahameha II (Liholiho) 123–5, 167,
        169
Kamahameha III 169, 173, 175
Kamamalu, Queen 124–5
Kamchatka 34, 66, 79
Kauai Island 66, 68, 80, 86, 94, 95, 96
Kaumualii, King 86, 94–7
Kealakekua Bay 67, 68, 70, 72, 76, 84,
        85
Keohuna (wife of a prince) 110
King George 80
King George III Island 7
King, James 70
Koa (Britanee) 69, 71
Kodiak Island 89
Kon-Tiki 19
Kotzebue, Otto von 96

language
    learning 41, 50, 53
    missionaries' achievement 124, 146,
        164, 178
    Polynesian complexity 4, 47, 48, 144,
        170, 194
Lewis and Clark Expedition 87
Liliuokalani, Queen 193
London 158, 186
    crime 47, 104, 154
    foreigners 26, 114, 118–21, 124, 125
    news arriving 31, 138, 142
    ships at 124, 130, 139, 140, 141, 151,
        180
London, Jack 187
London Missionary Society 129, 139, 144,
        146, 150, 151, 166, 178, 186, *see
        also* mission and missionaries

Mackay, John 81
Madeira Islands 20, 36, 88
Makahiki 68, 69
Marae 105, 106, 109, 114, 115, 145, 147,
        148, 155–6
Marianas Islands 93
Marquesas 16, 20, 30, 99–100, 178, 182,
        183, 190
marriage 60, 57, 97, 124, 140, 155, 167,
        169, 170, 171, 179–80, 192, 194
Marshall Islands 20
Matavai Bay 37, 41, 64, 65, 117, 121, 131,
        132, 133, 135–6, 147–8, 179
Martin, Captain Henry Byam 175, 177,
        184
Matisse, Henri 187
Maugham, W. Somerset 189–90
Maui Island 17, 67, 70, 83, 103
Mauritius 20, 25
Meares, Captain John 80–1
Mexico 20, 77, 79
Metcalfe, Captain Simon 82–4
Metcalfe, Captain Thomas 82, 83–4
mission
    American Protestant 123, 168
        commercial influence 175
        cultural values 169, 170, 171, 175
        international effects 172–3
        occupations 168
        voyages 168; 71, 174, 175, 176
        women 169–70
    British Protestant 129–30
        commercial influence 149–50, 158,
            159
        cultural values 131, 137, 142, 152,
            153–4, 160, 164, 169
        divisions 182, 186
        historical value 146, 151
        international effects 178–9
        occupations 130–1
        voyages 130–1, 132–3, 138,
            139–40, 151
    French Roman Catholic at Hawaii 172
        expelled 172, 179
        international effects 172–3, 180–1
        Tahiti 179
    Spanish Roman Catholic 133
        abandoned 136

treaty 134
voyages 133–4, 135
missionaries
American
Bingham, Hiram 168
Holman, Dr 169
Jones, John C. 169
Lyman, Sarah 171
Richards, Mr 176
Thurston, Asa 168
British
Armitage, Mr 158
Bennet, George 151
Broomhall, Mr 143
Cover, James 132, 138
Crook, Mr 153
Elder, Mr and Mrs 147
Ellis, William 124
Eure, John 129
Eyre, Mrs 138
Gyles, Mr 149
Henry, Brother 136, 143
Henry, Mrs 143
Lewis, Thomas 140–1
Nott, Henry 146, 147, 151, 152
Platt, Mr 157–8
Pritchard, George 178, 179
Tyerman, Daniel 151
Wilson, Mr 151
French
Caret, Padre 179
Laval, Padre 179
Spanish
Geronimo, Padre 134
Narciso, Padre 134
Rodriguez, Senor 135–6
Moerenhout, Jacques Antoine 179, 180, 181
Moorea Island 51, 52, 53, 132, 135, 147, 148
Morrison, James 53, 55, 57, 136
Morton, Lord 35
Moxeley, Mr 106

Native Americans 21, 79, 88, 99, 100, 118, 191, 184
Nautilus 137, 138
Neva 89, 90
New Cythera 13, 29

New South Wales 74, 90, 143, 149
New Zealand 15, 16, 17, 27, 28, 35, 65, 85, 117, 118, 121, 122, 166, 178, 188
Norfolk 145
North America 21, 22, 79, 100, 118
Northwest Passage 65, 66, 67, 71, 76, 79

Oahu 66, 86, 90, 94, 95, 96, 98, 103, 124
Obearea, Queen 11–13, 29, 42, 115, 117
Obeyesekere, Gananath 69
Olowalu Massacre 83
Omai 115, 117–23
Otkrytie 95
Otoo (also Tu and Otu) 132, 134, 135

Palea 70, 72
Pandora, HMS 29, 50, 60
Papeete 179-80, 181–2, 183, 184–6, 187, 190
paradise 19, 51, 91, 117, 175, 187, 194
Paris 23, 104, 112, 115, 174, 182, 183
Parry, William 120
Pauillac, Bordeaux 99
Paul V, Pope 69
Paulet, Lord George 172
Pelew Islands 26, 27
Perseverance 147
Peru, 19, 20, 133, 135
Petit-Thouars, Admiral Abel du 180–1, 182, 183
Philippines 15, 26, 77–8
Phillips, Molesworth 72, 73, 74
Pickney, Francis 11
Pitcairn 21, 149, 165
Plymouth 36, 88, 118, 121
Podushkin, Lieutenant 95
Polynesian gods 17
Hawaii 66, 68, 69, 102–3, 104
Tahiti 54–5, 104, 141–2, 144–5, 146, 147
Pomare I, King 132, 137–8, 143, 144–5
Pomare II, King 144, 146, 147–9, 150, 153, 162, 165, 177
Pomare III, King 177
Pomare V, King 187
Pomare dynasty 147, 148, 156–7, 165, 183, 180–2, 185, 186

Pomare Vahine, Queen 154–5, 165, 177
population
   Hawaiians 103
   decline 174, 192, 194
   migration 15–16, 18, 19, 20
   Tahitians 52–3, 188, 190
   decline 152–3, 155–6
Port Jackson 143, 147
Portlock, Captain 79, 81
Portsmouth 34, 130, 139, 151
Proctor, James 10–11
Puget, Lieutenant 86
punishment
   Britain 56, 142, 154
   Polynesians 46, 47, 53, 55, 57, 83,
      104, 138, 153–4
   sailors 10–11, 37–8, 41, 44, 75

Queen Charlotte 80
Queensland 117

Raiatea 46, 51, 52, 58, 115, 117, 118,
      199, 121, 122, 143, 147, 161,
      180, 182, 183, 185
Ralston, Caroline 108
Reed, Andrew 186
Resolution, HMS 65, 70, 71, 73, 75, 79,
      118, 121
Reynolds, Sir Joshua 120
Ricord, Mr 176
Rio de Janeiro 37, 91, 139
Rives, Jean 124
Robertson, George 3
Roquefeuil, Camille de 98–9
Rousseau, Jean-Jacques 24, 116, 119
Royal Admiral 143
Rurick 96
Russia 31, 87–8, 89, 91, 94–6
Russian-American Company 88, 95–6

Sahlins, Marshall 69, 105
St Helena 20, 30
Sally 141
Samwell, David 70, 135
Sandwich, Earl of 119, 120, 121
Sandwich Islands 167
Sannack Island 89
Scheffer, Georg 95–7

sexuality, free 42, 50, 63, 103, 111–13,
     165
   Hawaii 70, 165, 170–1
   Tahiti 13–14, 42, 60, 82
   trade 5, 6–7, 66, 99, 105
slavery 35, 116, 149, 158, 189
social class and status 47, 113
   Hawaii 52, 74, 90, 105
   Tahiti 52, 53–4, 105, 157–8
Society Islands 15, 16, 18, 46, 51, 131,
     183
Solander, Dr 34, 119, 120
Solomon Islands 15, 20, 30
song 58, 112, 163, 187, 188, 193
South America 19–20, 99, 118, 13, 137,
     139
Southern Continent 3, 4, 29, 35, 49, 118
Spanish Pacific 20, 30, 35, 77–8, 85,
     133–5, 136
Starbuck, Valentine 124–5
Stavers, Captain Francis 151
Stevenson, Robert Louis 187, 188, 189, 190
Stevenson, William 106
Sydney 137

taboo
   abolition 148, 161–2, 167–8, 169, 175,
     191
   chief's power 45, 54, 70, 76, 84, 173
   definition 54
   environment 21, 54, 72, 92
   European 27, 71, 83, 150, 154, 173
   female 63, 108–9, 113, 155
   male 48, 61
   social 56, 57, 58, 68, 105–6, 148, 179
Tahaa 51
Tamena, Queen 90, 109, 193
Tamato, Chief 147
Tahitian Wars, alliances 53, 144–5, 147,
     177, 180, 183
   Christians v. Pagans 147–9, 156, 165,
     177–8
   effects of 46–7, 63–4, 147, 152–3,
     155–6
   foreign influence 7, 64, 117, 133,
     144–5
   French war 180–6
   inter-island 52, 115, 122, 134–5, 183

missionary involvement 137–8, 143, 145, 147–9, 182, 186
tapa 8, 63, 68, 109, 120
tattoo 49, 56, 57, 110, 161
Taut, Chief 147
taxes 68, 92, 93, 105
Tayweheerooa 121
Terito, Queen 147
theft
  definition 24, 47
  Hawaiian 72–3, 74, 75, 82–3
  limited 71, 80
  sailors 9–10, 11, 37, 41, 44
  skill 47
  Tahitian 4, 43, 44–6, 134, 145, 165
  westerners 125, 154, 175
Thomas, Richard 182
Thompson, Mark 57
Tootahah 42, 45
Tonga 65, 121, 145, 188
Treaty of Protection 186
Tromelin, Admiral de 173–4
Tubuai 131
Tupia, Chief 117
Tuscon 151, 158

United States 87, 169, 173, 174, 176, 193–4
Upufara, Chief 148
Urban VIII, Pope 69

Valparaiso 99
Vancouver, Captain George 85–6, 87, 125
Venus 145
Venus, transit of 30, 44
  goddess 13
Vaitua, Princess 187–8
Vindictive, HMS 181

wages 33, 34; loss of 36
Wallis, Captain Samuel 25, 41, 42, 62, 115, 121

  career 4
  discovers Tahiti 3, 7, 29, 31
  firearms 4, 6–7, 8, 133
  punishments 10–11
  Queen Obearea 11–12, 42
  women 5–7, 9–10
war casualties
  Hawaii 73, 75, 83–5
  New Zealand 27, 118
  North America 100
  Tahiti 25, 44, 115, 148–9, 183, 185
wars
  American Independence 23
  Anglo-American 1812 123
  Cold War 190, 193
  First World War 190
  Maoris 28
  Marquesas 99
  Napoleonic 87, 98
  Second World War 190, 193
  Seven Years War 30
  see also Hawaiian and Tahitian wars
Watman, William 70
weaving 63, 77, 90
Welch, William 10
West Indies 16, 50, 88, 149, 189
whalers 90, 179, 181
  Hawaiian crew 123
  Kamehamehama II 124
  missionaries 130, 132–3 139–40, 141, 142, 151
Williamson, John 74
Wilson, Captain James 130
work
  European 113, 129, 131, 158–9
  intensification 91–2, 98, 149, 159, 174–5
  necessity 51, 71, 102, 123, 129, 189
  manufacture 7, 46, 47, 63, 78, 159
Wyllie, Mr 176

Young, John 84–5, 92, 94, 95, 124, 167